OJAI VALLEY'S VETERANS STORIES

VETERAN'S STORIES OF THE

OJAI VALLEY VETERAN'S OF FOREIGN WARS, POST 11461

PHOTO COURTESY OF HOWARD GILBERT

COVER PHOTO COURTESY OF HOWARD HANSEN
MARCHERS LEFT TO RIGHT:
CHUCK BENNETT, JULIO CONTRERAS, HANK BAST AND
BRYAN MORGAN

COVER DESIGN AND ARTWORK: CHUCK BENNETT

ACKNOWLEDGEMENTS

■■■■■■■■■■■■■■■■■■■

The Book Committee

The book, Ojai Valley Veterans Stories, is the concerted team effort of Chuck Bennett, Sanford Drucker, and David Pressey. The specialized skills and talents of each member of the team were critical to the writing, production, and distribution of the book. David Pressey helped develop the original historical and biographical material. Chuck Bennett designed and formatted the cover and the presentation of the written material along with technical skills in production. Sanford Drucker brought his business talents, including marketing, and community networking abilities into the final equation. This team consulted, formulated the pattern for the book, and discussed each facet of its creation over a two-year period.

Our Veteran Contributors

Special thanks and appreciation is given to the Ojai Valley Veteran men and women who were so supportive in contributing their stories to the Book. Collectively, their stories represent an oral history of the 20th Century as experienced at the human and personal level.

Dr. Joyce Kennedy, Ph.D and Director Emeritus

The Book Committee is especially grateful to Dr. Joyce Kennedy, Ph.D., and Director Emeritus of the California Northridge State College Extended Campus for Ventura County. Dr. Kennedy, a veteran herself, gave invaluable assistance in editing and offering suggestions on the development of the text. Dr. Kennedy's extraordinary academic background plus being a published author of military history provided the Book Committee with sound advice.

Stephanie Hodges, Consultant

Stephanie Hodges supported the team effort by conducting individual follow up interviews, taping the oral histories, technical field work, and reformatting the oral histories of each participant, as well as ongoing participation in committee planning and decisions.

OJAI VALLEY'S VETERANS STORIES

33 stories
from military veterans
of the Ojai Valley's VFW Post 11461

Written and Recorded By
Charles A. Bennett
and
David E. Pressey

Committee
COMMUNICATIONS, INC.

First printing June 2003

Published in the United States of America by Committee Communications, Inc., P. O. Box 343, Oak View California 93022

Library of Congress Control Number:

Publisher's Cataloging-in-Publication Data

Bennett, Charles A. and Pressey, David E.
    Ojai Valley's Veterans Stories
    Oak View California, Committee Communications, Inc.   2003

       Includes Index and Bibliography
       ISBN 0-9709324-1-3

DISCLAIMER
    This book is designed to provide interesting stories concerning various individuals involvement in past American wars and actions. The information provided is solely that of the presenters and cannot be verified to truthfulness. It is sold with the understanding that the publisher and author are not engaged in rendering legal, accounting or other professional service. If legal or other expert assistance is required, the services of a competent professional should be sought.
    It is not the purpose of this manual to reprint all the information that is otherwise available to the authors and/or publisher, but to complement, amplify or supplement other texts. You are urged to read other available material for a broader understanding.
    Every effort has been made to make this book as complete and as accurate as possible. However, there may be mistakes both typographical and in content. Therefore, this text should be used only as a general information.
    The purpose of this manual is to educate and entertain. The authors and Committee Communications, Inc. shall have neither liability nor responsibility to any person or entity with respect to any loss or damage caused, or alleged to be caused, directly or indirectly by the information contained in this book.
    If you do not wish to be bound by the above, you may return this book to the publisher, within 90 days of purchase, for a full refund.

Notice: The information in this book is true and complete to the best of our knowledge. It is offered with no guarantees on the part of the presenters, writers or Committee Communications, Inc. The authors and publisher disclaim all liability in connection with the information in this book.

    The Ojai Valley's Veterans Stories is available at special quantity discounts for educational use. Special books, or book excerpts, can also be created to fit specific needs.

THE LIVING MEMORIAL OF THE MILITARY SERVICES AND MEMORIES OF THE FAMILIES, FRIENDS, AND VETERANS OF THE OJAI VALLEY VETERAN'S OF FOREIGN WARS, POST 11461

FOREWORD
■■■■■■■■■■■■■■■■■■■■■■■

T his book evolved out of biographical material of VFW family members, friends, and veterans of VFW Post 11461. Initially, interviews were conducted for material for the local newsletter. Articles were limited in scope and detail. Some members then suggested that these interviews would be excellent material for our monthly programs where local students and friends were invited to hear the various presentations. A serendipitous discovery was made. No longer was the Post a group listening to minutes and financial reports. As the membership learned about one another, the camaraderie and interpersonal relationships was enhanced. A new respect and admiration developed among the comrade veterans. It was discovered that the membership of this Post represented some facet of American history for the last sixty-five years. It was truly amazing how this small community with a small Post should have such a microcosm of world history at our fingertips. Much of the history discussed is from the perspective of the writers and historical view points of the membership. You will note different view points but with one common thread of patriotism. This is what makes America.

Unpolished and unvarnished, the individual experiences were told by each veteran without the refined expert training in public speaking. Their comments gave voice to long cherished and buried memories. The reports evoked humor and sadness as the good and the bad was explained in simple extemporaneous conversation. The comrades listened in awe as they related to the pain and pride, the suffering and resentments, the pleasures and the comradeship experienced by all veterans. They told how it was, not like some academician would explain. The freedom of expression without the restraint of a politically correct environment gave us an understanding of the feeling of what it means to be a veteran. We found a commonality of emotions.

When most of the veterans had made their presentation, it was discovered that our Post was what Sanford Drucker had created, "A Living Treasure," which is now a growing partnership with Rotary International. It was suggested that this treasure of unvarnished experiences told with candor and emotion should be published.

When most veterans served their country, it was a common thing. It was uncommon not to have served in the military. As the years have passed into decades and sickness and age have thinned the ranks, we have discovered that only fifteen percent of all American men have ever served in the Armed Forces in any capacity. Not only that, the general public has lost some of the understanding of what it meant and means to serve your country.

There is a sense of urgency in this Post to publish these historical experiences before it is too late. Already, four of our comrades have passed away and several others have entered nursing homes. We are racing the clock to ensure that our legacy of experiences, memories, emotions, and yes, attitudes are not lost to our community and posterity. This is a book for our families, for veterans, for current active and reserve personnel, and indeed, our very nation.

The Mission of Ojai Valley's Veterans Stories

All veterans understand the meaning of the word "mission." Within the military definition, the word "mission" is the ultimate commitment to duty and service to your country. It is an absolute commitment that can claim one's health, comfort, well being, and indeed one's very life. It is a sacred duty to those sworn to uphold and defend the Constitution of the United States of America and those rights and liberties granted the free citizens of this great democracy.

As a Veteran's of Foreign Wars Post, our mission is to preserve, protect, and promote those causes for which we served. We exist to transmit those values of democratic government, to promote the veteran's well being, and transmit to the general population what it means to be a veteran. Concurrent with our activities in support of veterans, we endeavor to support our active duty and reserve duty military forces that are defending this nation today as we defended this nation in the past.

Sanford Drucker has said, "We are the living representing our comrade dead if they could speak."

Chuck Bennett has said, "I help living veterans and serve in veteran's organizations for those who never came home. I promote patriotism to America. I would hope they would do the same for me if I had never come home"

Julio Contreras' service to veteran's is his memorial to his brothers who died after serving our country in the United States Marine Corps.

The continuing patriotism and belief in our nation's destiny underlies the commitment of all the veterans of this Ojai Valley Post.

There are lessons to be learned from the preservation and sharing of our individual and collective memories of what our service means to us. By understanding the past, a democratic society may avoid the pitfalls of erroneous and unwise political decisions. Hopefully, as we fulfill our mission herein, we will be promoting the common good of our community and our great American Nation.

*This book is dedicated
to the individual and organizations
who demonstrate daily
what American Patriotism
and support of our Constitution
is all about.*

CONTENTS

#1: VETERANS OF THREE WARS   5

#2: VETERANS OF TWO WARS   35

#6: VIETNAM WAR ERA 315

BIBLIOGRAPHY: 393

INDEX: 395

WORLD WAR II

■■■■■■■■■■■■■■■■■■■■

*T*he roots of World War II can be traced back to the rise
of nation states and the development of Western
European Colonialism. Starting with Columbus and
the discovery of the New World, mercantilism was an
accepted practice whereby conquered and colonial nations
and people were in economic subjection to the nations of
Western Europe.

*Three great powers came into national existence during
the 19th Century. Though these nations had existed as
fragmented principalities of kindred people for several
thousand years, it wasn't until around 1871 that Germany
and Italy were born as modern states. Japan had been an
isolated hermit kingdom until 1853 when the United States
Navy, acting as a diplomatic advanced party opened Japan to
the world beyond and the modern age. These three great
powers with burgeoning populations occupied territorial
masses relatively devoid of many essential raw materials
necessary for building themselves into world powers. They
looked around the world and saw that all desirable colonies
on the six continents of the inhabited world were already
possessed by other European nations. Free trade was not an
option and the colonial empires were closed to trade with
new nations.*

*The desire for colonies and national prestige and wealth
that came from colonialism stimulated development of a
new form of nationalism and mythology that sought to
justify their rights as a nation to conquer other nations.
Mussolini developed the myth of the new Roman Empire.
Beating his Fascist drums promoting Italian expansionism,*

he justified an attack on Albania, and Greece, Libya, and Ethiopia. This new nationalism was mean spirited and aggressive. It trampled on the rights and freedoms of the conquered people. Conquered people lost their freedom merely because Mussolini wanted what they possessed. Italy became a classic robber nation. Germany was a basket case after World War I. The German people were suffering from an unjust Treaty of Versailles, a treaty that produced a most egregious inflation and outright hunger among the peoples of the German nation. In desperation, the Germans turned to radical and extremist politicians who promised a painless solution to their problems. They elected Adolf Hitler to the German Parliament. Once elected Hitler proceeded to dismantle every visage of the nascent democracy government. Like all aggressor government, a myth had to be created. The myth propagandized in Germany was the idea that they were a super race, a master race. Mankind was reclassified from the Aryan Super Race to an inferior race including the French called the Alpines, and the most inferior of human races being the Mediterranean. All other races of human kind were classified as subhuman. Once Germany bought into the Hitlerian mythology, Germany began an active and expansive program of aggression against neighboring nations. Their race superiority doctrine justified programs of enslavement, extermination, and genocide. Propaganda slogans combined with a terror state reduced the German population to unwitting accomplices in this program of world conquest. Lebenstraum and Nach den Osten (Living Room and To the East) became slogans for military advances into the Balkans and Russia. Existing populations were scheduled for extermination or relocation. Thus World War II began. At first, the Western Democracies did not understand the magnitude of this threat from the German Nazis and the Italian Fascist. It was almost too late when finally Western Democracies began to fight back in a global war. In East Asia, Japan was experiencing national-istic growing pain which were reinforced by a military war machine unseen in Asia since the days of Genghis Khan. Japanese mythology developed the theory of the superiority of the Yellow race and the attended nationalistic religion of

Shintoism coupled with emperor worship. Japan had defeated China in aggressive actions in 1895. In 1905, Japan destroyed the Russian fleet in the Far East. In the 1930's Japan struck at Manchuria and China. While playing a cynical game of peace diplomacy in Washington D.C. the Japanese attacked the United States at Pearl Harbor. Ironically, these three aggressor nations became the Axis Partners in carving up the world. The fury of these nations struck at the heart of the liberties of a free people. The abuse and cruelty adminis-tered on innocent populations was unheard of among civilized nations. It is into this cauldron of world war that our veterans of Post 11461 were called to duty. Before this war was over, our veterans had fought in every corner of the globe. Stan Schneider was on Guadalcanal. Sanford Drucker was fighting in Alaska; Howard Gilbert was with the 10th Mountain Division in Northern Italy. Howard Hansen served on ammo and fuel ships from Guadalcanal to the Adriatic as well as the dangerous waters of the Gulf of Mexico. Sebastian Catarroja fought the Japanese in the Philippines as a Filipino Guerrilla and later served in the U. S. Army. Tom Mahon served in the 82nd Airborne in Central Europe and Germany. Phil Culbert serviced bombers on Tinian in the Western Pacific. John Magill directed aircraft from bases in India and Burma; Lester Peterson served in the Artillery in the frozen Aleutian Islands. Elton Perkey fought through New Guinea from Hollandia to Biak. Jim Rodgers, a professional soldier, served worldwide.

This book tells the story of these ordinary men, local friends and neighbors in the Ojai Valley. But buried deep within their hearts and minds are the memories of their experiences in the fight for the survival of our American Nation and the freedoms we continue to enjoy.

VETERANS
OF THREE WARS

■■■■■■■■■■■■■■

W.A.B. "BART" HANCHETT

WWII, KOREA– THE RELEASE OF THE PUEBLO CREW,
AND VIETNAM

Foreign policy is conducted through three dissimilar channels. Diplomacy is the first and preferred channel providing that nations negotiate in good will and good faith. But when negotiating with "Tiger" nations with a hidden agenda, diplomacy must be conducted with knowledge gathered by the intelligence community. Rational and democratic nations can not rely on reason when negotiating with the aggressor nations of the world. The aggressor nations tend to respect power. Therefore the democracies must have the might of the mailed fist hidden by the velvet glove of the diplomat. When diplomacy fails, war is the ultimate arm of foreign policy

The Cold War was such a time in history. No one could trust the communists with all their nefarious schemes for world control. At times, the Cold War became hot as in Korea and Vietnam. Other times, servicemen and intelligence operatives were engaged in constant surveillance of enemy activity, especially the Soviet Union, Red China, and North Korea. AWAC planes constantly flew off shore; U-2 spy planes photographed every inch of Russia and satellite nations until Gary Powers was shot down. Intelligence ships bristling with electronic equipment constantly monitored enemy activities. The stakes were high. The threat of thermonuclear war was an ever-present danger. When AWAC planes disappeared or planes were shot down in this Cold War, the unfortunate Americans simply vanished from planet earth. They were the living sacrifices for the defense of the nation. Often the relatives grieved alone and in silence for the lost Cold War warriors because their disappearance was classified, top secret, a non-event.

If American agents or operatives fell into communist hands, their fate was fierce torture and ultimately ignominious death. On one occasion, the capture of an American intelligence ship, the U.S.S. Pueblo, by North Korea was too big of an event to ignore. Too many lives were at stake; yet, the communist slave state of North Korea was anxious to wring every confession and every detail out of the hapless Americans captured. Long after the communist intelligence apparatus had exploited the captives, the communist used the event for maximum propaganda mileage throughout the communist block and wavering third world nations.

Into the North Korean cesspool of hate and fear and international intrigue, the United States began to negotiate with the Communist North Koreans for the release of the Americans. The North Koreans held the trump card for they held the Americans captive. The event took place at Panmunjom, across from the "Bridge of No Return" on the truce line in Korea. A team of tough American military officers was given the daunting task of negotiating. Our Veteran of Foreign Wars comrade, Bart Hanchett, was one of those negotiators. In his own words, this is his story:

Growing up in Military Schools

I was born in San Francisco in the children's hospital. I was the older of two children. My Mom died when I was 12, and my dad was the Vice President for General Motors, Oldsmobile Division, so I spent most of my younger years in Military Schools. One school was in Lake Elsinore, California. It was actually fun. I remember that we used to sneak out and swim across the lake to meet girls. We had it all planned out. They would have a change of clothes for us and everything. It was kind of crazy though because it was a couple of miles across the lake! My graduating class had only 11 students in it.

First, Off to the Navy

After graduation, I enlisted in the Navy. I was sent to the U.S.S. Boxer, an aircraft carrier. We were deployed to the South Pacific during the Japanese occupation. It was the end of the war, and we were part of the clean up crew.

Back to the U.S., College, and R.O.T.C.

When I returned to the United States, I decided to go to college at the University of Arizona, to get a degree in Business Administration.

It was 1948, and I needed money. So I enlisted in the ROTC, where they gave you $27.00 a month! I entered ROTC as a Junior because I had already served in the military. While still in college, I was called to active duty during the Korean War in 1954.

Hawaii, My Future Wife, and on to Korea

After serving in Korea I was sent to Hawaii with the 25th Division (Tropic Lightning Division) that had just been pulled out of Korea. It was there that I met my future wife. I was detailed to deal with civilian sales representatives that bombarded the military with their wares. My future wife was one of only two female sales representatives. She sold me 270+ televisions for the Army! She has always been persuasive. I returned to CONUS and spent several years in Air Defense of SAC bases

Cold War Assignments and race riots

Upon my return, I was sent to McCord AFB in Washington State, where I married Jane, the same television sales girl who sold 270 TV sets to the Army. We were sent to El Paso where I received more training, and then on to Pforzheim, Germany for four years. I couldn't speak

German, but Janie could. While in Germany, my unit built a fire station and a Kinderheim, an orphanage home for the Germans.

Upon returning to the United States, I was assigned to attend The U. S. Army Command and General Staff College at Fort Leavenworth. Upon completing the course, I was assigned as Operations Officer or S-3 for a Nike-Hercules Air Defense Battalion outside Chicago and was slated for promotion to Lt. Colonel. This was during the mid-1960's when race riots were breaking out in cities across the United States. I had a problem on my hands when three of my soldiers were knifed to death. One was knifed while getting a pizza and two others were knifed while catching a ride on the EL(Elevated Railway). As the situation deteriorated, rioters burned a police car outside the Nike-Hercules base and were threatening to come over the fence. I had ordered the soldiers not to shoot unless the rioters actually came over the fence. It was a tense situation because if the rioters had breached the base, they could have access to weapons, explosives, and munitions. I was up for promotion in two days. As I left for duty, my wife Janie told me, "If you're gonna get killed, it had better not be tonight!" She thought I should at least be promoted first. Of course, that was a little "black humor" because she was really worried about me and I was worried about the troops. I made it through the riots okay, and was promoted the next day. It is sad to think that the people we were defending were the killers of three of my soldiers.

We then moved to Colorado Springs, where I headed up the Nuclear Inspection Division and was trained as a nuclear weapons designer. I was appointed as " Chief of the Nuclear Division.

The Face of Communism

Later, I was one of the officers selected for the task of negotiating with and investigating the North Koreans. They had captured one of our military ships, the U. S. S. Pueblo. It was an unarmed recognizance ship that was gathering information in neutral waters off the coast of Korea. During our negotiations with the North Koreans, it was discovered that the one gun on board had not even been uncovered, let alone fired! My title was Chief of the Joint Observer Team and I investigated incidents along the Demilitarized Zone when they were in violation of the truce. Negotiations were in an atmosphere of consummate hostility and in an atmosphere of immediate threat to the fragile armistice. Korean communist negotiators were an arrogant in-your-face hard-nosed people known for stonewalling, threatening, lying, and always creating untoward incidents for propaganda to improve their position. The Korean Red Army was conducting numerous infiltrations across the DMZ (Demilitarized Zone) designed to intimidate the United States military negotiators, and our South Korean allies. It took 12 months from the time the U.S.S. Pueblo was captured to the release of the imprisoned crew. Negotiations were started after the capture. During that time, an American EC121 radar plane was shot down and the crew captured as well as a helicopter with two pilots who strayed across the DMZ in error.

The Chief Mortician and His Merry Mad Monks

I was called the "Chief Mortician" and my compatriots were known as the "Merry Mad Monks of the DMZ." (Demilitarized Zone). Of course, this was an unofficial organization. When we discovered a point of infiltration in violation of the Korean Armistice, it was my job to photograph any bodies or remains with their clothing, weapons, and other accouterments useful in identifying the enemy. It took me over two weeks to get to the point where I could stomach the stench and the site of rotting bodies. I remember the North Koreans at Panmunjoun used to toy with us, by coughing in our faces. They knew we were afraid of getting tuberculosis. General Woodward of the Army required that all guards had to be six feet tall or over! The negotiations were very tedious and frustrating. The official language designated for the negotiations was Chinese. The Chinese language has the most detailed and exact symbology. So all dialogs had to be translated into Chinese, then in the respective language. Usually, when we would ask a question, we didn't get an answer until two or three meetings later.

Simultaneously, we conducted negotiations for the Pueblo crew in the "Neutral Nations Conference Room," where we got real-time answers regarding Korean activities. The two negotiating processes assisted each other. Finally, an agreement was reached and the American crewmen were released.

Traumatized Americans Released

After enlisting in the Navy, at the end of WWII, Bart Hanchett went through R.O.T.C at Arizona State to become an Artillery Officer. This picture was taken after his experiences with the Pueblo crew release in Korea.

PHOTO COURTESY OF BART HANCHETT

Across a river from Panmunjom was a cluster of trees where the prisoners were instructed to cross the "Bridge of No Return" in single file twenty feet apart. Commander Lloyd Bucher was released first so he could identify each man as he crossed. The men were silent, afraid, and traumatized. The Koreans had told the men that if they looked right or left or made any exclamation, the whole repatriation would be stopped and any prisoner not across the bridge would be returned to the Communist prisons.

One prisoner was dead. The Koreans returned the dead seaman in a crude wooden coffin, which they shoved off a truck causing the lid to pop open revealing a yellowed corpse. Commander Bucher identified the corpse as Seaman Hodges of his original crew. The prison experience was one of unmitigated terror and torture for the American sailors. The Koreans would beat and torture the men until they were almost dead, and then they would be allowed to recover only to begin the process of beatings and torture all over again.

Cleansing of the Communist Stench

Upon their release, the Red Cross gave the men a package of razors, soap, toothbrushes, etc. The men took out the soap, clutching each bar as if it was a precious gift. On the way to meet the press and General Bonesteel, the men asked to stop at the latrine. When I let them out, they all immediately began taking showers. I could understand that they wanted to rid themselves of their horrible experience, but I caught a lot of flack for making the General and press wait!

After my tour in Korea, I was then sent to the Pentagon, where I was the Chief of Personnel Division.

Back to the Field – My Third War, Vietnam

I really didn't enjoy being at the Pentagon at all. I really wanted to be in with the troops, so in 1971, I volunteered to go to Vietnam. I was sent to MACV Headquarters in Saigon where I was the Chief of the Field Operations Division for CORDS. Every day, I would go out in CIA planes and helicopters. I would visit provinces, basically to just check out what was really going on. The U.S. military had been removed, and we worked around the clock, seven days a week. I would gather information and brief, gather information and brief. The only reprieve was the Continental Hotel next to the BOQ. The food was of French influence, and quite good, so on Sundays, I could go over there because I didn't have to be at work until 8:00 am.

After returning from Vietnam, they tried to put me into the Pentagon again, but luckily I was sent to Fort Belvoir, Virginia, where I was Chief of the Nuclear Division in the Nuclear and Chemical Surety Group. I saw nuclear weapons approved to safeguard anti-ballistic missile systems for the Sprint and Spartan systems.

After the Military

In September 1975, I retired from the military. But I didn't stop there. I decided to return to college, this time to get my degree in my area of expertise. I had spent the better part of my life in Mechanical Engineering, so that is what I studied. Five years later, I had my Masters. Janie and I and our three children lived in Virginia until we made the decision to move west again. Our choices were Colorado Springs, or Ojai. I was offered a position in engineering in Ventura, so Ojai it was! We have lived here since Father's Day 1981.

Still at Work and Still Volunteering

Jane and Bart Hanchett, 2001.

PHOTO COURTESY OF BART HANCHETT

I worked for VSE Corporation as an Engineer, then for Advanced Technology. I was recruited by American Management Corporation to run their Ventura County office. I designed an Anechoic Chamber, which was a testing device for HARM Missiles. I eventually built my own consulting company, which I still run today. I also am a volunteer computer specialist rebuilding computers for Sunset School in Oak View, giving kids the tools for tomorrow.

Few Americans including combat veterans have ever had the experience of negotiating with the communist face to face. Through Bart's experience, we get a feeling of the cruelty and callousness of the enemy. Listening to Bart helps underscore the blessings of freedom and the sanctity of human life in a free and open society. The Korean War is long over, but the Communist oppressors in North Korean continue to offend civilized people. His experiences help remind us that we need a strong military defense against the Tiger Nations of the world where the only right is might.

■■■■■■■■■■■■■■■

CLARENCE "ED" HISER

SAILOR, ARMY ARTILLERYMAN, SEABEE

AS TOLD BY HIS BROTHER, DICK HISER

Some men become servicemen as a matter of duty and circumstances. The citizen soldier is the legendary military man that fleshes out the Armed Forces in times of crisis. Then there is another class of person, different and unique, the serviceman that comes from a tradition of military service where service is held in high esteem. This is the story of the Hiser Family Military History and Ed Hiser's continuation of and contribution to that history. Ed died last year and he has now become part of the continuing thread of the family tradition.

From the Revolution to Vietnam—A Patriot Family

The Hiser family began fighting for America in the Revolutionary War where the German immigrants shouldered a Pennsylvania rifle to stop the British. John Hiser served as a private in the Pennsylvania Militia at the age of 17, entering service in 1776. For his service, he received a pension of $25 dollars a year during the last six years of his life. Another Hiser, who was an officer, was paid a little better. He received 4000 acres of land for his service as an officer. How's that compared to $150 for six years received by Private John Hiser! The Hisers were in service again in the Civil War and the Spanish American War. William Hiser served with Teddy Roosevelt's Rough Riders in 1898. He was a Private in Company E of the Oklahoma Volunteers. Another Hiser was killed in the Filipino uprising in the early 1900's. He was killed by a spear when his pistol failed to stop the Moro native. Later, the 45 caliber pistol was introduced for the express purpose of stopping a fanatical Moro dead in his tracks. The 45 created hydro-static shock that could kill instantly. Incidentally, the Moros were Moslems as they are today, and members of our Armed Forces are once again active in trying to suppress the Moro's continuing terrorism.

Father gassed in World War I

Our father did his service in the trenches of World War I as an U.S. Army sergeant. He served in the Americal Division with General Douglas MacArthur. He was gassed in the European action, but recovered sufficiently to lead a fairly normal life. He was a sergeant in charge of the motor pool. By his example of military service, he set the tone for his boys who all volunteered in life long commitment to America and the Constitution.

Family Life
in Southern California in the 1940's

There were three boys and a girl in our immediate family. In 1919, our dad got a job with the Edison Company, so the family lived in a little cabin in Bouquet Canyon, where he worked as a mechanic. Eventually Edison moved us to Ventura. We later moved to Meiners Oaks, behind the old red and white market, which is now where the water company is located. Our grandfather also worked for the Edison Company. He was an engineer. He engineered the Santa Paula Edison station, and the Casitas Springs Edison Station as well.

First Brother into the Navy—Bill Hiser

William Hiser was the first of the Hiser boys to volunteer for the United States Navy in World War II. He set the pattern of for the younger brothers who chose Naval careers, including Ed Hiser and Dick Hiser.

Bill Hiser on his return from duty in the Pacific during World II

PHOTO COURTESY OF DICK HISER

Second Brother, Ed Hiser —Booted out of the Navy

Clarence "Ed" Hiser, was second in the line up. Clarence's middle name was Ed. He didn't like the name Clarence, and it was also too long, so we just called him Ed. He was born on December 21st, 1925, in Watts, California.

Ed hated school, so he seldom attended, and when he did, he was always getting in trouble. He usually skipped school and went duck hunting or fishing down along the pier in Ventura. It was a time when fish and game were more plentiful in the Ojai Valley. It was also a time when getting a job and making a living were more important than finishing high school. When World War II broke out, Bill, our oldest brother, went and enlisted. He served as a serviceman on a ship. Ed decided that he was going to join the Navy too, so he joined in 1942. He had a slight problem though. When he entered boot camp in San Diego, they found out that he was only fifteen, so they shipped him back home! He waited until he was probably one day after he turned 17 and enlisted in the Navy again.

U.S. Navy career in World War II–Tarawa

Ed served during the war on four different ships: the U.S.S. Breton CVE 23, the U.S.S. Jason ARH 1, the U.S.S. Norris DD 895 and the U.S.S. Gunnison. Ed was a coxswain or boatswain. Later, he was a ship serviceman until he was wounded during an amphibious operation on Tarawa. Tarawa was one of the early Marine landings in the Gilbert Islands where we were fighting against the Japanese. The assault on Tarawa was the beginning of a whole series of amphibious operations leap-frogging across the Central Pacific. The men of these early landings experienced heavy casualties because they were just developing the tactics and strategies for assaulting fortified beaches. It was a trial by error and the servicemen suffered heavily during the learning process. It was at Tarawa that the Navy and Marines learned how to coordinate naval gunfire with air strikes, followed by assault waves of Infantry and then by larger landing craft carrying artillery, armor, and supplies.

After being wounded in the leg, Ed was sent back home and was stationed in San Diego. He re-enlisted and met his wife. While on leave and visiting his parents in Ojai in 1949, he was "drafted" by the U.S. Forest Service to fight a major forest fire in the Los Padres National Forest. He also was married in 1949. After his discharge from the Navy four years later, he moved to Meiners Oaks with his wife and children.

The Korean War
— Army National Guard Artilleryman

Ed joined the Naval Reserves after World War II, but the long commute for drills in Santa Barbara were so time consuming that he switched to the California National Guard Artillery in Ventura. The artillery battery met in an old industrial building off Garden Street in Ventura. Almost immediately, the Korean War broke out, so on September 1 of 1950, Ed was federalized and sent to Camp Cooke, California. Today, Camp Cooke is called Vandenberg Air Force Base.

During the Korean War Camp Cooke became a training center for 50,000 troops, many of whom were shipped to Korea as replacements and fillers. The core of the National Guard component was kept intact at the insistence of General Daniel Huddleston, the divisional commander who did not want the Division fragmented and dispersed. General Hudelson wanted the Division to fight as an intact 40th Infantry California National Guard Division. After almost a year of section, battery, and regimental combat training, the Division was shipped to Japan as occupation troops and provided security against an anticipated Russian attack of the Japanese Islands. The California politicians were fond of saying that the California National Guard would never fight on the field of battle; only draftees and regular army troops would be sent to Korea.

In early January, Clarence found himself loading an APA troop landing ship in Yokohama Harbor. His ship sailed south and around Japan to link up with a massive naval convoy headed for Inchon, Korea. Unloading at Inchon, Ed's Division moved quickly to the front lines relieving the 24th Infantry Division.

Clarence "Ed" Hiser upon his return from Tarawa

PHOTO COURTESY OF DICK HISER

He was assigned as part of a forward observer team, which was positioned with division infantry on the MLR or front lines in January of 1952. As part of a Forward Observer team, Ed helped adjust artillery fire into Chinese bunkers and troops in the field.

The 40th Infantry MLR or front line was a relatively shallow defense consisting of foxholes and bunkers. A concerted attack by Chinese forces could easily penetrate that line except for the constant artillery bombardments and air strikes that kept the Chinese forces at bay. While working with the Forward Observer team, Ed was shot in the arm by a sniper, so he returned to the US. He was discharged as a Sergeant First Class.

Rest between Wounds and War

For a while, Ed worked for a movie star named Rory Calhoun. Rory had a ranch up in Rose Valley. He played in Western movies during the 40's, 50's, and 60's. The

Hiser family was into horses and we kept our horses up there. Rory decided to donate the ranch to the Boy Scouts, so Ed went to work for the Forestry Service. He ended up being stationed at Lake Piru. He had five kids at this time. He met up with some guy there and decided to go into business with him, building big powerboats. The business partner wasn't too honest, because he took all the money, and took off. So Ed went back to ranch work as a foreman. In 1969 there was a big flood and they had to helicopter food in. Life was kind of rough on the family up there in the mountains, so they moved back down to Ojai. Ed re-enlisted in the Navy with the Seabees as a heavy equipment operator.

Third Wound Ends Ed's Career

By this time Ed had six kids including two grown sons. One was serving in the Marine Corps and the other in the U.S. Navy. Ed reenlisted for the third and last time. He was deployed down to Diego Garcia in the Indian Ocean and other similar isolated posts.

Luck runs out
—Shot in the face and shot down

When the Vietnam War began, he signed on for three tours of duty in the war zone. Ed was pushing his luck and every thing seemed to happen in threes. On his third deployment to Nam, he was wounded. He was hit in the mouth with shrapnel. They loaded him on a plane in Da Nang to be sent to Tokyo, but the plane was shot down right after they took off. So they had to ditch that plane. He survived and was reloaded onto another plane. Ed ended his Vietnam tour of duty at the Naval Hospital in San Diego. His last duty station was at the Naval Air Station at Lemoore near Hanford, California. While Ed was there, he got pneumonia and he suffered a collapsed lung, so he received a medical discharge. Three wounds in three wars, three Purple Hearts and a Bronze Star qualified him for retirement. Ed packed his medals and sea bag and retired to serving as a Federal Police Officer for the next ten years up in the Medford, Oregon area. He was a member of the VFW Post 11461 and the American Legion Post 482 in Ojai. On January 9, 2001, Ed passed away. Six children and ten grandchildren survive him.

A soldier's uniform tells his history. Patches tell of the branch of service. Hash marks tell the length of service. Overseas hash marks tell of the years that he served overseas. His chevrons and insignia tell his rank and authority. The ribbons tell of wars, battles, wounds, places of service, and awards for courage. The uniform is a symbolic record of achievement. Today, there is a mantel in the Hiser home. It is graced with the family coat of arms, a Pennsylvania rifle, patches, ribbons, awards, Purple Hearts, the Bronze Star, chevrons, and hash marks. It is his family's place of honor for their father's service. It is their memorial to their Dad, a courageous soldier, sailor, and Seabee.

Clarence "Ed" Hiser's military achievement wall at his home before his death.

PHOTO COURTESY OF DICK HISER

JIM RODGERS

WWII, KOREA AND VIETNAM
— PROFESSIONAL SOLDIER AND AIRMAN

Jim Rodgers has experienced the greatest era of American history, progress, and change. From his early life in Texas to his retirement in Ojai, First Sergeant Rodgers has witnessed history first hand. Indeed, he helped make history, real history of real men and women ignored in the modern textbooks. He tells it as it happened.

A Little Bit of Family History in the Wild West

My family was all from Texas, true pioneers of the state. I have five sisters. I was the only boy. One of my family members was known for arresting John Wesley Harden at the height of his career, after he had killed more than 46 people. John Wesley would just kill people for no good reason. Like one time, he was in a hotel, and a guy in the next room was snoring, he fired through the wall at him...things like that you know. Wild Bill Hickock was supposed to be afraid of him. He was just mean!

So anyway, my Granddad was born during the Civil War, and he and several brothers came out of the Confederacy. My Granddad's nickname was "Big Ed." He never weighed over 130 pounds in his life, and he was about five foot seven. It was a joke because "Little Ed," his first cousin, weighed over 240 pounds and had real trouble finding horses that he could ride! But they were buddies. Granddad was City Marshall at 18.

One day he had to go down into the river bottom to arrest this Black fellow who was picking cotton. He went galloping off to arrest him—this was Big Ed. So when the guy saw him coming, he just lay down on his cotton sack and said, "Okay Mr. Ed, I know what yah wan, here I is, go head an rest me." So Big Ed picked him up and said, "I'll be back in a little bit." Big Ed went back and got Little Ed. They caught up with the Black guy, and they were thinking that they were going to have to drag this guy up and haul him off to prison. But the Black guy jumped up and swam across the river. It was in full flood at that time. Anyway, it was a joke about "Little Ed" and "Big Ed."

The Great Depression Hits Texas

I was born in 1920 in Hico, Texas. It was on the railroad. Most of the roads were dirt. I was born in my great-aunt's house. She was a nurse, a sister to my grandmother, who was a schoolteacher. My Grandmother was not my Grandfather's first wife. His first wife died in childbirth. So anyway, when the railroad died in the 30's, the town died. My parents had met during the oil-boom in the 20's. I remember as a child, seeing my first lynching. I was nine years old, and I had snuck out during the night. I saw them take a guy out of the jail, and they lynched him. Times were different back then.

We always had cars though, even though it was the Great Depression. We were living on an oil lease in West Texas. My Daddy got a job as supervisor on the oil lease. About that time, the bottom dropped out of the oil industry, and the ranchers went bankrupt too. But we owned a house back in Eastland. It had indoor plumbing and everything! But it burned, and the insurance didn't pay for anything because the insurance companies had gone bankrupt. And we wound up out in Coleman County with my Grandmother and Uncle Roy Sanders, my mother's oldest brother. It was a little two-bedroom house. But, like so many people during the depression, we still owned an automobile, and we went to school. I was about ten, and I learned to write. We lived there for about two years until my Daddy could save up enough money to buy some property in Erath County, Texas. We grew up there, and I got through the tenth grade.

I would go to school and find whatever books I could find in the library, and I would read them all. I had taught myself to read when I was about four or five years old. They put me in Kindergarten because I was reading the funny papers. It took me a long time to re-educate myself because when I would read, I would learn words by how they looked. I had never heard them spoken, and they weren't teaching in school, what I was reading. Like the Bible, I read the entire Bible when I was nine years old! I went into Stephensville to high school, and I just couldn't cut that. I read everything. My aunt had sat me down when I was about seven years old and straightened me out in math.

So, I quit high school, because we weren't speaking the same language. They wouldn't teach me what I wanted to know. I wanted to know so many things and people wouldn't tell me. My Dad didn't talk either. I took the GED, and later I also took the college GED, and breezed through that, so I had an equivalent to two years in college.

I Wanted to Go Places

I had three uncles who were WWI veterans. They wouldn't talk a whole lot about it. I lived in the country outside Stephensville when I quit school at 15. I wanted to go places. I was curious about the world. A guy who was living in our town came home from the Navy without a leg. He had been a sailor and he had lost his leg in a motorcycle accident. He had lots of stories! He had a good life, he got paid, and he got to go places and see things! And that's when the bug kind of bit me. I hitchhiked over to Dallas. I used to hitchhike or ride freight trains everywhere; that way I got to see more. Anyway, I didn't think much of the Navy, and when I walked into the courthouse, the Navy office was on the 3rd floor, and the Army office was on the 1st floor. And that's why I wound up in the Army—I didn't have to hike up two flights of stairs to the Navy!

The Machine Gun Cavalry

I was 18 years old and weighed 117 pounds. They shipped us to El Paso and loaded us all up on the trucks, took us to Fort Bliss, and unloaded us. They then divided us up according to our weight. Those that weighed over 140 pounds were on one side, and those under, on the other side. None of us weighed much over 160, because it was the Depression. The reason they did that was because Cavalry horses are lighter than artillery horses. That was our classification system in those days! We went through 12 weeks of recruit drill, and were assigned to Machine Gun Troop, 1st Cav Div.

This was 1938. Twelve of us went in, but four "went over the hill" That meant, that if you couldn't cut it, you just went over the hill. It was peacetime, so nobody said anything. There were still chain gangs building Skyline Blvd. in El Paso during this time. I started my career in Texas at Fort Bliss as a cavalry soldier on October 25th. When I say cavalry, I don't mean mechanized armor—I mean horses that carried the pack 37-mm anti tank guns and heavy 50 caliber machine guns. But that wasn't what I wanted to do. I wanted to go! Not just from here to there on a horse either, so I transferred from the horse cavalry to the Army Air Corps at San Antonio Texas. I got down to Randolph Field, and they asked me, "What can you do?" I said that I could drive a truck, cause I had gotten my drivers license when I was 16. They said, "Can you really?" And I had a soft job until December 1939 when I was shipped to Moffet Field California.

Boy, Did I Get To Go Places with the Army

In 1940, after spring training, we were on a convoy, it was a practice thing, and we went to Medford, Oregon. Colonel Eakers had arranged with somebody for the camp location. We went out and camped on the Rogue River. We took mattress covers made out of canvas; wet them in the river, held them up to the wind, until we had a big sausage-type thing. Then we'd tie them up, lie on them, and shoot the rapids down the river, long before they had ever thought of what they do now. We had to make our own fun. We didn't lose anybody; we all made it.

Jeeps and Jeep Drivers, A Novelty

Right before I went up there, I saw a big ad for somebody that was making some Jeeps. Jeep came to California in 1940. The word "Jeep" came from the Ford Model, "GP—General Purpose," that's why we started calling them "Jeeps," short for GP. We got two of them. We would do 300 miles up Mount Tamalpais near Petaluma, and stuff like that. Testing. Anyway, one day our First Sergeant insisted on driving me. Normally, I wouldn't let anyone drive the jeep because I was the motor dispatcher, but those days were during a transition between the "old army" and the "new army." I was "old army."

Later, Colonel Eakers had gotten a hold of a thorough-bred mare that was bred. He didn't know it when he got her at the time, but she had a foal, so he had a small stable built on the far side of the field. He put the horses down there, and he was having a time with them. He heard that I had been in the Cavalry, so I was taking care of his horses. That was a pattern of my life all through the Army. I could do anything that needed to be done, and I never worried about rank.

I went through two wars as a Corporal, because I didn't need a rank. I always knew how to get along. Anyway, the First Sergeant got someone to say, "Oh let him drive the Jeep." So, he took off with his company clerk, and they got around the far side of the field, and sure enough, they drove off the embankment! Neither one of them was hurt, but it demolished the Jeep. So now we only had one Jeep. And from that day on, you had to be vetted before you could drive that Jeep. That was the Jeep we drove up to Medford. When we got there, the editor of the newspaper, the publisher and their wives, were all invited out to be wined and dined. And of course, they wanted to ride in the Jeep. So I took them on a wild ride up and down the river banks, and I picked a low spot in the river and we went sailing down there into the water! I got my picture in the paper and everything. Good publicity! That was Medford.

I was happy, taking care of the Colonel's horse, driving up and down and all around, as a motor pool dispatcher.

While working in supply at Hamilton Air Base, I had to drive supplies down to Martinez where the Navy was repairing two destroyers that had returned from their war. These were British Navy destroyers that had been traded to Britain in exchange for America's right to use British bases for 99 years in the Caribbean. The ships were shot to pieces. While we were delivering supplies, we could see workers removing bodies of British sailors who had been trapped in the ship. The scene was a precursor to the war America was about to enter.

Life between Hitches

I was discharged from the Army-just two months prior to the attack of Pearl Harbor. I headed for Texas! On my way home I stopped off in Las Vegas, which was a boomtown then. They were building Hoover Dam. I did a little gambling, but I didn't do so well. I had two silver dollars in my pocket, and I was hitch hiking near El Paso one day. I was arrested and taken to jail because I was a white male; it was assumed that I was a draft dodger fleeing the country!

Draft dodging in World War II was a serious crime. Military service in wartime was a duty and responsibility. To avoid military service was considered a shirking of duty. Many men were trying to cross the Mexican border to avoid the draft. It irritated me that I would be considered a draft dodger, so I wouldn't tell them anything! I said, "I just got out of 3 years in the Army, what do you mean you're picking me up!" They hauled me in and dropped me off at the Sheriff's station. I had seen the chain gangs down there, so I decided to haul my discharge papers out. The officials realized that I was honorably discharged and was too young for the draft anyway, so they released me.

The Infantry

I got back to Texas. I had just missed the cut-off date for the draft by just one week, so I was sure that I would get orders any day. When I had been home two weeks, my oldest sister got married. While on the way back to her new husband's home, the guy that was driving the car had an accident and wrecked the car. A day later, Pearl Harbor was attacked. The driver of the car died. My brother-in-law was able to stay out of WW II because he got a lick on the head, and my sister suffered two compound fractures of both femur bones.

All of a sudden, things were kind of tight with money because there wasn't any health insurance. Daddy and I went down to Fort Hood. He was a carpenter, and I got on with a concrete crew. We worked about eight weeks. We sent our entire checks home. When we were all done there, I still hadn't heard anything regarding the draft. I was getting restless, and was tired of waiting around, so I just went on over and rejoined the Army.

Because of my prior military experience, I was assigned to a training command and reception center with the rank of corporal. I re-entered service as basic Infantry cadre. I had a high AGC score, the Army equivalent of an IQ test. Captain Skelton, a WWI veteran said, "You can't just sit here, you really ought to do something!" I said, "Okay, well I don't want the Infantry" because I had gone through the Infantry Non Commissioned Officers School while I was sitting around running the Bachelor Officers' Quarters. And boy, they put you through it! I liked the information, but I didn't want anything of the Infantry, so I chose air cadet training. But I was unable to complete the course because I had a middle ear problem. It ended my cadet status, but not before I had six months of training at Texas A and M, an equivalent to two years of college. I was transferred to Lowry Field in Denver.

There was always something going on. I was sent from there to the Mojave Desert. From there, I was shipped to England as an aircraft armorer.

U.S.S. Argentine to England

We went over on the U.S.S. Argentina. It was a passenger ship that had been converted. It was double loaded, meaning that every bunk was filled, and the same number of men also slept on deck. We would rotate back and forth. It took us 12 days to get to England, but it wasn't too bad. We came under torpedo attack. Fortunately, I was sleeping on deck that night! We made it okay though, no big deal. I was still surplus at this time. I was assigned to command a base defense detachment, improvising an air defense system. We had four squads armed with fifty caliber machine guns for use as anti-aircraft defense. Our anti-aircraft batteries had been shipped to Europe after the invasion.

Buzz Bombs over England

The "buzz bomb" attacks were occurring over England at this time. For those unfamiliar with the term, the "buzz bomb" was a missile system developed by the Germans late in World War II. It was basically a ballistic missile designed to terrorize the British people, and it packed a warhead that was quite destructive. The Royal Air Force had developed a tactic whereby a chase plane would get close to the wings of the "buzz bomb" and flip it over causing it to go out of control. The explosive impact was quite a blast! The Battle of the Bulge was raging and the army was desperate for Infantrymen—so I volunteered for Infantry training for deployment to France and later to Germany.

Tidworth Barracks-Military Prison

I had my basic infantry training at Tidworth Barracks--also a military prison for U.S. military personnel. This was my fourth time in basic training. They didn't need us right away so they put us on prison guard. I remember asking one Black guy, while I was taking a break, "What the hell did you do anyhow?" He said, "That M---- F----, I didn't like him." I said, "Who?" He said, "That First Sergeant." I said, "Well, what did you do?" He said, "I cut his head off. I say, I cut his head aaaawwwl the way off!" They were criminals! With an Army of millions of people; you will have some criminals in there.

Anyway, that didn't last very long and I was still surplus, I didn't belong to anybody. So eventually, they broke us up into groups of 12. World War II had just ended. I was stationed in France as an Air-force squadron, supply sergeant. We began our deployment back to the U.S. through Antwerp in a dense fog. My bunk was deep in the hold of an old Liberty ship below the waterline. Our ship was lightly loaded and had only roughly three hundred troops so we bobbed up and down like a cork.

Even though the war was winding down, a lingering hazard of naval warfare persisted. Many floating mines were still in the North Sea and ships were being lost as the mines came loose and drifted into the shore and shipping lanes. During our return everyone was on edge. We ran into a storm in the North Sea, and every time we heard the clinks and bangs of the storm, we were all sure that the vessel was going to explode. At first, we were a bit sedated, as we were able to stash some liquor aboard the ship. But that ran out in a few days—with the exception of one soldier who had a large bottle of champagne, which he was saving to celebrate with his wife when he got home. We had all been expecting a thirty-day furlough when we returned home. But four days outside of New York harbor, we received word that the atom bombs had just been dropped on Japan—and that they had surrendered! That fellow opened that bottle of champagne and we celebrated then and there!

The Cold War

Even though World War II was over, the threat of war was not over. The United Nations had been fractured by an East-West confrontation. The United States wanted a return to peacetime and quickly demobilized, but the Soviet Union was in an expansionist posture. Soviet troops were occupying the Eastern European countries and had moved massive tank forces up to the borders of the free western European nations. Every GI in Europe was in harm's way as Russia rattled the saber, and the occupation soldiers in Germany were particularly vulnerable and expendable!

The Texas Navy

Back home, I got out of the Army—again! I worked at a few odd jobs. I was working in construction in Freeport, Texas and struck up a conversation with a guy that owned a shrimp boat. I said, "to hell with construction work!" and I went to work out on that shrimp boat. It was fun! Take a case of beer down there, and we'd go out two or three days. That was when I went to work for the "Texas Navy." You see, there were foreigners from Louisiana and Mississippi, and they were shrimp fishing in Texas coastal waters. It was because they had just discovered these big "golden shrimp" that only come out at night. And here they come, these big old thirty-foot trawlers. They'd go in and strut through our little shrimp fleet, and off they'd go back to their home ports.

The Texas Fish and Game Commission came down and they would assign an agent to selected boats. One night, we nailed one guy. He was a Greek guy out of New Orleans. He came charging down through there, we hailed him, he answered. The Fish and Game agent stood up and hauled up the Texas flag, and boarded him. That was how I was part of the "Texas Navy!" Anyway, I got bored with that and I found myself rounding up sheep on horseback. It really wasn't for me, so I decided, once again, to enlist in the Army.

Back in the Army in Various Assignments

When I re-enlisted, they asked me what I would like to do. I decided to go into the Transportation Corps. and I wound up at Newport News, Virginia. I was then sent back to Germany to serve in the Constabulary Corps. They still had horses in the Constabulary, and they did police patrol work on horses. I thought, Oh hey, that would be great!" I had been away from horses for a long time, so that was what I wanted to do. This other guy who was with me had had enough of being in the action, and he decided he would like to be a clerk and serve behind as desk. Anyway, I wound up in the clerk's school because of my high AGT score. I was sent to the Constabulary unit back with the horses!

I wound up in ECOM Headquarters, as high as you could go and was eventually assigned as Chief Clerk of the Transportation office of the European Command Center. I was responsible for scheduling U.S. military prisoners, war brides, soldiers, and army families for shipment to the U.S. There were thousands upon thousands of war brides from Berlin alone at the time of the Berlin Airlift when the Soviets blocked all land and water routes into Berlin. One famous prisoner that we processed for return was the infamous Axis Sally. She was an American traitor who broadcast propaganda for the Nazis during the war.

I continued working with the Transportation office until my enlistment was up, then I went back to the States and I was due for re enlistment again. I asked for the Counter Intelligence School at Fort Halibird, MD. More schooling at Army expense and then we volunteered to go back to Germany where friends had advised me that a new assignment was waiting. I knew that something was going to happen. I thought it would be better to be in Europe, so that if the balloon went up, I could submerge myself in the population. I worked with the Adjutant General's office with European Command, processing personnel within the civilian employees of the Army. Many of these people were reserve officers who were being classified and slotted for mobilization in the event of war with Russia--which the entire military assumed was about to occur. This new mobilization created many opportunities and good jobs in the command structure.

Things Were Heating Up In Korea

Later, I was transferred to a Recon Company of the 1st Infantry Division, "The Big Red One," headquartered in Erlanger, Germany. We were sent to the Czech border where we found ourselves eyeball to eyeball with the massive Soviet Army! Later at Graffenwehr, I trained troops for CBR warfare (chemical, biological, and radioactive warfare). I then became Chief Clerk in the G-3 section of the 1st Infantry Division. I decided that I needed to settle down and I thought to myself, "I've been in the military 12 years, so I had better get moving." So I became a Master Sergeant. In those days prior to specialization, a regular army career soldier could find himself in almost any assignment imaginable. NCO's had to be flexible. As the result, my service in Europe ran the gamut. I helped set up training commands, worked in communications, served in Division Headquarters of the "Big Red One," and helped dispose of German chemical munitions.

Missile Defense Command – On to Korea

Back in the States, I was assigned to a medical command doing schedules and editing training documents. I didn't much like that assignment, so I decided to go to the Nike Air Defense School at Fort Bliss--where I had started my career as a horse cavalryman back in 1938! I spent the next few years in the Nike Missile Battalion Operations section—but restless and anxious for new challenges, I interviewed for Sgt. Major for KMAG (Korean Military Advisory Group) with subsequent assignment to Korea. My final years of military service were served once again as First Sergeant of the Headquarters Missile Battalion in Pasadena and as Safety Officer for the missile defense group. In 1963 I retired and moved to Oxnard. Then in 1971, I moved to Ojai because my wife wanted to get into the Arabian horse industry. From the horse cavalry to an infantryman, to air cadet, to military advisor, to missile man—I have lived a lifetime of military versatility and experience. It was the way it was in the old Army.

Finally "Kicking Back"

I retired with the rank of First Sergeant (E-8), and finally earned the right to "kick back" and enjoy a restful retirement. I have served on three continents, backing the military policies of this nation for over three wartime periods. I served the veterans of Ventura County as the Veterans Service Officer for 10 years. And for six years, I worked at Point Mugu in procurement and disposal of government property. My other assignments included work with EDD and the Ventura County Sheriff's custodian division. As a member of the American Legion, I continued to look after my "troops," as the American Legion claims officer. As a professional soldier, I continue to provide leadership and advice to my citizen soldier comrades in the veteran's organizations.

My last employment was as a hospital representative for the American Legion. I worked for six years at the VA Clinic in Santa Barbara, CA from which I retired in 1985. This was my fourth retirement.

Master Sergeant Jim Rodgers, back in his 1963 uniform (at retire-ment) for the 2001 Ojai Independence Day parade, shows his appreciation to the Air National Guard for allowing older retired Vets to ride on their trucks in the parade.

PHOTO COURTESY OF JIM RODGERS

VETERANS OF TWO WARS

■■■■■■■■■■■■■■■■■■■■■

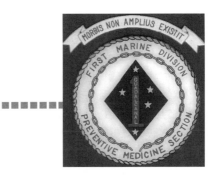

DICK HISER

KOREA AND VIETNAM
—NAVY CORPSMAN, THE ULTIMATE SERVICE

Many young men do not relate to the artificialness of modern education. Once they learn to read, write, and compute they see no purpose in many of the mundane courses of modern public education. Their inner being is a bundle of pent up energy and curiosity about the world. They want action and adventure but are frequently without purposeful direction and sufficient motivation. For countless generations and millions of young men, military service has provided the outlet for their need for action and adventure coupled with direction and purpose. For those young men who can accept the discipline and withstand rigorous training, the military has turned many youth into focused and responsible citizens.

This story is about Dick Hiser, raised in the rural atmosphere of the Ojai Valley of the 1940's. It was a time when everyone in the valley knew everyone else. The school system was the same with the emphasis on course work that confined the active and the restless to a classroom seat six hours a day. Dick Hiser came from a long tradition of men of action as the Hiser family had been fighting America's wars back to the Revolutionary War. But the fact that there is a family tradition does not always translate into complete comprehension of what military service entails and the risks involved. Military service can be the most disciplined of all human activities and the end result may be fatal, negating all the beneficial advantages of training and discipline. This story documents the evolution of Dick from an unsophisticated and unfocused youth to a highly educated and highly trained Medical Corpsman and medical technician. As he evolves in maturity, he evolves in his commitment of service to people and society.

Born at Home in Ventura

I was born at home in Ventura, during the Depression on May 2nd, 1933. It was the worst year of the Great Depression. It was a turbulent year in the world scene. Nations were in turmoil. Roosevelt had been elected in the United States and Hitler had come to power in Germany. I was number three in the line up of Hiser children. When I was twelve years old, we moved to Ojai, it was 1945. World War II had just ended. I was in the fourth grade at Ojai Elementary. I started working when I was just a teenager.

One job was as an oil driller, off Ventura Avenue in Ventura. My uncle was in the oil business. I had a midnight shift, and it was cold and miserable. I was out there on one of those rigs, and some guy was up above me pulling pipes. He said, "Oops!" and he dropped a wrench, and it came right down and knocked my hard hat right off. After that I said, I quit, I'm going home!

Another job I had was planting and picking cotton up in Cuyama. It was a summer job; it must have been 110 degrees out there. I did what they call "choppin' cotton." We had to space the plants out chopping out the weeds.

Oh boy, after 12 hours of that, for a whole summer, the Navy started to look like a pretty good alternative!

In Nordhoff High School When Korea Starts

I was going to Nordhoff High School, the local high school for the Ojai Valley. I was in the eleventh grade and the Korean War started heating up. My friends were discussing enlistment and the pending draft upon graduation. There were four of us. One day in September, we decided to meet in Ventura at the recruiting station. We agreed that we'd all go in the Navy. Well, I was the only one that showed up! So, while I was waiting for my friends, there was this Navy Recruiter. He was a pretty smart fox. As an enlistment NCO, it was his mission to obtain recruits. He certainly knew how to entice youngsters to sign the enlistment papers. He said, "You go ahead and fill out the paperwork, and when your buddies get here, they can go ahead and fill them out then." Well, none of them showed up!

Number Three Son to the Navy
—Mom said, "Oh no, no!"

So I just went ahead and signed up, seeing how I was there and all. Then he told me that I had to catch a bus at 4:00 in the morning in Ventura, because I needed to take my physical in Los Angeles! I went home and told my mom, and she did like all moms do, "Oh no, no." she cried.

Well at that time I was a skinny kid, I only weighed about 118 pounds, but I got through my physical, and they put me on an train to San Diego, bound for boot camp. The put me on this awful train. That thing had more cracks and leaks in it! The wind just blew right through it. It was like a left over from the early Western days, the vintage train used in the days of Jesse James.

It seemed to take forever to get to San Diego, over a day and a half from Los Angeles to San Diego! One of my buddies finally got there the next day. But we didn't get to get together because he was in another company. For the next 22 years, the Navy owned me—body and soul.

Korea and Cinderella Liberty in Yokohama, Japan

When I got out of boot camp in late October, I went aboard ship. It was a troop transport ship. As the Korean War wound to a close, I was in Pusan, Korea aboard the U.S.S. Mitchell off-loading troops, standing watch, and helping to maintain the ship as a Boatswain Striker. I spent several months just sailing from San Francisco to Hawaii, Okinawa, Guam, Formosa, Korea, and Japan. While we were off the coast of Korea, we got shot at. We had gotten in just enough to get shelled, so we had to back out about a mile, then we went further down to drop the troops off and headed back to Japan.

Village scene on Okinawa

PHOTO COURTESY OF DICK HISER

I remember my first trip into Yokohama. I was probably eighteen or nineteen years old, and in Yokohama you could drink because there was no age limit. Well, like so many young sailors, I got drunker than a skunk, and we were on "Cinderella Liberty." That meant that you had to be back aboard ship before midnight. As a kid here in Ojai, I used to do a lot of swimming up at Wheeler's Gorge or Matilija Lake. I loved to swim! So between where the bar was and the ship was tied up, there were about seven canals you had to cross. On the way back, I decided that I wanted to go swimming. Crossing over one of the canal bridges, I decided to dive into the canal and go for a swim. In the dark, I thought I was diving into water, but I ended up in the middle of a sampan, a small Oriental boat. Being judgment impaired from my youthful indiscretion, I would have broken my neck if I hadn't been so relaxed! I later learned that Oriental waterways are not the most healthful for swimmers. But I finally got back to the ship without further problems.

To Formosa (now Taiwan)

We made a trip into Formosa, which is now Taiwan. This was in 1952 - just seven years after WW II had ended. I would have thought that the Japanese would have hated us. But they didn't. The people were just as friendly as could be! One day, I was climbing a ladder with a five-gallon can of "red lead" paint weighing about fifty pounds. The ship took a roll, and I slipped and fell down the ladder, and that can of paint came down on top of me. Luckily, it didn't come open, but I was injured and I had to be hospitalized. So they took me up to sick bay. While I was there, I noticed that the "Docs" got to sleep on six inch mattresses and could stand watch inside of sickbay instead of up on the bridge, which was a cold and miserable place. We had to sleep on hard canvas, so it didn't take much prompting from a Navy Corpsman to talk me into becoming a Corpsman.

Navy Corpsman at Camp Pendleton

I put in for Hospital Corps School. I had been aboard ship for about two years. Time flew so fast during those years. Hospital Corps School was like four years of college, crammed into twelve months. I had left high school because I was not into books and study. Suddenly, I was thrust into study and learning more intense than anything I had ever experienced in public school.

Unless you have experienced such a disciplined and difficult military school, you have no idea of the intellectual demands. Suddenly, I was shifted into high gear and was studying with an intensity I never expected of myself. However, I could see the purpose behind the rigorous instruction. I was studying to learn to save human life. After completing Hospital Corps School in San Diego, I got assigned to Camp Pendleton in the orthopedic ward. We were treating Marines coming back from Korea.

I was stationed at Camp Pendleton for about three years. While there, I developed an interest in clinical laboratory work, so I put in for Lab School.

The Human Sub Chaser

I mentioned before, I used to love to swim. We used to go down to Carlsbad, and there was a cliff along there with a beautiful little beach. We'd get a bonfire going and have a few drinks. It was fun. I was only about twenty years old at this time. Three of us went swimming. While down at the beach swimming, a submarine surfaced off the coast. It was on maneuvers from San Diego. I said, "Hey I'm going to swim out to that sub, I'll race you guys!" So we hit the water, and were swimming' away! I kept swimming and looking back, and pretty soon I looked back and there was nobody back there.

I finally made it out to that sub. Boy did it seem like it was a long way out there! An old guy came up to me and said, "Here, have a cup of coffee." Well, we got to talking and I asked him how far off the shore they were. He said, "Oh, about 2500 yards." Pretty soon the public address system came on and said, "Were getting under way." So, I jumped back into the water with a Mae West life preserver.

I looked back at the shore and those guys on the beach looked like ants. I was a long way out in the ocean. I got just outside the breakers and a big black fin started circling me. I finally got into the surf, and it left. I got up onto the shore and I said, "Okay you rats, where you been?" They were drinking, and they said, "Here's your five bucks, you won." They thought I was crazy. I still have that coffee mug from the sub. I did some crazy things when I was a young sailor!

More OJT – Pathology and Morgues

Through OJT or on-the-job training, I became involved in pathology and assisted in the morgue. We examined corpses from babies to 90-year-old people. I saw Marines who had gone out and been in car wrecks from being drunk and stuff. A lot of times I had to get the bodies ready for the pathologist to do autopsies. I've never really talked much about that part of my military experience. From there, I transferred to Point Mugu in Ventura County. My new duties included service as a crash crew member and ambulance duty. I also served in Santa Cruz and San Nicholas Islands, both off the coast of Southern California, and eventually Point Arguello.

Dick Hiser as a young Navy seaman

PHOTO COURTESY OF DICK HISER

You Mean the Marines Do Not Have Medics!

Though I was quite savvy about the military, I was totally ignorant of one fact. I did not know that the U.S. Marines don't have their own corpsmen. I didn't know that Navy Corpsmen were the ones that provided direct medic support to Combat Marine Infantry. That was a shock to me especially since I had not planned on a career in the U.S. Marine Corps! One day, I just found myself up to my eyeballs in Marine Infantry training, learning to read maps, firing weapons, compass reading, amphibious landings, and medical treatment of wounds and injuries.

Most of my sea duties were with the Marines. Of course, the Navy Corpsmen had to learn about the Geneva Convention and how it applied to Corpsmen. However, Americans discovered that the North Koreans and North Vietnamese did not respect the Geneva Convention and Corpsmen were fair game for communist gunners.

Training and More Training while Seeing the World

Next, I was assigned to sea duty. My unit was with an amphibious unit referred to euphemistically as, "Preferred Sea Duty." Like all things military, the title had nothing to do with reality, least of all, my preferences. The title really meant that our unit was always on the alert for deployment to some hostile area. After training at Camp Pendleton I attended additional training at Camp Fuji in Japan and Camp Swabb on Okinawa. Eventually, I received orders for lab school in San Diego.

Most of the sailors I served with were in the 18 to 22 year old age bracket. At age 29, married with one child and two step-kids—I didn't have it so easy. I had to study twice as hard. Those others guys were going out and whooping it up every night, but I had all these responsibilities.

I ended up being the Adjutant because I had the most rank, and I graduated 7th in the class. Not bad considering there were 21 of us in the class. Surprised the heck out of me! When I got out, the blood bank wanted me, and the chemistry department wanted me. I decided to work for the chemistry department. At that time, they had just started automated chemistry testing using blood panels, made by Technicon. I stayed there a long time until we got new orders.

Preventative Medicine in Naples, Italy

Prior to Vietnam getting so hot and heavy, the Navy had what they called the Bureau of Personnel. They handled all the orders. So the Bureau of Medicine and Surgery took over the assignments and the rotation of Corpsman. Anyway, the orders came in. At that time, you went to a ship, to Vietnam, then back to a ship, or visa versa. Well seven orders came in. Four of them were to a ship, two of them were to Vietnam, and one was to the Naval Hospital in Naples, Italy. So guess who got Naples, Italy?

It was supposed to be a four-year tour, so the Navy sent my family and me over to Italy where I served in Preventative Medicine for Naval Forces in the Mediterranean. I hadn't been there two months, and they cut my tour down to two years. But I had already moved my whole family over there. While there, the War in Vietnam became a hot war. Suddenly, my life and services received a new direction—again. The priority needs of combat Marines took precedence over the operation of a preventative medical clinic in Italy.

They must have thought I was an Admiral

So I was deployed to Vietnam so fast that I arrived in the combat zone in Class A uniform with my hash marks, stripes, and ribbons decorating my uniform--dress blues. It was July, and it was so hot! But still in that uniform, they sent me in a Jeep to north of DaNang. We had to go through all these checkpoints.

By the time we got to the third checkpoint, we were receiving unfriendly fire. The Viet Cong must have thought I was an Admiral or something. There was an Army Captain heading back on a tank, and he threw me his flack jacket. They made me take my blues off and some guy gave me a camouflage thing to put on and a helmet.

Overrun by Viet Cong

We lived in huts called "hooches." I had been there about six days when the North Vietnamese overran us. They were all running around in their black pajamas, yelling and screaming about three o'clock in the morning and they were shooting at us. I ran for the door at the triage station, and I heard this thud. The next day I discovered that it was a mortar that had slammed into the bunker just above the door, but it hadn't gone off. Next, a 500-pound bomb was jettisoned into the trenches; the detonating charge exploded, but the bomb didn't. A Viet Cong with a flag came over the parapet and some WW II sergeant started yelling, "Kill that son-of-a-bitch!" So somebody did. In a couple of hours, the fight was over and VC women came to pick up their dead. The Marines did nothing as they let the Viet Cong women retrieve their dead relatives.

Hiser in Vietnam

PHOTO COURTESY OF DICK HISER

Over the next year I worked at the firebase assigning corpsmen to the patrols. Occasionally I assisted the U.S. Marines as they set up a defensive screen around the firebase. Patrol action was dangerous because of the ever-present ambushes and lethal mines blowing up in our faces. The life expectancy of a Corpsman in Vietnam was very short. It was something like four-to-one compared to the other guys.

I also worked in a mobile medical unit called "B Med." We had to go all over South Vietnam, checking out all the natives. I saw every parasite you could think of. And the area we were in had been defoliated with Agent Orange, so we were all exposed to it. I ended up being on the front-line for about ten months.

Buried Alive in Paperwork

When my time was up in Vietnam, I was reassigned to the Naval Hospital in Saint Albans, New York. We lived out on Long Island, and I was working out at the lab, but there were seven other lab-techs waiting to get in. So I ended up working in outpatient records. This was about the time that Champus, a medical program for service people, was introduced, so I had to convert all the files to the new Social Security system. I had seven guys working for me, and twelve civilians. There was something in the neighborhood of 18,000 records; we were buried alive in paperwork. They estimated that it would take two years to complete the job, but it only took us nine months. I got a Navy Commendation medal for that!

When my enlistment came up, I thought long and hard about it. I decided that I would re-enlist if I could get back to the West Coast. But they told me that if I re-enlisted that I would have to spend four more years in New York. So I decided to get out. I was still in the Fleet Reserves for another seven years, so I had to maintain a sea bag and remain on standby. After years of Military schooling in highly technical subjects, with years of supervision of men and women, and a lifetime of experience applying my military education with 22 1/2 years in the military, I had to come back and finish my last year of high school! I took and passed the GED along with California History. After all the years of Navy schools and training, it seemed a little crazy! In fact, it was almost silly after the fact.

Home to Ojai and a Medical Lab Job

This was 1972. We moved back home to Ojai, and I eventually got a job at a medical lab in Ventura. It was called Automated Analytical Laboratory. I told them about my experience on the old Technicon machines, so they hired me and also ordered up all new automated analyzing machines. The fifty thousand-dollar machine did twenty-two tests at one time. Based on the fact that I had worked with similar ones in the military. I worked there for twenty-two years until Unilab bought the company.

They moved the Lab to Tarzana, and I decided that I didn't really want to drive that far, so in 1994 I retired. I had the company buy me out because I had owned shares in the company.

I continued to do volunteer work in a whole host of organizations including, but not limited to, the Mended Heart Association, Ventura County Veteran's Employment Committee, Veteran's representative for the Municipal Advisory Planning Commission later known as the Private Industry Council, the Ventura County Veteran's Memorial Committee, American Legion, District Commander as will as the State and National Representative for the American Legion. I was the Adjutant of the Ojai Post of the American Legion and past Commander of the County Council of the American Legion. I served on the Ventura County Veteran's Memorial at the Ventura County Government Center. I'm currently Sr. Vice in our VFW Post 11461.

The U.S. Navy transformed Dick Hiser from an unfocused and restless youth into a Navy Chief with all the responsibilities, authority, and experience necessary to carry out his medical mission as assigned. He accepted the risks and nearly loss his life in Vietnam when a mortar shell and then a bomb failed to explode. Many were not so lucky. In the history of warfare, the Infantryman has been called the ultimate soldier, but in reality, the ultimate soldier may be the Navy and Army Corpsmen who save lives while enduring the hazards of the battle. Dick was that ultimate military man.

STAN SCHNEIDER

WWII-GUADALCANAL, AND KOREA

War has not visited the shores of the contiguous United States since 1865. Few Americans today really understand the magnitude of fear and despair that gripped the soul of the Nation in the early dark days of World War II. It was a time when the entire West Coast of the United States was exposed to Japanese aggression. There was cause for great fear as most of our Pacific Fleet lay in ruins at Pearl Harbor. The American and Filipino Armies were destroyed in the Far East.

The British were annihilated in Hong Kong and Singapore. Nationalist China lay in ruins and the Dutch were forced out of Indonesia. The Japanese war machine conquered from the Alaskan Islands to New Guinea and from the Solomon Islands to Manchuria. The relentless aggression threatened India and the island gates to Australia.

As Japanese forces were marshaling for the conquest of Australia, America drew a line in the coral sands of Guadalcanal. The Japanese incursion was a war without mercy for a defeated foe. The victims, civilian and military, were treated with the utmost cruelty and barbarity. There was no sanctity of life, no fair play, no Geneva Convention. In this caldron of terror and oppression, the remaining U.S. and Australian forces assembled to defeat the Japanese.

The whole Pacific was a war zone with no rear area. All participants were vulnerable to enemy attack by land, air, and sea. And as is typical of modern war, the battle sites were in the most God- awful terrain imaginable. Our G.I.s had to fight malaria, dengue fever, elephantiasis, weather, and the perils of the sea. This was the situation when Stan Schneider was called to service.

A One Parent Family in Connecticut

I was born on May 14, 1922 in Norwalk, Connecticut. In my family, we had five children, two sisters that were older, and two brothers. I was the oldest of the three boys. We were all about two to three years apart. We lost my mother when I was eight years old. My father kept the family together with the help of my two older sisters. At one time they thought they were going to put us all in an orphanage home—but he said, "No way!" My Dad was good. He used to work two jobs to keep a roof over our heads and keep us fed. He would leave in the morning, then go back and forth to each job to keep us going. He belonged to the National Guard back home. I went to school up until my last year, then I got out and I went to work. I didn't graduate.

Barely In the Navy When Pearl was Attacked

Since my father was working so hard, I figured I needed to get out and work too. Then on October 1, 1941, I enlisted in the Navy. It was in New Haven, Connecticut. I said to myself, "I don't want to get in the Army, I don't like the Army!" So me and my buddy, on the Sunday of the Pearl Harbor attack, were in the Navy. When I got my orders, I went to Great Lakes, Illinois for boot camp.

Thank God we didn't stay there too long because it was COLD! From there they sent us to Treasure Island, San Francisco because that was the receiving point where they assigned you to a ship or whatever.

We waited there…it wasn't for too long…maybe a couple of months. They divided us up, and I ended up being one of thirty sailors who were transferred to the Marine Corps.

A 20 year old Stan Schneider in 1942 just before WWII duty.

PHOTO COURTESY OF STAN SCHNEIDER

Loading Transports in New Caldonia

We didn't know where we were going. They just called it "The White Poppy," a code name. They didn't want the Japanese to know. Our outfit was called "SCAT" South Pacific Combat Air Transport. (Later, when moved to Ventura, I saw the buses called "SCAT," I said, "Hey, they stole our name!")Anyway, we boarded a cargo plane and were dropped off on our first island. I spent my first Thanksgiving overseas. As a matter of fact, a funny thing happened, we were having turkey, because it was Thanksgiving Day. They had the turkeys flown in, but they left them out in the hot tropical sun and nobody knew about it. We all got diarrhea! You should have seen the sight of all of us running to the latrine the whole day! A Thanksgiving I will never forget! That was on New Caledonia in the South Pacific.

We loaded the transport planes. It was interesting, because the planes didn't have ammunition or guns or anything. All that they had were life-jackets. They would fly maybe 100 feet above water. The way they got away with it was, when enemy planes came diving, they needed time to pull up so as not to crash into the water. They couldn't fly low enough to get to our planes. The planes would carry in supplies and later on the Army nurses came in. They would go out with them and bring back the dead and wounded Marines.

Air Raids—Condition Red

I can still remember my first air raid. We had tents and I was in a bunk. All of a sudden we heard "condition- red!" I said, "What the hell is 'condition-red'?!" What it was, was it meant that everyone needed to get to their foxholes. All the lights were out, and we were all grabbing our clothes…what happened was I grabbed clothes, but they were somebody else's. They were so big I couldn't run! Anyway, we ran to the foxholes and all of a sudden we saw all the anti-aircraft fire going up in the air. What happened was the Japanese planes—we used to call them "washing machine Charlie," because their planes sounded just like washing machines - were all of a sudden dropping flares - Taking pictures of the ships. We were more scared of our anti-aircraft fire than we were of the Japs! After a while, we got so used to the air raids, that half the guys wouldn't even go in their foxholes.

Espiritus Santo in the New Hebrides

As the Japanese were driven back, my unit moved to Espiritus Santo in the New Hebrides. One day while we were standing in line to get our mail, I saw two buddies that I went to school with! It was the strangest thing. Who ever thought you'd see three boys from my hometown in one place. They both got killed later. One was a gunner and got shot down. And my other buddy was on the U.S.S. Helena, and the Japanese sunk that ship.

I remember one day when we were supposed to get seven days of R&R (rest & relaxation). We were all sitting there in our uniforms, all pressed...we were saving our cigarettes and candy...whatever we could get. We were thinking,"Oh boy, we got seven days!" I think I was second or third on the list, to go to Sydney, Australia. And son-of-a-gun, they canceled all the leaves. I thought, "You got to be kidding!" What happened was the 403rd Air Wing from the Army came in and took over. So we got pushed to Guadalcanal. Some of the guys became kind of crazy. One guy went running around with a machete, saying that he was going to kill everyone. It was there that I was assigned to the First Marine Air Wing loading C-47's for Marine and Army ground units.

PHOTO COURTESY OF STAN SCHNEIDER

Though the islands were secure, residual Japanese forces were still present. Day after day, my unit loaded planes for the fighting areas ensuring delivery of supplies supporting the forward troops. In addition to my supply duties, I was

SCAT planes being loaded.

assigned as a firefighter to protect the planes on the ground in the event of attack. Living conditions were miserable in the tropical jungle climate with daily doses of salt tablets, atabrine, and heavily chlorinated water from warm lister bags. We lived in Quonset huts and the food was monotonous and limited. I still have an aversion to Spam and warm beer. I can also still remember the smelly land crabs, disgusting scavengers. Some of my buddies contracted malaria and one fellow got elephantiasis. Day in and day out, the transport planes carried out supplies and returned with the wounded and dead.

Bougainvillaea in the Solomon Islands

The last Island we got orders to was Bougainvillaea, in the Solomon Islands. As the war was progressing, we had to get closer and closer to the enemy. I ended up serving over there for three years, five months, and 19 days. Then we got our orders, pretty late though because you had to have so many points to get shipped back. We went back to Guadalcanal.

Treasure Island, San Francisco

We got on board ship and sailed into Treasure Island, San Francisco, waiting on orders again. Then maybe a week or two later, we got our orders. They said to report to Hogan Naval Air Station. There they were supposed to give us a 30-day leave, so I hopped on a train and went back to Connecticut. When my leave was over, I hopped on another train and ended up in Vero Beach, Florida— Naval Air Station. The war was just about over and it was 1945. I was the storekeeper, it was like a quartermaster and my job was to keep things rolling. One of my jobs was to inspect the gasoline that came in because gas was very scarce. When the trucks came in, I had to get on top and make sure they hadn't put water in the gasoline. I had to siphon off so much and check it. If the fuel was okay, then we let them through.

I don't know any girls –

Right after I had gotten to Florida, my younger brother came home from the war. He asked me if I could come home to visit. Well, I had just gotten off my 30-day leave, so I went to the Red Cross, and they got me a seven-day emergency leave. I came home and he said, "Come on, let's go out dancing." I said, "But I don't know any girls!" I had been away for over three years. He said, "I know two girls, maybe you'll like one of them." I said, "Well, let's see, we'll ask your girl friend's mother which one is the best." And she said, "Sydell." "Okay, I'll go out with her," I said. So we, Sydell and I, went out, and almost every day while I was home. Then my leave was up and I got shipped back to Vero Beach again. Then all of a sudden she said that she was coming down because her friend lived in Florida. She came to West Palm Beach, and they stayed in a hotel.

So she is Jewish and I'm Catholic —What the Heck?

We were going out each night. So one day we decided, why don't we just get married? "What the heck, since you're here now!," I said. Well, we didn't want to tell our parents because she was part Jewish and I was Catholic. We were married, and because I was a non-commissioned officer, we could live in a trailer on the base. But I think you could only stay there 30-60 days, so then they pushed us out. We went and got a room in downtown Vero Beach until finally, I got my orders to go back to Connecticut on March 16, 1946.

PHOTO COURTESY OF STAN SCHNEIDER

Recalled for the Korean War

Schneider's Korean War duty was on the U.S.S. Tutuila.

One year later on April 25, 1951 I was in the reserves, and I got my orders for the Korean War. I said, "They can't take me, I've got a family and kids and all!" But they took me all right! I ended up in the Brooklyn Navy Yard, awaiting orders. I got my orders and boarded a train to report to Maryland. And from there I got on board a personnel ship that took us to Norfolk, Virginia.

I was given shore patrol because I was a non-commissioned officer. My job was to make sure that people behaved themselves, because it was not a Navy ship.

"Man Overboard!"

Three quarters into the first day out, it was getting dark and we were about ready to have chow. All of a sudden we had a call of "man overboard!" They said that they thought one of my Navy men had jumped overboard. I said, "You gotta be kidding, not our guys!" So we circled the ship, and sure enough, it was one of our Navy guys. But I don't think he wanted to commit suicide too much because he had used the Navy trick of blowing up his pant-legs like a pontoon. Anyway, we picked him up and put him under guard. I asked him, "Why did you do that, you crazy young squirt?" He said, "Because I had a fight with my girlfriend, and I wanted to end my life." I said, "You gotta be kidding! Now you're in trouble! You jumped ship, your under military guard, they'll pick you up in Norfolk and you'll probably go to jail." But I'm not sure what happened to him because that was the last time I saw him.

We finally ended getting orders to the U.S.S. Tutuila. It was a repair ship, and it was our job to help anybody who had problems. But I never did get on board. What happened was they went out for a trial run and they were rammed by a merchant ship. They towed the ship in; we got on board and ended up in Baltimore for repairs. As soon as we got back, they discharged me. So I never got to Korea!

The Grocery Biz and Affordable House

That was 1952, and I started working in the grocery store industry, A&P's and stuff like that. We rented a place for a while, and we lived with my wife's brother one time...and I thought that that was a heck of time, so I decided that we needed to go out and buy a house. So I bought some land for $1,500.00! I had a buddy of mine…he said, "Look, I got the place for you. It's an empty lot, corner of a cul-de-sac…if you want it, give me $500.00 down and it's yours!" I said "Okay." Then I got in contact with one of these contractors, and he said he would build our house for $16,800. So that's what we did. We sold it for over a quarter of a million when we left Connecticut! The house was very nice. It was a Cape Cod style, nice corner lot, plenty of land. We weren't on top of one another. I retired at age 66. I had lost most of my family in Connecticut by this time, so we decided to sell our house.

Off to California and Grandchildren

We moved to California on June 29th, 1988 to be close to my grown children and grandchildren. The way we ended up in California is that my daughter, Sheryl, was going to school in New York. One time when she went to Washington D.C., she went to a USO dance. She met a young man that was an officer in the Army. My daughter called me up and said, "Guess what Dad, I found a guy, and he's just like you!" I said, "Well great, then marry him!" They got married and moved out to California because Bob, her husband, was from Fillmore. They bought a house in Thousand Oaks because Bob is the Senior District Attorney for Ventura County, and my daughter is a school guidance counselor in Ventura and is also working on a Ph.D. I have two grandchildren from them, both of whom are college graduates from San Diego. My son, Stan, is working on his Ph.D. at Humboldt State.

Epilogue

I will never forget my eight years in the Navy. I have been a Life Member of the VFW post 11461 as well as a local officer. Over my 31 years in the VFW, I have served as commander of a major post in Connecticut, and I am now serving as the Quartermaster for the VFW in Ojai.

Old Navy Prayer-

"O Lord God, who alone spreadest out the heavens, and rulest the raging sea; Take into thy almighty and most gracious protection our country's Navy, and all that serve therein. Preserve them from the dangers of the sea and from the violence of the enemy; that they may be a safeguard unto the United States of America, and a security for such as pass on the seas; that the inhabitants of our land may in peace and quietness serve thee our God, to the glory of thy Name. Amen."

WORLD WAR II
EUROPEAN THEATRE

▬▬▬▬▬▬▬▬▬▬▬▬▬▬▬▬▬▬▬

▪▪▪▪▪▪▪▪▪▪▪▪▪▪▪

VIRGINIA ALLEN

– U.S. ARMY NURSE CORPS

Service "brats" are a unique breed whose lives are set apart by the very nature of their parent's military service. That can be good or bad depending on the psyche of the child. Exposure to military service affects different children in different ways as they grow to adulthood. Some follow in their parent's footsteps accepting the life style of frequent moves to different assignments and duty stations along with long separation from family and loved ones.

Other service brats resent the discomforts and instability of military life and become indifferent to the motivations necessary to be a career soldier or sailor.

Virginia Allen was a unique child of the Army being born in the Philippines. She was imbued with that military spirit so familiar to many of our VFW comrades. She adapted and became the epitome of the finest traits of all good soldiers. Honor and duty were absolute givens in her life. She followed her West Point father into the military and became an Army nurse. This is part of her story.

I was an Army brat, the daughter of a West Point officer. I was born in the Philippine Islands in 1920 when my father was assigned to Stotsenburg Cavalry Post. The doctor who delivered me was Dr. Dufresne, the same Colonel that Dave, my husband, had coffee with over in Australia during World War II many years later. Stotsenburg Cavalry Post was renamed Clark Air Force Base. Like most military families, we moved from post to post and from one assignment to another. We even spent time at West Point where my father instructed in mathematics. I must admit that I admired the handsome cadets in their fine uniforms but I was way too young for them at the time.

As I grew older, my father was assigned to posts that were remote and in the isolated parts of the country though now with the growth of the country and modern transportation, they are not so remote. We were stationed at Fort Bliss in Texas, Fort Meade in the Black Hills of the Dakotas, and Fort Riley, Kansas. Many of the activities at those posts involved horsemanship and outdoor activities. At Fort Meade, I helped train horses for riding and polo. In the winter, I skied and ice-skated. We lived mostly on Cavalry posts with lots of horses because my father commanded horse cavalry units. Because of circumstances, I became an outdoorswoman.

Nursing Studies for Three Years —Then Joined the Army Nurse corps

I was ambitious and had aspirations of becoming a pediatric physician. I began my medical studies in nursing figuring that I would later transfer to a study of medicine. I studied nursing for three years and spent two years in premed at the beginning of World War II. With the advent of D-day and the U.S. Forces waging war on three fronts, Italy, France, and the South Pacific, trained medical personnel were in short supply.

PHOTO COURTESY OF GINNY ALLEN

There was a critical shortage of trained nurses to care for the mounting casualties. My father was serving in France and my future husband, who I had not yet met, was serving in New Guinea and the Philippines. Five of my associates from nursing school and I decide to join the Army Nurse's Corps. We left school because we felt that our country needed us at that critical time.

Ginny Morrison Allen(L) and three nurse friends during basic training in 1944 at Camp Carson, Colorado.

Rough Journey to a Field Hospital in France

We were sent to Camp Carson, Colorado for our military training which included training for gas attacks, a required training experience for all Army personnel at that time because of the experiences with gas in World War I. We were commissioned as 2nd Lieutenants in the U.S.

Army Nurse Corps. Upon completion of training, we were sent to England. From England we sailed across the English Channel. It was a very rough trip, and they were losing a ship a day from the mines that the German's had planted. The ship behind us was sunk from one of them. When we disembarked in France we didn't know where we were. Later, we found out that we were in Le Havre. It had been heavily bombed during the fighting several months before. From Le Havre, we loaded trucks to go to Reims, France to an Army field hospital.

Dad, with a Bottle of Champagne, Finds Me

As we loaded the trucks to go to our post, a Jeep came up behind us. This guy said, "Is there a Lieutenant Morrison here?" I said, "Yes, I'm Lieutenant Morrison." He said, "Your father is coming to see you tomorrow." All the nurses shrieked, "Your father!" I knew that he was in Europe, but I didn't know where because I just had an ETO (European Theater of Operations) number for mail. He showed up the next day with his helmet, his trench coat, and his 45 pistol on his hip, and a bottle of champagne! So we took my best friend Bess, who had joined the Army Nurse Corps with me, out to share that bottle of champagne.

My father had been assigned as G-4 in one of the Corps Headquarters groups, so he kept track of where we were. I was able to see him five times while I was over there, and that was really something else, especially for my mother, who was still back at home. It really helped her to know that we were close to each other.

Casualties From the Battle of the Bulge

The casualties from the Battle of the Bulge were just arriving. We were caring for the wounded men of the 101st Airborne Division along with German prisoners of war. Armed soldiers with locked and loaded weapons guarded the prisoners. I never really realized the depth of hatred in war until I was told by some American soldiers that if the guards were not present, that they would kill every German in revenge for all their buddies killed and executed by the Germans. This was a time when the Germans in the Battle of the Bulge had executed many American prisoners and those incidents were still fresh in the minds of the wounded men of the 101st Airborne. There was much anger and hatred.

VE Day, then Army of Occupation

After VE (Victory in Europe) Day, we were supposed to go to the Pacific Theater where the war against Japan was still raging, but they dropped the atom bomb on Hiroshima and Nagasaki. Japan surrendered. Then we got a call from the Occupation Army in Germany. The Army needed six nurses in the Army of Occupation, so the six of us volunteered. We were assigned to three different field hospitals in Germany.

From Daily Blackouts to That Well Lit New York Harbor and—the Statue of Liberty

We returned home to the States on a ship called the U.S.S. George Washington. It was a troop ship that had been fixed up like a hospital ship. It took us about eight days to go across the Atlantic Ocean. I will never forget seeing the Statue of Liberty. I tell you, I get goose bumps even today remembering it. All the lights in New York City were lighted. We had just been in Europe where blackouts were the order of the day.

It was wonderful to return to the normalcy of America after experiencing war. They even had a band playing to welcome us home. When I returned to the Army base, they asked me where I wanted to be stationed, and I said, "Someplace near the Pentagon, because my father is stationed there." So they sent me to Fort Belvoir, Virginia.

Scoffield Barracks, Oahu

A little later, they asked Bess, my girl friend and me if we would like to go to Hawaii. So we went to Scoffield Barracks, which is right in the middle of Oahu. We were there about a year and a half. Meanwhile I had been taking tests to become a Regular Army nurse because I had a Reserve Commission. I passed them all, but I was ready to get out of the Army. My Dad had just retired after 30 years in the service, so I went home.

In a Small Enough World, Well Friends Thought We Should Meet...

My parents had moved out to California to Sierra Madre, where my husband-to-be was living and working. I didn't know Dave at this point, but we had mutual Army friends who knew me very well after four years of service together. And they knew Dave really well through a n officer named Colonel Bertholet, who was in charge of ROTC. Dave had been in ROTC in college. Colonel Berkolett came to visit my Mom and Dad, and they started talking about David Allan. I guess they knew that he lived nearby, so they said that they would like to see him.

So my Mom went into the bank where he was working and she left a little note inviting him to dinner the next night. Dave came. And he just kept coming, and in three months, we were married! Of course, we were older and we knew what we wanted. I had four handsome officers over the years that had asked me to marry them, but I just wasn't ready. I'm glad I waited for Dave.

St Luke's Hospital, Pasadena

I got a job working at St. Luke's Hospital in Pasadena. We had three children in three years, two boys and one girl. We had planned the two boys, but Mary, the girl kind of snuck in there. One day Mary came up to me and said, "Mom, I overheard you saying that I wasn't planned." And I said, "Oh honey, after having two boys, by the time you came along, I was so thrilled to have a girl!" She's my best friend. We have five grand children now!

Fond Military Memories

For my service during the war, I earned the Rhineland Campaign Ribbon with two Battle Stars. Later, I was awarded the German Occupation Medal with other ribbons along with a captaincy. It has been a wonderful life. Dave and I have been together for 53 years and every morning, I still salute Dave, my husband, since he still outranks me!

Captain Virginia Morrison Allen with her father Colonel Charles Morrison at the Pentagon in 1947.

PHOTO COURTESY OF GINNY ALLEN

Virginia Allen is a kind and gracious woman who has devoted her life to service of her Country, her Faith, and her family. She belongs to several patriotic organizations and is a Life Member of the Ojai Valley Veterans of Foreign Wars Post 11461. Retired now, she remains active in the church and as a volunteer in the medical fields where she has special expertise. Her husband's story is included in this book in the Pacific Theatre section.

JOHN FAY

– *B-24 Navigator Over Germany*

Air power has been the key to America's victories since World War II. But air power requires superbly trained airmen gifted in mechanics, the sciences, and mathematics. Behind each aircraft is a small army of technicians and support personnel. Few air men ever actually man aircraft, but those that do, command more fire power than whole battalions of Infantry. Many of our comrades who fought on the ground in the last three conflicts starting with World War II can attest to the effectiveness of air power. Many comrades are alive today because air power saved them from annihilation. Those men who are on the cutting edge of air warfare manning the fighters and bombers are among the most courageous of modern warriors; yet, they are men of intellect and skill. Our comrade John Fay is such a man. This is his story.

My father was an associate in the Pacific Naval Air Base Contractors developing Port Hueneme in Ventura County. The family was living down in Central Los Angeles near Hoover Street. As World War II approached, Port Hueneme became an important naval harbor on the central coast. I had been attending Mt.

Carmel High School in the Los Angeles area until my senior year when the family moved to Ventura when my father was appointed Superintendent of Hueneme Harbor.

At Mt. Carmel and Ventura High Schools, I studied math and had especially fond memories of my Ventura High School math teacher, Margarite Scott. She taught me celestial navigation, an elective course, which turned out to be beneficial in learning to be a navigator.

At 16, Pearl Harbor Attacked —Army Air Corps Required High School

Pearl Harbor was attacked when I was sixteen years old. When I turned 17, my mother gave her permission for me to enlist in the Army Air Corps. That was in February of 1943. The recruiting office sent me to Los Angeles for the physical exam. Though I was a basketball player, I was somewhat underweight but otherwise physically fit. For some reason, I was afraid that my weight could be a problem so I ate bananas and drank lots of water just before getting weighed so I could increase my weight and qualify for the service. I was anxious to join the Air Corps.

Apparently, there was no weight problem, but the military wanted me to become 18 and complete high school before induction. While in high school, I worked on the railroad tracks with the Hispanic work crews and picked lemons. I graduated from Ventura High School in June of 1943. For Basic Training, I was sent to Camp Kerns, Utah which was south of Salt Lake City in the desert area. The training was rigorous but not of the caliber necessary to produce motivated soldiers. I was glad to leave that behind me, feeling that it had little to contribute to my future service.

Training in Santa Ana, Nebraska State, Kingman AZ, Hondo TX, and more training

The next duty station was at the Santa Ana Army Air Base, which was a first-class military installation. There we were tested for our qualifications for pilot, navigator, and bombardier. I qualified for both pilot and navigator, but the Air Corps especially needed navigators at that time so I became a navigator trainee. Training shifted to Nebraska State Teacher's College where we were trained on the old Piper Cub airplane.

Later, we moved back to the desert at Kingman, Arizona where we learned aerial gunnery. More training followed and then an assignment for navigation training in Hondo, Texas. There, the cadets flew in groups of eight to ten people in Beechcraft planes for practical application of our navigation skills. This was the final course before being commissioned a 2nd Lieutenant in the Army Air Corps. Many men were washed out even though everyone gave their best effort.

We were motivated and we were all volunteers. It was ironic that we received a lecture on fidelity to duty. We were told that if we deserted that we could be subject to the death penalty. I felt that was unnecessary considering the motivation necessary to complete flight school.

We Bomb Klamath Falls and San Francisco

It was June of 1944 and we were still training. Our last training assignment was in Boise, Idaho where we made practice navigation and bombing runs over various U.S. cities such as Klamath Falls, and San Francisco.

I'm an Military Officer but Can't Vote or Drink

Finally, we were shipped to New York Harbor to board a French liner called the U.S.S. Louis Pasteur. There were only ten aircrews aboard and 9000 Infantrymen and Engineers. It was election time in the United States and Franklin Roosevelt was running for his fourth term against Thomas Dewey. The age of adulthood was 21 so, I could not vote. But they needed an election's officer. Guess what? I was appointed election's officer even though I was too young to vote as were millions of other American servicemen.

More Training—B-24s Norwich, England

Upon arrival in England I was assigned to one of 13 B-24 bomber bases. I was near Norwich in Norfolk. Living conditions were minimal; we did not have heat in the barracks. With a short period of familiarization training, we were soon introduced to combat.

Three Missions—Then the Battle of the Bulge

By the time the Battle of the Bulge commenced on December 16, 1944, I had had three missions under my belt. The Battle of the Bulge shook up the whole Allied command since it was so massive and unexpected. There was a real danger that the Germans would push out the Allies and cut off their supply lines through Antwerp. The dangers intensified because the German armies were operating freely under the protection of fog and cloud cover.

The 101st Airborne was hanging on at Bastogne, but barely. Throughout England a vast air armada was sitting on the runways waiting to strike the enemy ground forces and drop supplies to the surrounded Army divisions. We waited until December 3, 1944 when the weather cleared. At that time, the most massive air armada ever seen in the history of warfare rose in a stream of fighter and bomber planes that stretched for 50 miles. This air armada flew over Bastogne as a morale booster for the ground troops.

Hit with Three Wounded Over the Bulge Area

Our fighter planes regained the battlefield initiative and struck hard at the enemy Panzer Divisions and supply lines. Cargo planes made waves of air drops of ammunition, food, fuel, and medical supplies to the troops below. The bombers gave tactical support to the ground troops. Flying over the Bulge area, we received heavy enemy ground fire. On one mission we were hit and three crewmen were wounded.

1Lt. John Fay (top center standing and bottom standing #2 from left). John and one other survived the emergency crash landing.

PHOTO COURTESY OF JOHN FAY

Only Two Survived the Crash

Six weeks after the Battle of the Bulge, tragedy struck our crew when we had left England and were flying over the North Sea. An engine caught fire and the pilot turned back to land. We were told not to jump until the pilot gave the jump command. As the engine and wing burned, some of the crew jumped without orders. They parachuted into the frigid North Sea. Rescue boats and planes raced from shore to save them but the cold waters killed them before they arrived. Meanwhile, the pilot was trying to keep the plane level so that when we reached land, he could give the order to jump. Only five men and the pilot remained in the plane when he gave the order but it was almost too late as the plane was only about a thousand feet off the ground.

I jumped and immediately pulled the rip chord. The pilot and three others crashed with the plane and died. Only two of us survived. I credit the pilot for being a hero. If he had not held the plane steady, I would not be here telling of this experience.

That crash was on my 14th mission. After that, I became a lead navigator for six more missions. We were awarded one air medal for every six missions. For multiple awards, you were given an oak leaf cluster. I earned the air medal and two oak leave clusters.

The B-24 Bomber, A Unique Fit, Yet Primitive

The B-24 Bomber was a unique aircraft. It carried more bombs, had greater range, and flew faster, but lower than the B-17. It could fly as high as 20,000 feet which was lower than the B-17's. The planes often dropped metallic chaff to confuse enemy radar that tracked our flights. For additional protection we picked up P-51 Mustang fighters which escorted us to the targets over Germany. That was an advantage. The conditions in the plane were primitive. It was necessary to fly in heated suits to keep from freezing. The interior of the plane was not finished. The ribs and skin of the plane were clearly visible.

Civilian Life and
Corporate Law in Ventura County

A man matures quickly in the service. I was 20 years old at the end of the war. I was anxious to develop a career so I started school at UCLA. I later transferred to Loyola Law School. In the meantime, I had met my wife who was a psychology major. We married in 1948 and she helped put me through law school.

John Fay, 2002

I graduated in 1950 and entered law practice in Ventura in 1951 doing estate work, construction, and corporation law as well as general practice. I was the corporate attorney for Southern Pacific Milling Company for 35 years. Over the years, I have been active in Ojai City affairs serving as Councilman, Mayor, Chairman of the Planning Commission, and City Attorney. I have also served as President of the Ventura County Bar Association, as President of the Ojai Civic Association, and President of the Ventura County Public Facilities Corporation.

John Fay has remained active well past retirement age. He has spent decades serving the Ojai community as a Councilman and as Mayor. His wife serves on the Ojai Planning Commission. He commutes daily to Ventura where he still practices law, mainly for long term clients. Committed to family, church, and community, he serves as an icon so typical of veterans. Service is an integral part of the veteran's nature.

■■■■■■■■■■■■■■■

HOWARD GILBERT

—THE 10TH MOUNTAIN DIVISION

What propels people and nations to engage in war against each other? How do nations and races stumble into such a morass of hatred and conflict that they are willing to sacrifice their sons and daughters on the altar of the gods of war? Of all human activities, why does war tear down everything sacred and holy and cause men to sacrifice everything for victory?

The most cogent answer to these questions relates to a nation propagandized by aggressive politicians who desire power and authority. But a blatant quest for power, authority, and domination will never be achieved without the support of the general citizenry. World War II started with small groups of fanatical zealots using ancient grudges to whip the flames of hate and hostility. Like many politicians, they played a blame game. It was an "us" against "them" mentality. They used the democratic system to achieve positions of power engaging in character assassination and eventually real assassination until the voice of dissent was silenced and constitutional government was suspended. After that the executive decree of the political leadership came from the dictator's dictates and will. The media were harnessed as an instrument of the state, lulling the people with good words and promises of economic betterment.

Hitler's Germany was a socialist state that put a cap on profits and demanded that land serve the communal interest first. The Nazi Party supported old age pensions while secretly supporting euthanasia of the aged, and the handicapped.. Investors were frequently targeted as enemies of the state. Profit was viewed as obscene. Education was harnessed to serve the national cause and garner support for the socialist ideology. All these goals were to be accomplished with minimal pain to the population. It was perceived that the economic interest of the German state was superior to that of other neighboring states and foreign people. In time the mythology of racism and economics justified the exploitation of other peoples and even German citizens who did not fit the definitions of the politicians. Initially, the blame for all the ills of the German nation was placed on Jews, but later, it extended to Gypsies, Slavs, Czechs, including the German citizen who dared speak out against the new National Socialist regime.

The civilized and cultured people of Germany were transformed into a nation indoctrinated into a mythology of a self-aggrandizing race that felt that the gods of the North had conferred upon them a destiny that included world conquest. So began World War II. Poland fell to the unholy alliance between the butcher of the East, Josef Stalin, and the butcher of the West, Adolf Hitler. Axis alliances and war soon transformed most of the European continent into subject people ruled from Berlin by one party and one man. All vestiges of parliamentary government disappeared. Even staunch allies of Hitler's power quest were quickly brought to heel.

When the evils of political oppression burst the bounds of rhetoric and invade the soil of free men and peaceful nations, ordinary men are called forth to stop the aggression. Howard Gilbert, from the national heartland, was just one of the millions of Americans who volunteered as Infantrymen. The Infantry was the cutting edge of a mighty host rectifying the wrongs created by political statism run amuck

The Restless Family

I was born on July 7th, 1916 in Rein, Colorado. I was one of three children. I was the only boy, number three in the line-up. In the early years, my parents were farmers. My father got some government land, and he proved out the claim. We stayed there five years and grew mostly alfalfa for horses. We had irrigation because this was in Colorado. I don't remember living there though because we left when I was two. My father was the sort of person where the grass was always greener on the other side of the fence. We moved a lot. I guess I'm sort of like him.

I have had several businesses, kept them ten years, and then did something else. So my life has always been like that. I changed occupations every ten years. We moved to Arkansas, and from Arkansas, to Kansas, and from Kansas to Illinois. In Illinois my parents had a restaurant called "The Streeter" in 1924. We started different restaurants in different towns at that point in our lives. We eventually ended up in Joliet, Illinois. We had two restaurants there while I was attending school. We lived there when I was 11 up until I was 14. We lived in the Italian district. The strange part about it was that all the children that I played with only spoke Italian. I heard a lot of Italian. When I went to Italy years later, most of the language came back to me. From Joliet, Illinois, we moved to Ottawa, Illinois. We stayed there quite awhile. We stayed put, oh, eight or nine years. Actually, when I got old enough, at about 18 years old, I left home and went to Ohio.

Sightseeing
14,000 Miles of the USA for $194.00

I went to Ohio with friends. They were brothers, and they were from there. We all had pretty good jobs. It was piecework, and we were making pretty good money, so we bought a car, a new 1937 Plymouth. The three of us took off and went to California. This was during the depression. We were gone three months and we drove that car 14 thousand miles in three months! When we got to California, we leased a gas station out on Crenshaw, which today, is about in the middle of Watts, California. We ran that for a while, until one of the brothers got homesick. We sold the lease to the gas station, luckily, and we went down to San Diego. One of the brothers and

I met a couple of high-school girls so we stayed there a week and ran around with them. We were headed back home to Ohio.

We took the southern route, down through the Gulf Coast, through the Everglades, and over to Miami, and back up to Clinton, Ohio. All in all, we were only gone three months. We figured out how much we had each spent, and I had only spent $194.00! That included money for gas, food, and motels. Motels were $1.50 for three of us. It was quite an experience. We got jobs at American Steel Package Company in Continental, Iowa. Again, it was piecework making condensers for little radios. They don't make those anymore. The three of us were pretty good. We were actually the top three fastest in the whole plant.

We made the most money, and back in those days, we were making a hundred bucks a week! That was a lot of money because the postman was making only twenty-five a week. I worked there for about three years. I met my wife and we were married in 1937. She was from Pleasant Bend, Ohio. The other two boys stayed at the American Steel Packaging Company, and I went to Westinghouse Corporation to build bombers for the war.

Army Basic and the 10th Mountain Division

As the war progressed I made the decision to join the US Army. My daughter was six years old, and my wife and I talked it over, and made the decision. My basic training was in Camp Walters, Texas. Afterwards, I was shipped from Texas to a port of embarkation in Maryland. It was strange, because 36 hours later, I'm on a train going back to Texas! I had been sent to the 10th Mountain Division. In order to get into a Mountain Division, you had to have three letters of recommendation saying that you could ski, mountain climb, or have a background in forestry. Most of the men were college graduates because their folks had money to do stuff like that. President Harry Truman said that he wasn't too sure about the Mountain Division because they were a bunch of college kids! Anyway, we trained there with mules for about six months. We were Mountain Infantry. These mules were great big government mules. We were an elite army unit and we were being prepared for specialized mountain combat so the training was exceptionally rugged. We marched 1500 miles in 17 weeks!

As our training progressed, I elected to become a mortar man. A mortar is simply a tube mounted on a base plate with two legs that supports the tube. Attached to the legs is a system of screws for elevating and traversing. Mortars fire at a high angle and have the explosive power of light artillery. As is an old army custom, the lightweight men tend to carry the heaviest weapons and I weighed 128 pounds. I guess I was the perfect size in Army logic. With a rucksack, ammo, personal weapons and mortar, I was often lugging 90 pounds or more of equipment. The Army, during World War II, consisted primarily of foot soldiers. Two feet and a strong back were the prime movers.

Zigzagging Through the Straits of Gibraltar

When training ended for the Division, the Mountaineers were shipped across the Atlantic on the U.S.S. United States. It was a two-stacker, and there were 13,000 people on that boat! They used to bring prisoners back on that ship, so there were bars across the bunks, in what are called, "state rooms." It was an exciting voyage. We crossed the Atlantic by ourselves, so we had to zigzag all the way so the German U-boats wouldn't torpedo us.

When we came to the Straits of Gibraltar between Africa and Europe, two British destroyers met us and escorted us into Naples. You know how people talk about premonitions? Well, while we were offloading the U.S.S. United States, the Captain asked me to carry some of his stuff for him. We stopped, and he turned around and looked back at the ship and he said something that I never will forget it, he said, "I really hate to leave that ship." Well, he was killed later. He was a good Captain. There, we loaded into small coastal boats so that the Germans wouldn't torpedo us.

We went up the Italian coast to Pisa, the city of the Leaning Tower. We could see the Leaning Tower in the moonlight. We thought that we were going to leave the next day, and I said, "Well I want to see it up close!" So four other guys and I stole out to see it. We didn't know it, but we didn't need to sneak out, because we ended up staying in the town for four days! That's the Army for you. They never do things quite like they say they are going to. We then got our equipment, and went directly into seven days of combat.

Double Time in a Foxhole or Die

It was snowing when we arrived in Italy and we didn't have any blankets. To stay warm, we'd dig a two-man foxhole, and climb in it together. The military was supposed to have sent snowshoes, but we never got them. We had shoepacks, which were oversized rubber and canvas boots. They would get wet and our feet would freeze. So, we had to take off the shoepacks and put them close to our bodies to dry out. To keep our feet from freezing, we would double-time in the foxhole. We'd take turns doing that.

As part of General Mark Clark's 5th Army, the 10th Mountain Division fought its way through mountain villages and rugged terrain. The mules that we had trained with were shipped overseas with us, but we never saw them. The Italians had mules though, and we'd pay them a dollar a day to carry our equipment through the mountains for us. When the mountains got too rugged, we would carry all the equipment on our backs. I was in heavy weapons, 81mm mortars. We would put a mortar at the foot of the mountain, and fire over it. There was always one person, usually the staff sergeant, in the observation tower at the top of the mountain. We'd string sound power phone wire from there to the guns. We had six guns. They would call the fire orders back and we would fire. We were fighting against the German Gothic Line in the Dolomite Mountains. Two divisions had already been beaten back and could not take the Germans. They thought that 10th Mountain troops could do it, because it was a long sloping mountain. When they sent us into combat, they sent us up without any ammo in our rifles because they didn't want us firing on the way up, giving away our position. The Germans woke up with GI's all around them! In three weeks combat, we lost 900 men killed and we had 3000 wounded. There were 15,000 men in our division. For every soldier that was on the front line, there were 29 soldiers in back, backing him up and supplying him. We fought around the clock, seven days a week. You slept when you could. One time, I went 72 hours without sleeping.

PHOTO COURTESY OF HOWARD GILBERT

The Pangs of Hunger

Upper Canole Valley, Italy

The conditions were pretty bad. We ate K and C-rations, and sometimes we didn't have any food. One time, we didn't have food for over seven days. My wife had sent me some dextrose tablets that I shared with the guys. The British were on our left and the Brazilians were on our right. So I said, "I'm going to go and try and get some food." I went out towards the Brazilians and when I came upon them, they were sitting in shallow foxholes about two feet deep with their upper torsos fully exposed. They were all lying over dead. They had our old Army uniforms on with overcoats and in each overcoat pocket they had K-rations. So, I tipped them over and got their K-rations. I must have had ten or twelve boxes. I got to thinking that maybe the Germans had booby-trapped the bodies. They used to do that. They would even booby-trap their own troops. So I quit taking K-rations and went back.

Two days later, our First Sergeant finally made it up with some food for us. One time I remember seeing a little

Italian lady with a sack of food. She said that she wanted to go over the mountain because her bambino was over there. We told her that we couldn't let her go, so she started running. We couldn't let her go over there, because if they caught her, they would ask, "What's over there?" So I told the men that when she starts running to put some rounds at her feet, but don't hit her. So, finally she decided that she didn't want to go over the mountain anymore! She went back where she came from bawling.

You see, they had all been ordered out of the villages previously because the area was going to be shelled. But people didn't want to leave their homes, just like anybody else. They wouldn't leave, so they had to suffer the consequences. A lot of people were killed for that same reason. Those things happen. The Germans almost succeeded in kicking us off that mountain.

I didn't know it at the time, but I was just on the other side of the mountain from Senator Bob Dole. He was a replacement officer and was badly wounded after a short time on line.

Firing British Long Tom Artillery

We had a British Long Tom gun. I remember one time when it was firing at a German convoy that was leaving. It was about seven miles down the road. This Limey said to me, "Hey Yankee, you want to fire this bloody gun?" and I said, "Oh sure." So I went over there. It had a pulley with a striker on it. He told me, "When you pull that, cover your ears." Well, it hit before I could cover them, and oh boy, my ears rung for a long time! The shells were so big in that thing that you could actually see them when they fired. Each one of them weighted 103 pounds! They had something like an 11-mile range. We fired those things around the clock. We had an aiming stake that had a light on it, so when it was dark they could aim correctly.

(As Howard Gilbert told his story he paused slightly. It was obvious that there was still that residue of inner pain from painful memories. He commented on how they passed wounded and dead American buddies and comrades but could not stop to help them. He said he just hoped that the Medics would pick them up. He was under orders and had to keep moving, after all, he could be among the dead and wounded himself at anytime from the effective and intensive German artillery and mortar fire. At times, they would stop and dig in with their entrenching tool. While dug in, they would be harried by German patrols that were reconning the positions for subsequent artillery barrages. Howard said that they lost many officers who were often sent up to the Observation Posts, Observation Posts being prime targets for enemy action.)

British Long Tom, Howard is on the right.

The Civilians in Italy

Periodically, we got a five-day rest period in the rear areas including Florence, Italy. The conditions were horrible. People were starving. People were so hungry that they had eaten all the dogs and "roof rabbits" to be found. The term "roof-rabbit" was an Italian joke, another name for "cat." Italians were driving American weapons carriers when the troops on line were unable to secure replacements for weapon carriers destroyed. Things were very confusing.

Some Were Faked Out—and died

As my unit approached the Po River, we boarded small boats on a moonlit night. Enemy M109 aircraft spotted us and dive-bombed. But apparently, they had expended their ammo on another target so we survived. A few of the men jumped into the Po River before they realized the planes had no ammo. Some of them drowned.

One time we were billeted in Northern Italy and we were staying at some palace with a winding stairway. My boys were staying in a room up at the top and there was this wooden commode-lookin' thing outside. We had a fireplace, so I said, "Go get that commode and bust it up and burn it." So they did. A week later "Little Junior" and I had to go back because we had left some ammo at the foot of the stairs. When we got upstairs, there was some Limey there with a pad and pencil. He said, "Was there a piece of furniture up here?" And I said, "Yep, why?" "Well you've gotta pay for it!" he said. I said "What?!…You gotta be kidding!" I couldn't believe it! We had to pay for anything that got destroyed during the war, unless it was a Fascist's home. Every Italian home that was damaged or destroyed, U.S. taxpayers paid for it to be replaced.

We Were So Tired...

When we were in Northern Italy, we marched 24 miles in the rain until we came to a little town called Malseseine.

Some of the guys were so tired that they went to sleep standing up! While we were there this German came up to me and asked if I spoke German. There was a guy in our division that did; we called him "Willie the Clump." I said, "Hey Willie, there's a guy here that wants to talk to you, and it's a German." At that point, we were so tired that we didn't even care. This German guy had four buddies in a house on ahead of us. He wanted us to take them as prisoners because they were afraid that the Italian partisans would come out of the mountains and kill them. We were so tired that when we came across some German barracks, we decided to stop and rest. One of the Italians told us that the Germans had left at around 5:00 at night, and it was now 11:00 at night. So we decided to go in and get some sleep. We were all lying down, just about to sleep, and some guy says, "I wonder if they booby-trapped this place?" Half the guys were so tired that they didn't move a muscle, "Whatever," we thought. So we just went to sleep.

The Germans Surrender

The war in Italy ended when we were in Malseseine, and many of the Germans came down through the Brenner Pass and surrendered to us. They didn't want to surrender to the Russians, so they hiked all that way to surrender to us. Our duty was to put them in a compound in Villa Franka Airport. They put up a fence and put the Germans in there until they could be sent back. They sent them to the United States actually. We treated them well. They didn't want to fight anymore than we did. We'd take their guns and stuff away from them. We had a pile of Italian Lira, German issue money, piled up, thousands of dollars worth. Some of the guys were clever enough to take some of that money and turn it into American Occupation Lira, then into American dollars. I never did though. While we were doing that, we were called up to Trieste, at the top of the boot, because some skirmish was going on up there. But nothing ever came of it.

Our Division had taken numerous prisoners of war. While escorting "the walking wounded," one German officer who was 29 years old said to me in very good

English, "I've been on the Russian Front, in France, and now in Italy—I'm glad I'm captured, I'm going home." In my heart I was glad also because I was not one of the 4072 10th Mountain Division men killed or wounded in the North Apennines and Po Valley Campaigns.

The Long Way to Home – Then On to Japan

The war was over, so they put us on boxcars and we rode down to Naples. Mussolini had some barracks there, so we stayed in there until our ship came in, which was supposed to be in a day. It didn't come, and it didn't come, so I decided to go visit a friend who lived in Naples. He was a dentist. So I went down there, and I climbed the stair. I asked, "Is Dr. Kemal around?" Some sailor said, "No, he went home yesterday." We must have passed each other! They put us on a boat headed for home. The boat was double loaded. We used to draw straws for the bunks. If you didn't get the luck of the draw, you had to sleep on deck in the rain. It rained every night

Relief for the War Weary – Japan Surrenders

Two days out of New York harbor, the war ended in Japan. I can't describe what it felt like to see the Statue of Liberty—to really be home. I went home for 30 days and then back to Camp Carson, Colorado. I was ready to get out of the Army. I had enough points actually. So the Commander of the post said, "Sergeant, I need a supply Sergeant." I said, "Sir, I don't know anything about…" "You don't have to know anything about supply, you've got a Corporal over there that's been over there a year, you've got a supply officer, that's your job!" So I couldn't get out of the service until I got somebody to take my job. They had POW's at Camp Carson—Prisoners of War. My wife and daughter came out, and we had an apartment at "The Garden of the Gods," at the foot of Pike's Peak. Just like a job, I'd go to work everyday and issue firearms for the guards. I did that for about three months until one day I had to go down to the supply room to get some clothing for an officer who was taking some prisoners back to Germany. I ran into this Sergeant and he said, "I just re-upped for three years." I said, "Hey come on with me," so we got in the Jeep and I took him in to show him the supply room, then I took him in to see the "old man" And I said, "Sir, this is Sergeant so-and-so, and he just re-upped for three years." The old man nailed him! That poor guy—he had re-upped because he wanted to leave the camp, and he ended being snagged into my position. That's the only way I got out of there! From there I went to Ft. Leavenworth and was discharged.

26 year old Howard Gilbert at the end of the War.

PHOTO COURTESY OF HOWARD GILBERT

Epilogue

In 1991 I went back to Italy to visit that mountain where I had fought. During battle, all the trees had been blown off from shellfire, so the way I found the spot again was by looking for a big square house with all the corners shelled off of it. It had been right above us, so I knew that my gun position had to be at the foot of that building. And sure enough, the divot made by the mortar was still there. You know the war was not all bad. We made our own fun. I took pictures everywhere I went. One time, I took the film in to be developed because we were supposed to be in that town for four days. Well, the next day, that had us move out, so I didn't get to go back to get the pictures. Two years later, I got a package from some Sergeant with a note that said, "I thought you'd might like to have these." I always took that camera with me, even in the foxhole. If I had a pillow, I would put the camera under it. One day I forgot it. I decided to go back and get it, which was dangerous because I had to move through artillery fire. We had already covered that ground, so the enemy was firing long-range shells in that area. But anyway, I went back and got it, so that's why I have pictures.

We sang songs while we were marching; this was one:

NINETY POUNDS OF RUCKSACK
(Tune and theme from Navy's "Bell Bottom Trousers")

I was a barmaid in a mountain inn
There I learned the wages, the misery of sin
Along came a skier, fresh from the slopes,
He's the one who ruined me and shattered all my hopes.

CHORUS
Singing, ninety pounds of rucksack, a pound of grub or
two
He'll schuss the mountains like his daddy used to do.

He asked me for a candle to light his way to bed
He asked me for a kerchief to cover up his head
I being foolish maid and thinking it no harm
Jumped into the skier's bed to keep the skier warm.

CHORUS

Early in the morning before the break of day
He handed me a five note and with it he did say
Take this my darling for the damage I have done
You may have a daughter, you may have a son
Now if you have a daughter, bounce her on your knee
But if you have a son, send the bastard out to ski.

CHORUS

The moral of this story, as you can plainly see,
Is never trust a skier an inch above your knee.
For I trusted one, and now look at me,
I've got a Bastard in the Mountain Infantry!

Civilian Life after the War

After service I owned a bowling supply company and a bowling alley with a cocktail lounge. I also worked as a foreman in the construction of the San Onofre Nuclear Plant at San Clemente. I raised my family and buried the sorrows of the war until recently. I realized that it's really too bad that people don't really know what war is like. You can go back, even a hundred years, to the wars before us. Those guys did more and suffered more than we ever thought of suffering. As far as war is concerned, it accomplishes nothing. In war, people lose everything. They freeze to death. They starve to death. But nobody understands the futility of war. They just keep doing it. Hopefully this book will help wake people up!

Howard Gilbert, 2002

PHOTO COURTESY OF CHUCK BENNETT

Howard treasures each day of life he has been given. He is thankful that he has survived the carnage of war and returned home alive and uninjured. He realizes the gifts of family, children, and grandchildren and all the opportunities in this great and good land. He remembers in sadness those young soldiers who died or were forever disabled and disfigured by war, young soldiers who never lived to enjoy the blessings of life. At eighty-six, Howard is forever young in attitude and physical vigor. Each day he contributes his work and efforts to the Habitat for Humanity, to his Church, and to his family, activities of gratitude for the life he was spared. He is a staunch supporter of veterans and veterans' organizations. He remembers his departed comrades and treasures his brotherhood with living comrades who have shared the battle.

HOWARD HANSEN

— *COMBAT MERCHANT MARINE* — *WW II*

Ignoring the politics and justification for modern warfare, war becomes a game of hunting and being hunted. Essential to this game is supplying the fighting forces with all the accouterments of war. Supplying war materials is essential to victory. WWII was a global war. America's supply lines were the ships of the Merchant Marine. Immediately upon the United States entering the war the German and Japanese submarine forces launched attacks on all U.S. Merchant Marine shipping bringing the war to the coast of the United States. Hundreds of Merchant Marine ships were sunk and thousands of mariners died in the violent warfare carried out by German U-boats off the coast of Texas, Florida and the Eastern Seaboard. German subs hid in the mud of the Mississippi Delta stalking American shipping. In the nature of war, the Merchant Marine was the hunted. All of America's fighting forces depended upon them for their supplies of war. Day and night the mariners stood their watch and manned their ships never knowing when a torpedo would strike. Obviously, Merchant Marine ships that carried munitions or gasoline were exceedingly dangerous.

This is the story of Howard Hansen, Merchant Mariner.

Construction Worker in the Aleutians

I had been working on a civilian construction crew in the Aleutian Islands before World War II. The climate and working conditions were miserable to say the least. It was cold, wet and windy in the summer. The winters were beyond comprehension with the cold, ice, snow, and those frightful Willawalla winds.

Foreman Beheaded

We were given the opportunity to transfer to construction work on Wake Island, a small island in the mid Pacific where the climate was warm and balmy. A number of workers were selected along with the foreman. Unfortunately, when the Japanese attacked the island, the construction workers were taken prisoner and it was reported that the foremen were beheaded. I was later told that the captured workers spent the war as slave labor in Japan and never received compensation for their years of servitude from the United States or Japan.

This was before World War II, but by the nature of our work, the military was preparing for something. I did not get to go to Wake Island. Instead, I returned to Seattle, Washington.

Enlisted into the Merchant Marine

Shortly after the Japanese bombed Pearl Harbor, I enlisted in the Merchant Marines. I was sent to Port Hueneme in Ventura, California for boot camp. Though I was a Merchant Marine, the training was essentially like Navy boot camp. We trained at rifle and pistol ranges in the sand dunes between Ventura and Port Hueneme. The area is now covered with expensive beachfront homes.

First Assignment, Texaco Oil

Upon completing boot camp, I received my Seaman's papers and signed on a Texaco Oil Company ship sailing from San Pedro, California through the Panama Canal and the Caribbean Sea to the East Coast. As soon as the ships transited the Panama Canal into the Caribbean, we were in a war zone, the severity never fully understood by the American people. German U-boats operated freely and at will. They even sank banana boats in the harbor at Limon in Costa Rica. Merchant ships carrying fuel and war supplies were prime targets.

As soon as the ship entered the Caribbean, a U-boat was stalking my ship when an U.S. Navy sub-chaser began to drop depth charges all around my ship. Unfortunately, the explosions were so close to the ship that the boiler room was damaged and the ship had to make an emergency run into Guantanamo, Cuba for repairs. Three ships from that same convoy were sunk in the Florida Straits. I guess we were lucky to be in Guantanamo at that time.

From there, I was on various ships hauling gasoline and oil out of Texas and to the East Coast. U-boat activity was heavy during the next six months and the Merchant Marine sailors took more casualties than any other branch of service at that time. Hundreds of merchant ships were sunk.

German U-boats Off American Coast

Often, German U-boats would lie in the mud of the Mississippi River Delta watching for loaded tankers from Texas. Upon spotting a loaded tanker low in the water from cargo, the U-boats would attack, often within sight of the U.S. mainland. I have passed fellow American seamen on rafts in the water. We could not stop and help because of the extreme dangers from U-boat attacks. I served on ships all over the world during World War II. I was on ships delivering ammunition and/or fuel to New Guinea, the Solomon Islands, to the Battle of the Coral Sea, Guadalcanal, Tinian, and Saipan. That is where I served in the Pacific.

The Most Dangerous Areas...

The most dangerous areas I experienced were in the Gulf of Mexico, the Caribbean, and along the Atlantic Seaboard of the East Coast of the United States. The worst action experience by the Merchant Marine was often in sight of our own shores. I made ammunition and gasoline runs through the Straits of Gibraltar into the Mediterranean Sea and up the East Coast of Italy to Brendesi. My supply ships supported Mac Arthur in New Guinea and the American troops in Sicily. I delivered aviation fuel for the bombers that were raiding the Poliesti Oil Fields in Romania, which was under German control. For one thousand days and one thousand nights, I sailed the worldwide oceans and seas in support of our fighting forces in most major battles of the war.

Merchant Marine was Part of Armed Forces

During World War II, the Merchant Marine was part of the Armed Forces. The Merchant ships had weapons such as three-inch and five-inch guns. Though our mission was supply, we had limited means of defense. After the war, we were ignored and forgotten as veterans. We petitioned Congress to be recognized year after year. Many of us joined the Merchant Marine Veteran's Association and after years of lobbying, Congress finally recognized the Merchant Mariners of World War II as being veterans. Our final recognition came through Congress in 1988. Sadly, this recognition was too late for many Merchant Seamen who died while waiting for recognition and veteran's benefits.

After the War

After the war I became a tool and die maker for experimental aircraft in the aerospace industry. I married and settled down to the routine of civilian life. But for the rest of my life, I was active in the Merchant Marines Veteran's Association and was involved in the re-activation of the Merchant Marine memorial ship, The U.S.S. Lane Victory now berthed in Los Angeles/San Pedro Harbors. I joined the Veterans of Foreign Wars as soon as a post was activated in Ojai where I served as Chaplain and Buddy Poppy Chairman. Though I am not what you would call a churchgoer, I do believe in God and hold my departed Merchant Marine comrades in my memory and esteem. I know what they endured and suffered.

Charred remains of an American Seaman on the flying bridge of the U.S.S. Pennsylvania, hit by German U-Boats,

PHOTO COURTESY OF U.S. MERCHANT MARINE ASSOCIATION

Howard passed away before this Story could be completed

Howard was knowledgeable in the history of his unique branch of service, a service that goes back to John Paul Jones. He was very proud of that service's contribution to global victory, yet Howard was a humble man who merely wanted recognition for his branch of service and its contribution to the success of American Armed Forces in World War II.

Two weeks before Christmas in 2001, Howard passed away at the age of eighty. His comrades from the VFW Post 11461 met at the Santa Paula Cemetery to honor him and support his family. The Rev. Dave Pressey of the Anglican Church, and also a VFW Post member read the burial service from the 1928 Book of Common Prayer. The ten members of the Post stood at attention as VFW member Chuck Bennett presented the American flag to Howard's widow in token of appreciate of Howard's service as Merchant Seaman and veteran of World War II.

Howard had wondered how many good years he had left. He was active to the last. He was full of ideas for enhancing the veteran's organizations to which he belonged.

Howard was of Norwegian/Viking descent and jokingly he spoke of his end. He said that when he died, he should be given a Viking funeral. He reminded us that all good Vikings were given a funeral on a Viking ship; which was set ablaze and set sail upon the open seas. As a seaman who spent 1000 days and 1000 nights on the high seas during World War II, he might have qualified as a Viking Warrior. In the spirit of the Viking warrior, the Valkaries, the women warriors, would carry his body up to Valhalla. There, in the heaven of the heroes, he would be revived to fight another day. Of course, Howard was just joking for he was really a Christian man. Though he was not into organized religion, he maintained his Norwegian faith and belief. He was not narrow in his faith for he had a spirit of toleration for mankind.

Howard Hansen stayed active in the VFW right up until he died.

Howard had many interests in his retirement. He enjoyed gardening where he raised fine tomatoes and other vegetables. He had built the house in which he lived. He was an excellent photographer and electronic repair technician. On the 4th of July of 2001, he walked the entire Ojai Parade taking pictures of the VFW Color Guard and the National Guard trucks filled with his comrade veterans. Howard took the picture on the cover of this book. He was always there for the men who had borne the battle, his comrades in arms. He always was there for funeral services of fallen comrades. The Veteran's Day Massing of the Colors Ceremony at Ivy Lawn Cemetery was especially important to Howard. He was constantly trying to raise the profile of veterans in the community. Howard's life was a life of giving, constructive work, service, comradeship, and community involvement.

OTTO HEINO

WWII— WAIST GUNNER ON THE FLYING FORTRESS

America's industrial might and righteous indignation are potent powers when unleashed against an aggressive foreign foe. One of the great ironies unique to America is the diversity of people drawn from the unwanted and dispossessed peoples of the earth. This diversity has become a unity bound by a system of government that creates loyalty through the rule of a righteous law guaranteeing freedom, justice, and opportunity for all.

Europe, with all its ethnic and religious conflicts, has often failed to understand American unity despite the flaws in the practice of the ideals of a beneficent government.

The Axis powers of World War II feared America's latent power and might. Germany had seen how American industrial might and resolve tipped the scales in the stalemate of World War I thus bringing that war to an end.

America entered World War II because of the Japanese attack on Pearl Harbor. An otherwise pacifist America was transformed overnight into a unity of purpose to rectify a wrong and restore a proper relationship among the nations of men.

Many innovative tactics and machines were perfected in the subsequent war years, but perhaps, the most significant instrument of modern warfare was the airplane.

Airplanes require technology and production skills beyond the requirements needed by basic infantry or artillery. Nowhere was America's industrial might more critical than in the mass production of fighter and bomber planes. Ultimately, it was air power that brought both Germany and Japan to their knees as bombers devastated their armies and industry as well as the infrastructure of both nations.

As fast as Allied planes were shot down, a continuous stream of replacement crews and new planes, bigger planes, and more technically superior planes replaced them. But planes do not win battles alone. Trained and disciplined airmen win battles.

In Europe, the unrelenting attacks of B-17's, known as Flying Fortresses, destroyed Germany's ability to wage war. The story of Otto Heino is the story of one of these airmen who flew forty missions as a waist gunner (a gunner located on the sides and middle of the B-17) on these planes.

I was born of Finnish immigrant parents who had first come to America at the turn of the century to visit relatives in Boston and Pittsburgh. My mother was a Laplander from the far frigid north of Finland where her family raised reindeer. They were herdsmen in a reindeer economy. My father was from a dairy farm near Helsinki, Finland.

Mom and Dad
—Bootstrapping Farmers from Finland

When my father graduated from high school at the age of 16, he traveled to America for a vacation. My mother traveled to America to visit relatives. They did not know each other at the time. The steamship passage was relatively inexpensive at the turn of the century. My father played drums for a Finnish Cultural Dance Hall where he met my mother. They soon married and settled in east Hampton, Connecticut where father worked in a foundry. Both of my parents were very thrifty and soon bought some land, built a house, and purchased some cows.

Eventually, they bought a bigger farm in New Hampshire. They had a large family of six boys and six girls that provided the labor force for the dairy, milking the herds of cows and processing the milk. In addition, they raised top quality Timothy hay to supply the local racehorses. During the summer, the farm produced truck crops such as potatoes, tomatoes, and corn. It was a large farm.

I did not want to be a farmer so I saved my money and went into the milk hauling business while still a teenager. I obtained a loan from the local bank and was able to obtain a bond for performance of my contracts. The bond was a requirement of the business.

1-A = 8th Air Force Gunnery School, Las Vegas

War was raging in Europe and Asia and our country had initiated a peacetime draft prior to America being involved in World War II. As is typical of so many hard working farm boys, I was in peak physical condition and was classified 1-A which guaranteed my induction into the service. But I didn't mind. It was prior to Pearl Harbor. I was called to service and sent to the 8th Air Force Gunnery School in Las Vegas, Nevada. At that time, Las Vegas was a small town with only one gambling hall and an open-air rodeo. It was really a little bit of a town, hot, windy, and dusty. There was no air conditioning at that time and we just endured the desert heat.

Later, I was sent to Great Falls, Montana where I was assigned as a waist gunner in a B-17 Flying Fortress. I was considered a good gunner and could score up to eighty hits out of a hundred firing at the target sleeve being pulled by another airplane.

A Flying Fortress with Three Tons of Bombs

All the B-17's had ten man crews, which included the pilot, the Co-pilot, a navigator, a bombardier, a radioman, and the gunners. It was so heavily gunned that they called it a Flying Fortress. The plane carried three tons of bombs except when the planes flew to Berlin. Then they carried only two tons of bombs because they needed more fuel to fly that far. The planes flew at 220 miles per hour fully loaded but accelerated to 235 miles per hour as soon as the bombs were dropped. I could really feel the upward surge of the plane as soon as the bombs were dropped.

1942—England, Flying "Old Crow" to Germany

I arrived in England in 1942 and within a week, we began to fly missions over Germany in a Flying Fortress named "Old Crow." The name had nothing to do with the crow bird. The name referred to the beverage we drank upon completion of our missions. When we returned from a mission, we were cold from the high altitude flying and cold from the fear of the mission. Our nerves were on edge. The flight surgeon called it our medicine. It would warm us up and settle us down. The airmen who did not drink ended their service with severe emotional problems from the fear and trauma of the experience.

Fear was an ingredient of every mission. One waist gunner was so frightened that he failed to fire his machine gun even under attack by ME 109 Messerschmitts. I reported him because he was a danger to the entire crew of the plane. I wanted a fellow gunner who would do his duty.

Flying in the Lower Box—"Tail End Charlie"

We usually flew in a formation called a box. The most experienced crews flew in the lower box. The lower box received the most attention from enemy fighters and flak. The German fighters had a limited airtime; apparently, they were short on fuel, so I have been told. The second box of B-17's flew in the Mid-level box and the most inexperienced crews flew at the highest level. I flew in the lower box most of the time and was in the lead ship or what was called "Tail End Charlie."

Our planes had a very high casualty rate, I do not think that the Air Force ever released the true figures but it was often forty percent casualties on a single mission, especially in the early days of the air war.

Bronze Star, Purple Heart —and Credit for 22 Planes Shot Down

I had a good eye for shooting and am credited with downing 22 German planes as recorded by the attached cameras. About this time I was awarded the Bronze Star along with my Purple Heart Medal. However, I always aimed at the engines and not the pilots. Sometimes, a German pilot would wave to me as he bailed out.

Shot Down After 23 Missions

My plane was eventually shot down after my 23 missions over Germany. I was somewhere over Leipzig Germany. The Anti-Nazi German Underground resistance that was in close contact with American intelligence operatives rescued three of us. We hid in cellars, hay stacks, traveled at night walking by foot or traveling in horse drawn carts. We went through France and over the Spanish Pyrenees where we were picked up by small British craft that took us back to England.

Bailed Out a Second Time—While Landing!

Our planes were frequently shot up during each mission. One time, we were shot up so badly that the brakes didn't work and the pilot announced that we were going to overshoot and crash at the end of the run way. The plane was bouncing wildly and when it bounced up, I dropped out of the bottom. I timed my drop so the rear wheels wouldn't run over me. The plane was going about fifty or sixty miles per hour. I was badly bruised and beat up by the fall. The plane crashed at the end of the runway, flipped over, and exploded. My fellow crewmen died.

The runways were constructed of steel mats and the ends of the runway were filled with water from frequent rains. I was constantly aware of the condition of the runway just in case of an emergency-landing situation. After my survival from the crash, I was given the name, "Super Man" by my comrades.

Shot Down Again!
—Almost Skewered in a Hay Wagon

In my 8th mission of my second 25-mission cycle, I was shot down again in the same area of Germany and rescued by the same group of the German underground. They said, "What, you again?" They prepared special papers and passed me off to German authorities as a deaf and dumb German. I did look German with my blond hair and blue eyes. My name was German sounding and that helped. Eventually, I made it back to England but not after one hayride where I was hiding and the Germans jabbed their spears into the hay searching for hidden people. They missed me.

Cruising at 60° Below Zero

As I commented, many planes were shot down or badly damaged by German planes and anti-aircraft fire. I was wounded in the leg just below the knee. I was lucky because it was just below the knee and I recovered. If the wound was an inch or two higher, I would have been crippled according to the doctor. Flying at high altitudes required sheepskin jackets and boots along with electric heater suits. It was sometimes 60 degrees below zero. If the power to our electric suit warmers failed while over Germany, it could have been fatal. The lower flight boxes flew at 23,000 to 24,000 feet where we were exposed to more intense anti-aircraft fire and fighter attacks, but as the war progressed and we had P-51 fighter escorts, the attacks and casualties diminished. The top flying box did not experience as many casualties. It was not uncommon for planes to have between 30 and 40 flak holes in them when they returned to base in England. When that happened, a new plane would be issued.

The Russians requested bomber support on the Eastern Front. I participated in several missions on the Eastern Front receiving two medals from the Russian Government.

As the war and casualties continued, there was a shortage of trained pilots so women began flying the

Flying Fortresses from the United States to England via way of Labrador, Greenland, and Iceland.

One of the world's most famous potters lives in Ojai. His amazing military past is little known.

PHOTO COURTESY OF OTTO HEINO

Developing a Philosophy for Life

During the war I developed several ideas for the future of my life if I should survive. I wanted to become an independent person and not have to take orders from anyone. I wanted to be a "self-directed" person. I never wanted to have to take orders from anyone again. I developed a philosophy, "Never hurry, never worry."

While on leave in England, I took advantage of several unique opportunities that influenced my later life. One time I worked for 20 days in the Rolls Royce factory. I fell in love with the Rolls Royce Motor cars and determined that some day I would own such a car. Today, I have a Rolls Royce, which is a source of great pride in the sense that I achieved my youthful ambition.

A Visit with England's Foremost Potter

Another time while I was on leave, I visited Bernard Leach, England's foremost potter. I visited for nine days between missions. That experience influenced my future life.

California, Marriage and a Potter's Life

Upon returning home, I took advantage of the famous GI Educational Program enrolling in the League of Arts and Crafts School in Concord, New Hampshire. When my principal teacher moved to California, I followed and eventually taught at the University of Southern California for two and one half years and 13 years at the Chinard Institute.

However, the demand for my pottery became so great that I resigned to become a full time potter. When I married, I married a first generation American whose parents came from Sweden. Sweden and Finland are neighboring countries. My wife was a potter also and developed schools, curriculums, workshops, and seminars in the pottery field. She was very much into helping people develop their skills and talents. She traveled frequently and worldwide. We were married for 47 years when she died of cancer in 1995.

Like most people of Finland and Scandinavia, I was raised a Lutheran and attend church on Easter, Christmas, and New Years. I miss my wife but have appreciated life. My life is my work and my work is my life. I work at my creations everyday even though I am 83. I take no medicines. As I said during the war, if I got out of the war alive, I would become a potter and this I am.

Otto Heino is world famous for his mastery of the art of pottery and his unique yellow glaze, but few people know of his roots and his wartime service.

Tom Mahon

– 82ND AIRBORNE INFANTRY

Located in the East end of the Ojai Valley near the slopes of Chief Peak and the Topa Topa Range of mountains sits a quiet house deep in the orange groves of the Ojai Valley. The fragrance of the orange blossoms fills the air. What peace and tranquillity permeates the atmosphere! The grounds and landscaping give evidence of the quality of person who lives in such a setting. Tom Mahon, one of our Veterans of Foreign Wars, occupies this exquisite place in the Ojai Valley. The peace and tranquillity is in stark contrast to Tom Mahon's early life as an Infantry Platoon Leader in the famed 82nd Airborne Division of World War II. This is his story -

I was born February 22, 1923 in Oak Park, Illinois and raised with my younger brothers and sisters in Glen Ellen, Illinois. My father was a furrier in a family business started by his uncle. My later career choice was influenced by the fact that my father had been in the Army Air Corps in World War I and I had an uncle who was a military officer.

West Point, Where I Met My Girl Too!

Grammar school in Glen Ellen was followed by a Catholic Military High School in Aurora, Illinois. As West Point was my objective, I then went to a preparatory school in Washington D.C. The only problem I encountered in the West Point admissions exams was that I was underweight, which was corrected through adequate consumption of malted milks. Our entering World War II, in my first year, the program was accelerated to three years and so I graduated in 1944 with a degree in Military Engineering.

While at the Academy there was little leave, but people were allowed to come and visit. That is how I met my wife. She was a good friend of the sister of one of my roommates. I met her during my first year at West Point. We dated the entire time I was in school and wrote her while I was overseas.

He Chose Infantry

With graduation, desiring a combat branch, I chose Infantry and was sent for Advanced Infantry training at Fort Benning, Georgia.

Then He Chose Airborne Infantry

While I was there, a group of us decided to sign up for Airborne training to become paratroopers. There was quite a bit of physical exercise, and you had to have five jumps completed before you qualified. The last jump was a night jump. When it was time to go overseas, we boarded the Queen Mary and were shipped to Scotland then to France where I was assigned to the 82nd Airborne Division, the famous division that had just weathered many of the major battles in Europe during World War II.

Platoon Leader with the 82nd Airborne on the Rhine River

The 82nd Airborne Division was an outstanding outfit. There was a lot of loyalty in the unit - Lots of pride. The men were aggressive and very experienced. From Sicily to the Anzio Beachhead to the drops in Normandy and Holland to the Battle of the Bulge, these men had been through the war.

My first actual combat was leading my platoon on a patrol across the Rhine River. The crossing was uneventful, but on landing, we came under machine gun fire. The Germans were in an excellent position but for some reason decided to "bug out." The rest of our time on the Rhine River was relatively uneventful. The most interesting part being finding a typewriter with a manufacturer's logo the same as my wife-to-be's family name.

Tom Mahon went to West Point and then to Airborne Infantry. Gung Ho all the way. Looks are deceiving aren't they?

PHOTO COURTESY OF TOM MAHON

Racing to Meet the Russians at the Elbe River

Combat operations that followed were more like a race to the Elbe River where we met the Russians. There was relatively light opposition on this drive and we were generally able to be in a town for the night. At the same time the Russians were pushing from the East, fortunately reducing the number of Germans soldiers we had to fight.

Germans Surrendering

Just before reaching the Elbe River the Germans in our area wanted to surrender. They much preferred us to the Russians. In fact, some of them thought they would join us to fight the Soviet Union. The big issue seemed to be which of our senior officers would officially receive their surrender. In any event, my platoon was sent out to disarm them. As they came down the road we would order them to put their weapons on the side of the road where we were. They were more than happy to comply - they just wanted it to be over. For our part, everyone amassed a wonderful collection of guns.

Things went well until a tank unit came down the road. Since we were in no position to dismantle a tank and didn't know what to do with them, I just waved them through. We didn't do the same thing with one of their mobile commissaries when it came through.

S-2 and EM Club Officer

Shortly thereafter, the Division was sent to Berlin for occupation duties. I was then transferred to Battalion Staff as S-2, Intelligence Officer, with the additional duty of being in charge of the Battalion Enlisted Men's Club. At that time, one of the officers who had been with the 509th Regiment told me of a distillery they had run across in what was now the British Zone of Occupation. Needless to say there was a shortage of this commodity for the enlisted men. So I took a few men and headed for the Ruhr Valley with a 2-ton truck.

All the Schnapps You Want - 5¢ a Shot

The German who possessed the schnapps was convinced the British were going to find it and make medicinal alcohol out of it. This was his greatest concern! He had every kind of bottle in that place. Pop bottles, jars, anything he could find to put it in. We made three trips down to the Ruhr Valley. Just in case we ran into trouble, we had a soldier in the back with a Tommy gun, guarding it. On our third trip, on the way back to camp, the truck broke down in the Russian Zone. Well, the first tow-truck sent to get us couldn't tow the truck because it was so overloaded. We had to transfer everything to a new truck. We had to guard the schnapps heavily because it was like gold. When we arrived back at camp, I asked the officer in charge of the motor pool why he had given us a defective truck in the first place when he knew it was no good. He said, "Well, I knew it wasn't any good and I wanted to have it replaced." He thought he would have us do it! Despite all the trouble we went through, it was worth it because the Enlisted Men's Club was well supplied with schnapps. We sold it for 5 cents a shot.

Victory Parade March—5th Avenue, New York

In January 1946 the Division boarded the Queen Elizabeth and sailed back to New York Harbor. We then marched in the Victory Parade up 5th Avenue from the Dock to Grand Central Station from where we boarded a train to our destination for processing. Three days later I proposed to my wife-to-be and we were married shortly after.

I brought home with me the proceeds from the Enlisted Men's Club, which I just deposited in a bank and on arrival at Fort Bragg, North Carolina, I used it to start another fully equipped club with athletic equipment for the men. It was later that I was informed that everything should have been accounted for through the Finance Office. This was my first introduction to paperwork!

At Fort Bragg my primary assignment continued as Battalion S-2 until my transfer to Intelligence School at Fort Riley, Kansas.

I Jump as the "Wind Dummy"

Paratroopers were required to jump periodically in order to receive extra pay. To meet that requirement, a plane was sent to Fort Riley so that we could stay current in our paratrooper status. The people at Fort Riley decided they would watch, and set up stands for seating, with the cars parked close by leaving a relatively small area for the drop zone. To determine the effects of the wind, I jumped first and with no effort landed right in front of the stands. Unfortunately, the wind changed, and on the next pass troops were landing among the cars and stands. In general, it was a riot. Despite some of the rough landings I've never had any medical problems as a result.

No Housing for the Family - Time to Go!

On returning to Fort Bragg I was transferred to Division G-2. This was followed by a request to attend Harvard Business School. However, the Army decided that since my best grades were in mathematics, I should go to the Naval Post Graduate School at Annapolis, Maryland. Upon completion I was assigned to The University of Pennsylvania for a Masters Degree in Electrical Engineering. Unfortunately we couldn't find adequate housing for our growing family. So after five years of service I decided to resign and work for Mobil Oil Company.

Mobil Oil Company and a Master's Degree

While I was working for Mobil Oil Company I went to night school and earned a Master's Degree in Business Administration. Eventually I worked in the Foreign Trade Department in New York. Mobil had a subsidiary in Mexico called Mobil Oil de Mexico. They offered me a position as the assistant to the president of the company, so I moved my family to Mexico City, where we lived for two years. The people were really lovely, and we enjoyed living there. When it was time to return to the United States, I was scheduled for assignment in New York. We didn't want to go back to New York with the children with snowsuits and all that, so I resigned.

Off to Ojai, the Automobile Business, and Ventura County Auditor Controller

My aunt and in-laws had moved to Ojai, California so we decided to settle there. I joined the Chevrolet Dealership and eventually owned it. At this time I also served on the City Planning Commission. It was 1957 and Ojai was too small for two automobile dealerships. The Chevrolet Dealership didn't make it. Next I went to work for the Ventura County Auditor-Controller's Office where I worked my way up through the Department eventually being elected Auditor-Controller. In all, I spent 31 years working for the citizens of Ventura County. My wife and I raised 11 children.

Tom Mahon has led a rich and full life. He is modest when relating his achievements and accomplishments. He doesn't think there is anything special about himself. But very few people can claim the status of West Pointer, Airborne Combat Infantry Officer, and elected official of Ventura County's Office of Auditor-Controller, a multi-million dollar operation. With all his achievements, Tom Mahon raised 11 children.

WORLD WAR II
PACIFIC THEATRE

DAVE ALLEN

–THE FIGHT FOR NEW GUINEA

Behind each soldier with a rifle and bayonet is an army of support personnel that stretches back to the homeland. Many wars and many battles have been lost when this supply chain is destroyed or disrupted. Much of the strategic activity of war involves the interdiction of the enemies supply chain. Frequently, when armies are overextended and the supply chain is broken, the battle is lost.

World War II saw Japan, weak in natural resources, make a beeline for those areas of the South Pacific and Indian Oceans where the raw materials for war were available. Like a dagger, the Japanese armies and navies headed for Australia through New Guinea. It was in New Guinea where their juggernaut advance was halted in the jungles and on the beaches.

It was there that Dave Allen commanded supply units responsible for delivering the food, fuel, and munitions of war to the fighting front, at times a mere 28 miles away. This is the story of his life and experiences.

My mother was from Victoria British Columbia, and my Dad was from Bath, England. They met in Los Angeles while my mother was on the stage for two years. Dad came over from England at 17 years old, in October of 1883. He and two other of his brothers had been lifted out of school in England. His older brother and sister were born in Egypt because my grandfather was a cotton merchant there.

Grandfather Came to Altadena Area in 1877

My grandfather had made two trips over here before he moved the family out to California. They came by steamer to New York, then they traveled by stagecoaches for a bit, looking to see where he would like to settle. He decided that he liked Altadena, California. That's where my family came and settled. The pre-moving trips were in 1878 and 1879. The family came out later. He bought property in several different parcels, a total of 502 acres in Altadena. It wasn't called Altadena back then though, just the San Gabriel Valley. Pasadena didn't even exist. San Gabriel was where the post office was located, and it was the center of activities

My grandfather had retired from being a cotton merchant by this time, so he farmed the land. Some of it had already been planted in grapes and citrus. A lot of the land was just sagebrush and rattlesnakes. He cleared the land and planted it in citrus and grapes He also had a small distillery and winery on the property, and they sold lots of grapes to other wineries. Dad worked on the place when he came home from school. There were seven brothers and two sisters in my Dad's family, nine children in all. The youngest one was born after the family moved to California, and he was named Bernard Gabriel, for the two largest towns in Southern California—San Bernardino and San Gabriel. Los Angeles didn't amount to much at that time.

My Mom finished the equivalent of high school in Los Angeles, and then she went to New York, where she was on the stage for two years. She did mostly Shakespearean plays. She also went on the road with companies that traveled around the country. And I guess it was during one of those tours back to Los Angeles when she met my Dad. Dad liked to go to the theater and they'd often joke about it.

An old timer around Los Angeles would remember the Burbank Theater, which was on Main Street. Back in those days when they were dating and planning their marriage, the old Burbank Theater was a legitimate place. But when I was a kid, it was a follies joint. I don't know if it still exists today. It has probably been torn down. But I remember it. It was there on Main Street by the Pacific Electric Station at 6th and Main.

My grandfather died in 1886, but my grandmother lived until 1912! My father and one other brother managed the ranch because the older brother had gone off to Arizona—he was an old-time cowboy, with Indians mixed in too.

Dad, a Banker in Sierra Madre—1919

Somewhere along the line, between the time that Dad had arrived in the States in 1883, and 1906, when Mom and he were married, he had gotten into the mortgage and banking business. At the time when they were first married, he was working at a bank in Los Angeles but I think he had been in a couple of different banks previously. They lived in what was called Pico Heights near Pico Boulevard. It's kind of a run down neighborhood now.

They lived there until my two older sisters were born. Then they moved to South Pasadena where they lived in a rented house on Prospect Avenue, which is where I was born. My older brother was born there in South Pasadena and we lived there until they built a new house on Prospect Avenue next to where the Arroyo Freeway runs now. The house has been torn down, replaced by an apartment building.

Shortly after that, Dad started working in a bank in Sierra Madre, east of Pasadena. We moved to Sierra Madre in September of 1919, when I was just 2 1/2 years old. I remember some of the moving process. We moved into a rented house there and we sold the house in South Pasadena. I went to grammar school in Sierra Madre until the sixth grade. Then I went to Wilson Junior High in East Pasadena, which was four years in those days, seventh, eighth, ninth and tenth grades. Then I transferred to high school in Pasadena, then to Pasadena Junior College, which included the junior and senior year of high school, and two years of college.

I graduated and stayed on in the Junior College part for a couple of years. This was during the depth of the Great Depression, and to make matters worse, Dad had died just before I had graduated from high school. There wasn't a lot of money available. Before my Dad died, I had wanted to get a job, but my dad was very adamant and he said, "No, The family has enough to eat. You may not work and deprive somebody of a job that they may need in order to eat." I grew up not having any extra spending money.

Learned About Military Paperwork Early

I had become interested in ROTC prior to going to college, so I immediately got into it. I became Cadet Commander and led the Military Honor Guard in the Tournament of Roses Parade in 1937. It was a junior unit. In a senior unit, you could be commissioned as a Second Lieutenant or an ensign in the Navy, but there were no immediate commissions at that time. So I went to work in the bank in Pasadena, the 1st First Trust Savings Bank, which no longer exists. I was there for four years, and in the meantime I had completed requirements for Second Lieutenant in the Army, and was attending troop schools as they called ROTC in those days. I was doing a lot of correspondence work, and so on. I had already had basics in ROTC, even though it was a junior unit. I fully expected to be commissioned in 1940, but the wheels of the Army can grind very slowly at times. Then came the registration for the draft in October of 1940. I still didn't have my commission, so I registered for the draft at the Monrovia draft board. I was 23 years old at that point and the war had started in Europe, but America wasn't over there yet.

In January of 1941, the draft board picked fifteen numbers, and mine was included in it. I think the first fourteen had some sort of physical disabilities, or they were married, too old or something, I don't know. So anyway, here I was, supposed to go in the first draft from Monrovia. I went and told them, that I was supposed to be getting a commission at anytime, and that it was silly for me to go through all that, just to be discharged a couple weeks later. So they went along with it that time, and they deferred me. Then in February, the draft came again. Once again, I went to argue with them about this.

By March, I had a telegram from the Adjutant General that was addressed to me as Second Lieutenant. It said, "Contemplate ordering you to active duty, on or about, May 15th." I thought, "Well this is at least something, so I went over to the Draft Board with this telegram and they said "Well, could have typed this up yourself!" They were real nasty about it. Not long after that I got another order, a typical Army mimeographed order that I took over to them. And they said the same thing! "Well, you could have typed this up yourself." They wanted to draft me. I gave notice at the bank that I wanted to leave the 30th of April, and I figured that I'd have a few days before I'd have to leave for the Army. After that, I just ignored the draft board. I did the best I could and I figured if they come for me, "Oh well!"

When Las Vegas Was
Three Filling Stations and a Whorehouse

In May, I went to get my orders and they sent me for temporary duty at Fort Warren, Wyoming, which is in Cheyenne. I drove up there. The prices of hotels were very different in those days. I was living in Sierra Madre at the time, so I got in my car very early in the morning, and drove all the way to Salt Lake City without staying over. The only time I stopped was in Las Vegas, for gas.

Vegas wasn't even a wide place in the road then—there was the Union Pacific Station, the beer joints, three or four whorehouses and that was it!

After driving 711 miles, I got into Salt Lake and I remember, to this day, how pooped I was! I went into this hotel and said that I needed a room. When I registered I was very proud of this Second Lieutenant business. I put that on my registration. I was just dead tired and I went up to a beautiful room overlooking Temple Square. And I started thinking, "Gee, this is going to cost more than a couple bucks!" I'd stayed at the Fairmont and the Palace in San Francisco for $2.00 a night, and I was kind of worried about the price. But I thought, "Oh, just worry about it in the morning." I think I probably had five or ten bucks in my pocket, and a gasoline credit card.

There weren't other credit cards around in those days. I went to bed, got up in the morning, and looked at the rate chart. They used to always have a rate chart inside the closet door in the hotel, so I opened the door and I looked at it and it said, "THIRTY FIVE DOLLARS A NIGHT!" And I thought, "I don't have that! Oh boy, I'm going to be in the soup!" I had a checkbook, but I doubt I had that much in the checking account. I had some breakfast, and breakfast probably cost me 35 cents. When I went to the desk to check out, he said, "Oh, Lieutenant Allen, that will be $2.00!" I tell you, I was almost in a state of collapse! I said, "Gee, I was kind of worried because your rate card said it was a lot more than that" And he said "Military rates" With that, I drove on all the next day.

I was supposed to report on the 12th of May, and this would have been the 12th; they allow you travel time. I drove on to Laramie, Wyoming, which was just 15 miles short of the post. But, it was getting late and I didn't know where to stay in Cheyenne, so I went to a motel in Laramie. I put on my uniform when I was leaving, so as to report in uniform, and then I drove on and got there in the morning.

I'd Never Seen so Many Negroes...

My orders were just for one year of active duty at that time, so I was to stay at Fort Warren. I think my orders said, "Pending authorization of certain quartermaster units." So upon completion of that, I went to Fort Ord, California. I got there and reported to a guy that I ended up seeing some years later. He was a Major at that time. His name was Neil H. McKay. I reported to him, and he had a 1st Lieutenant at the desk beside him. I remembered that name for some reason, though I don't think I ever saw him again. Norby asked me if I had any problems working with Negroes, and I said, "No, I don't think so!" I thought to myself that the only Blacks I have ever seen were porters on trains, the garbage man, and some of the men that run elevators in some of the buildings. I knew there were some in school, as Pasadena had a fair sized Negro population.

So the Major said, "Norby, take Allen down to the 4th Regiment!" So, Norby jumped up, and saluted. I got in my car, and he got in his car and he led me to the 4th Regiment, which was a half-mile or a mile from the post. I'd never seen so many Negroes before in my life! There I was. There were white officers commanding the Black troops. Colonel Barbin was the regiment's commander. Nice guy. I met the other Lieutenants. I was there less than a month. I had arrived there just before the middle of May, and I left there on the 8th or 10th of June on a troop train

Quartermaster of a Troop Train to Fort Ord

On this early June morning, on a troop train to Fort Ord, there were fifteen Pullman cars—the old twelve section plus a compartment. Fourteen of them were full of white troops, and I had the fifteenth one full of Negroes. I was train quartermaster, which meant I had to get to the Post Quartermaster and get all the subsistence necessary for the trip. We traveled across what would have been the Union Pacific Lines, the Central Pacific Lines, Salt Lake, and then the Western Pacific. I've driven through it many times since, but that was the first time via the train. It was a beautiful trip down the Feather River Canyon and on down to Fort Ord.

When we got to Fort Ord, I was met by a Captain who said, "Where have you been?" We were expecting you several days ago!" I said, "Well, the troop train gets side tracked for everything." He said, "We aren't going to stay here, we're going down to Hunter Liggett." I spent a month at Hunter Liggett in a tent. Boy was it was hot and dusty! There were troops there just out of the draft center. They were mixed with all these old timers.

Battalion Supply Officer at Fort Ord

Here I had the job of Battalion Supply Officer. I had to provide rations for the battalion and then divide them between the companies. Then we moved to Fort Ord until early August, when the 4th Army was going to have maneuvers in Washington. We drove up with a truck battalion and camped on the way for several nights. We were up there for two weeks and it rained the whole time! We had tents to protect us from the rain, but the water just settled beneath the tents. We were always sleeping in mud.

Our job was to run our trucks to supply other units who were having combat exercises. Then we loaded up and went back to Fort Ord.

Quartermaster School at Camp Lee, Virginia

I got orders to report to Quartermaster's School in Camp Lee, Virginia. It was called Camp Lee at that time The troops were supposed to be there in early October. When the time came, we got in my car, put all our stuff in it and drove across the country. We stopped in New Jersey to see my older sister, who was living there. We spent a couple days around New York then we went down to Camp Lee. We were supposed to be there for three and half months. The school was interesting, but they treated us like a bunch of rookies, which I guess some of us were.

One nice thing was that they had tickets available for the Army/Navy game, which was in Philadelphia. I don't remember who won, but it was an interesting experience just because of the rivalry between the two. After the game we decided to go to the only restaurant we had heard a lot about, which was Book Binders. But we were told that you couldn't get within a block of the place in the evening after the game. So we ended up going to a place called Benny, The Bum's. That place was taken over by Navy Submariners. We were wearing uniforms, and needless to say, we felt very unwelcome. We stayed for dinner anyway, but I kept wondering when we were going to be torn limb for limb for invading their place! It was really funny. But we didn't have any problems.

"Freeze!, Put Your Hands Up..."

After that, we decided to head back to Virginia, but one of the guys wanted to see the Liberty Bell. I had been in Philadelphia once before, so I said, "Let's go, it's not very far!" So we drove over to Independence Hall. There wasn't any traffic around that late at night, and it was pitch-black. We parked the car right in front of the doors to Independence Hall. The four of us got out and pressed our faces against the glass, trying to see the Liberty Bell.

All of a sudden, someone behind us yelled, "Freeze! Put your hands up and turn around slowly!" Well, we already had out hands up, cupped around our eyes, trying to see in, so we turned around and there was a civilian guard with his pistol pointing at us. He said, "What do you guys think you're doing here?" We said, "Well, we just wanted to see the Liberty Bell?" He laughed and said, "Well, why didn't you just say so!" He hauled out a big bunch of keys, unlocked the doors, and turned on the lights! We got a personal viewing of the Liberty Bell, and then we went back to Virginia.

"War With Japan"—Declared

We stopped at one of those tourist home things that night because they didn't have motels back then. My mother was going up to New Jersey to visit my sister and she heard so much about Williamsburg and Jamestown that she wanted to go there. Williamsburg is an interesting place; you could spend a lot of time there. Afterwards, we drove back to Richmond because we were going to put her on a train to go up to New Jersey. We pulled up in front of the hotel, and the paperboys were screaming, "WAR WITH JAPAN! WAR WITH JAPAN!" That was the first I had heard of it. We bought a paper and took her up to the RFP station, and put her on the train to go on North. It was about a week later, in mid December when they gave us orders to go back to our organizations.

Motor Maintenance Assignment

Eventually, I received a telegram from the 4th Army, saying that I was relieved of assignment with the truck battalion, and that I was to proceed to Camp Roberts for assignment with the 83rd Quartermaster Company. I didn't know what the 83rd Quartermaster Company was. Camp Roberts was a huge place. There were 30-35,000 troops there! I was assigned to a motor maintenance organization. And most of the men had IQs of well over a hundred. I thought, this must be heaven, and it was...they were a wonderful group to work with. I went in as a 2nd Lieutenant, and there were two 1st Lieutenants in the company, at that time, a Lieutenant Waldon and a Lieutenant Sherwood. I was of course considerably junior to them.

Moving up the Ladder

This was during January of 1942. I was there at Camp Roberts until September. In the meantime there was an order from the Adjutant General that said that the reserve officers were being ordered to active duty. There were many Second Lieutenants who had been on active duty for a number of months who knew more about what was going on, than a lot of First Lieutenants just being ordered to active duty. Therefore, commanding officers could recommend 2nd Lieutenants for promotion to First Lieutenant without their having been in a year and a half, or three years as it was then. I was lucky, and I was promoted to First Lieutenant in March of 1942; then I was promoted to Captain by summer. I was very lucky, in that regard. Then we got orders for overseas shipment and in due time moved to Camp Stoneman, then to San Francisco at Pier 45.

To Australia on the U.S.S. Vernon

They put me on a ship that the Navy was operating, named the U.S.S. Mount Vernon. We had over 6,000 troops on it! I was lucky again, because I got in an A-Deck cabin that was supposed to have accommodations for three men. They had added cots, so there ended up being five of us total. But I was the first one to get in, so I got a bed by the porthole. We had our own bathroom and bathtub, but the only trouble was that there wasn't just the five of us as we first thought. Other people who didn't have their own bathing facilities, pleaded "Oh, can we pleeeease use your bathtub?"

Anyway, we had it pretty good, except for the food— It was vile! I couldn't believe it, because it was a ship that had been in San Francisco for several days. It could have been stocked with some decent food. There was no milk aboard, just powdered stuff. There were no eggs, nor fresh vegetables. Nothing! I couldn't understand it. I would have understood the lack of adequate food rations if the ship had been deployed overseas and was just returning to the United States, but not the other way around!

The troops were stacked three deep, and they were way below deck. I felt sorry for them, but there wasn't anything I could do about it. They actually had it a lot better than most ships. Some ships had guys stacked four and five deep. When we sailed out of San Francisco, I had finally heard where we were going. But I couldn't tell anybody, until we were out of port. I knew we were heading for Australia. You've heard a lot about convoys, and so on, but where were the other ships? Well, there weren't any! As we left the wharf, a destroyer came down from Mare Island, and one of the blimps came, so the two of us were sailing. And we thought, "This sure is nice to have a destroyer among us for our own private protection." Well, when we got out there, and the sun went down, the destroyer's whistle went "BOOP BOOP," and it turned around and headed back! It only went as far as the blimp did! So, we were on our own. The ship could go pretty fast, but we took the typical zigzag course heading southwest for New Zealand.

We were in Auckland for one day, and went ashore for a half a day. Half the troops were allowed off in the morning, and the other half in the afternoon. We had an anti-aircraft brigade on the ship, and they were getting off at Auckland. That left a little more breathing room from there on over to Sydney. A lot fighting was still going on up north, but we stayed south of that. The Corps Commander, Robert Eichelberger, was active for years in the Pacific War, and he wanted the ship sent to Port Moresby, but the Navy refused. They said, "No, it was too dangerous!" So they had to take us off in shore boats and small ferries. Thousands of troops offloaded the ferries and boarded troop trains. The troops were shipped to a place called Warwick Farms, which was a race course. The Australians are crazy about horse racing, so there are racetracks everywhere. It was raining, and they had Army canvas cots for us. But they didn't do much good because the ground was so muddy and soft that when you got on your cot you just sank up to the canvas in mud! We were there only a few days, and you can put up with most anything when you're young. It was all interesting—one big adventure.

1st Corps Ordnance and Motor Maintenance

By this time I had become acquainted with the Quartermaster. The Motor Maintenance Company had become the Ordnance Motor Maintenance by this time. We found out that we were going to be 1st Corps troops. That meant we weren't in a division, and we weren't in some other battalion. This Ordnance Major that I had become acquainted with in our travels told me that he had found out that my company was going to be in his Ordnance Battalion. So, would I be interested in going in and finding the Southwest Pacific Ordnance Headquarters to see if we could learn anything about where we were going. We didn't have any vehicles, so we caught a train into Sydney. We were in filthy clothes caked with mud.

The Grace building was part of the Grace Shipping Lines. WR Grace and Company had built this big, beautiful, modern, building in Sydney. And the Ordinance Officer had an office in there. We went in, and it was going to be a few minutes, before he could see us. We both needed to go to the rest room so we asked where the latrines were. We were standing at the urinal, side by side next to a great big Swede, and he started laughing! We said, "What's the matter?" He said, "See this? I'm going to have to tell my wife what they do with 'Royal Dalton' over here!" Royal Dalton is a type of fine china dishware, but there it was the logo for the urinal in the latrine! We didn't learn anything new from the Ordnance Officer though because he wasn't talking. So we went back out to Warwick Farms and loaded up on to trains.

In Australia, each state had it's own railroad, and the gauge of the track was different. You couldn't go from one side of Australia to the other in the same car. Anyway, we were on a train going up to Brisbane. When we got there, we had to get everything off of the train because all of the tracks to Queensland were narrow gauge. After getting back on the train, we went on up to Rockhampton, which is about 500 miles north of Brisbane.

Giant Roos and Paw Paws

The trains were little steam engines and they sounded sort of like teakettles. When they came to a hill, they really struggled. You felt you should get out and help push! I remember one time going along, just up a slight grade and we saw a lot of kangaroos of all sorts. And here was one of these giant roos, just going along beside the train. He was just going so easily, and the train was struggling. When we would stop at a station, there would be kids selling papayas and mangos. They called them paw paws. Some of the local women would have stacks of sandwiches and cold lemonade. Some were Red Cross; others just helped out of the goodness of their hearts.

When we got there, they built a mess hall for us and we set up camp. We were right next to a MASH unit- "Mobile Army Surgical Hospital." Sometimes early in the morning, while I was out checking out my unit, I'd see the

Colonel of the MASH unit, drinking his coffee. He would always invite me to come over and have a cup of coffee with him. His name was Col. Dufresne. Here I was a very junior Captain, and here he was this very senior Colonel Medic. I had been around senior officers before, but a "Bird Colonel" was something else, so I didn't always feel too comfortable visiting. He didn't make me feel uncomfortable. It's just an issue of respect.

We then moved our unit to an old abandoned orphanage, so I didn't see Col. Dufresne anymore. But that wasn't the last time that our paths would cross. It turned out that he was the same doctor that had delivered my wife when she was born in the Philippines.

I had been over there for six months. We have gone over in October of 1942, and it was now March of 1943. We were the First Corps troops, and during this time, the fighting in New Guinea was well under way. I received orders to leave my present assignment and to go to Port Moresby, which is on the south side of the island.

First Plane Flight, on a China Clipper, 200 Feet Off the Water and no "Sick Bag"

My transportation there was in a seaplane. It used to be a Pan American China Clipper. But the Army had taken it and was using it during the war. I showed up at the wharf where I was told to go. Pretty soon some Aussies showed up and said, "Aye mate! Are you going in the clipper?" I said, "I guess so." I had never been in a plane in my life, and I was not real fond of the idea. They said, "Well come on mate, get in!" There were only four seats in the plane. So I decided to sit in one of the seats. It was better than rolling around on the floor. Pretty soon another boat came in with one guy in it. He came in, looked around, and asked me, "Can we sit here?" I said, "Until we're told different." He sat down in one of the three empty chairs. Little bit later, the other two were filled up. We all sat there, bouncing up and down for quite a while.

Boatload after boatload came until the plane was very full, probably 150 people. Then there was some talk up in the cockpit as to whether or not we were ready to go.

But, no, we needed to wait for other personnel. Finally this other boat pulled up, with flags flying. Four men got out, and they were wearing suits and pants! They got in, looked around, found an empty spot on the floor, and sat down. The pilot started the engines and took off. We flew at about 200 feet above the water all the way to New Guinea.

That plane ride was so rough! I was sick the whole way, and they didn't have sick bags in those planes—at least not in the military. We got there, landed in the bay, and got off. And here was an Aussie band playing and flags waving. Then those four guys got up, and stomped out. It turns out, that they were members of the Aussie Parliament and we had usurped their chairs! Four guys. Four chairs.

After all that, I was pretty tired and dragged out, but I had to go hunt for the truck battalion where I was assigned.

New Guinea and the Planet Mars

I knew about as much of New Guinea as we know about the planet Mars. New Guinea was as remote a place as an American from Pasadena could imagine. It certainly was not a place to fight a war. It was a land filled with headhunters and cannibals, giant sea going crocodiles, poisonous snakes and insects, fevers of all types and descriptions, swamps and impenetrable jungles!

Commander and Port Authority for Port Moresby and Negro Battalions

The Japanese were within 26 miles of Port Moresby, and if Port Moresby fell, Australia would have been wide open for Japanese assault. In addition to daily tropical rains, the Japanese rained bombs on Moresby on a daily basis. As commander and Port Authority, my job was to deliver supplies to the fighting front up in the hills overlooking the port.

I showed up and it was another battalion of all Negro soldiers. They had had all kinds of political problems and I was relieving a guy that had practically gone nuts. They turned out to be a very good company. I was with them for nine months. In the eighth month though, another Major was assigned to the battalion. He was surplus and was sent up from Brisbane. There wasn't much for him to do, so he was assigned to be the sanitation officer among other things. Well this guy just started nit picking and driving everybody crazy! We called him "Super Sanitary Stottlar" He was driving us bats. Well, in a couple of weeks, he was called to the base headquarters.

Captain Dave Allen in New Guinea, 1944

PHOTO COURTESY OF DAVE ALLEN

When he came back, he came right to me, and he said, "We're both moving to the 394th Port Battalion." It was just down the road from us, but this battalion had had all kinds of problems! I guess we had done so well with the first unit that we were assigned to do the same for the new battalion.

Going Crazy and Court Martials

It was another all Negro battalion, and you want to talk about a mess! Their leader was the only white man in the battalion, and the poor guy was going out of his head running that outfit, so they wanted to send him back home to the States.

We went to this new battalion, and boy was it a mess! Stottlar didn't like this one little bit. He knew the right people to talk to get himself orders back to the States to go to the Command and General Staff School. I was left there as the only white man in an all Black battalion commanding as a Captain.

Stottlar was nice enough to give a recommendation that I be promoted to a Major before he left. This was before integration had really taken place, so the situation was a bit unusual at that time. That battalion was an administrative nightmare. There were at least 50 different court martial cases that had been opened, but never investigated. Most of the officers who had charged these guys in the first place had all left and gone somewhere else! Anyway, I was the investigating officer, so I had to go around and try and find out what had happened. I was able to close a lot of them because many of the guys who had been charged had been in custody longer than they would have been if they had actually been court martialed!

Keeping the Dispensary Open —Syphilis and the Miseries

Next, I was the Medic person in the battalion. The previous Medical Officer had been sent back to the States because he had a bad case of syphilis. Imagine that, the medical officer! Anyway, because he was gone, we were told that we had to shut down our dispensary. I started holding sick call myself. It was very busy because we were running the port. Twenty-four-seven! After a while, I started getting these guys with the miseries. I would send them to the hospital, and then afterwards, I would get disposition reports back. They would say, "Such and so, has been admitted for psychiatric evaluation—supposedly having symptoms of withdrawal."

Burning Crops of Marijuana

After about seven or eight of these reports, I really started wondering what these guys were having withdrawals from! So I asked my sergeant what this all meant. He said, "Well Major, you burned it all up!" I was confused, so I asked him, "Burned it all up! What do you mean I burned it all up? Burned up what?" He said, "You burned up their entire crop!" These guys had planted an entire crop of marijuana, and I had gone around doing weed abatement, and had burned it all up. I had thought that it was really odd that when I was burning, all these guys jumped up from an outdoor movie that they were watching. They saw me burning this dense brush area near the camp, and they all came running over, stamping it out as fast as they could! I couldn't figure the whole thing out at the time. Why did this area burn so much better than everywhere else, and why were the troops so frantic? Anyway, these men claimed they were having withdrawals, but in the end, the battalion straightened up very well!

Stacks of Human Skulls

There was never a dull moment over there. I remember one day a tug was towing a string of barges to Moresby when under threat of attack, the skipper cut the towropes and fled to the harbor. The barges drifted down the coast and ran aground. I commandeered a B-24 to find the barges and recover the supplies. We flew at treetop height over the ocean, jungle, and aboriginal villages. They had stacks of human skulls in their villages! We finally found the barges and towed them back to the port with all the supplies intact.

In August of 1944, my promotion to Major came through, but the administrative hassles were still going on. Soon after I was promoted to Major, the Port Commander, with whom I had been working closely for months, became ill. I think he was going back to the States, so the Base Commander said "Would you like the job?" and I said "Oh, heavens, yes! It has to be better than what I have now!" He said "I'll put you on temporary duty as a Port Commander." I still had this port battalion to work with and the truck battalions and all of that, but it was a lot nicer.

Mark That Experience Unstable and Hazardous

There were some interesting incidents in regard to working with ships. We had to plan when we were loading the ship, and we had to plan the layout for the cargo so that the ship was properly balanced. It was new to me, but I learned it quickly. I remember loading one ship and we were going to sail it that evening. Typically, five-hatch Liberty ships came because they were the workhorses of the transportation fleet. One time, we had a lot of engineer explosives to load, and we put those up in the #1 hatch at the bow. If there were some problem, it would blow the bow off and presumably the rest of the ship would stay afloat. We had already buttoned it up, as we called it; all the hatches were closed.

Then a kid Lieutenant from the base engineering came and said, "Colonel so and so told me to tell you that on the manifest, those materials should have been marked unstable and hazardous." I said, "You're telling us now?" So I had to get the stevedores back, and I unbuttoned the first hatch, off loaded all of it, and hauled it back to the engineer dump. We got it off, the trucks off loaded it and stacked it up. That night, all of that stuff blew up spontaneously! Boy was I glad that we got it off of the ship!

Off to Lingayen Gulf, the Philippines

Then on my birthday in 1945 and the end of the New Guinea Campaign, I sailed to the Philippines where I waded ashore at Lingayen Gulf. For modern readers, it is necessary to be reminded that in World War II, the whole world was subject to enemy action. Every time we crossed the Pacific, we were in real and constant danger from enemy submarines and aircraft. When assigned to a Port Battalion in the Philippines, we came under Japanese aerial bombardment with one additional hazard! U.S. Naval Forces in the area firing at enemy aircraft did not realize that their fire was hitting my battalion in the port.

The Big "Bomb Day" and Going Home

On August 6th, I was promoted to Lt. Colonel. It was a memorable day, because that was also "Bomb Day." We had dropped the atom bombs. We were told that we would soon be going home.

I had accrued so many points for rotation home that they were coming out of my ears. Within a couple of months, I boarded ship in Manila and headed for home. The food was really good this time. I got home the day after Thanksgiving. We sailed into San Francisco just as the sun was setting. The lights were coming on in the city and on the Golden Gate Bridge. They had a band and a boat to greet us. It was cold though! It was in November and we had just gotten back from the tropics, and we were wearing well-worn cotton clothing. We didn't want to go below deck though because we were home!

We couldn't wait to get on to American soil again, but when we got close to the middle of the bay, the ship dropped anchor and we had to spend the night there! We didn't go ashore until the next morning. A ferryboat came and picked us up and shipped us back to Camp Stoneman again for processing. Then we jumped on a train down to Fort MacArthur in San Pedro.

I got eight weeks leave because I thought that maybe I wanted to stay in the Army for a career. When my leave was up, I was assigned to Fort Mason in San Francisco. I hung out there while they looked for a suitable assignment for me. They offered me an assignment to go down to Uruguay. I said, "I just got home! I don't want to go to Uruguay!" I refused it. Then they said that they could use me at Camp Stoneman. But what I knew of Camp Stoneman wasn't too thrilling. But I went and worked as Personnel Officer until June. Then the Post Executive Officer was sent overseas, so they appointed me as Post Exec. That was the nicest job that I ever had in the Army. Everything worked just fine, but it only lasted two months because they decided to consolidate a few bases into one. They had a full Colonel running the new personnel unit, and I was the Commanding Officer under him. So when he left, I was the Personnel Center Commander. I stayed there from the summer of 1946 until October of 1947, when I decided to get out of the Army.

Bank of A. Levy, Trust Dept Manager, the Army Reserve and Marriage

I had served for seven years, so I decided that I was ready to go home to Los Angeles, to resume my career in the banking business. I worked and went to night school to earn a degree in economics at USC. I stayed in the reserves though, and received my promotion to full Bird Colonel. During my career in the banking business, changes in corporate structures along with the ever-present mergers caused me to look for new opportunities with expanded responsibilities in the banking field.

I met Bud Milligan of Bank of A. Levy, a prominent and successful bank in Ventura County. I developed and opened a trust division as the bank's first trust officer. Over the years, I became Senior Vice President, managed the trust department, and was responsible for managing the bond portfolio as well as many other activities.

I finally retired in 1980 from the position of Senior Vice President. I met my wife, Virginia, through some mutual military friends, and we raised three children. Virginia was a veteran of the Army Nurse Corps in Europe at the time of the Battle of the Bulge. She worked as a nurse for the men of the 101st Airborne Division.

Harold Breech

– THE B-29'S IN THE WESTERN PACIFIC

The men and women who lived the Great Depression, fought World War II, and were called back for Korea are fast disappearing as they go to their eternal reward and rest. They came from a different world with a different mind set. They were so poor and lived such hard lives. Opportunities were scarce and basic necessities were sometimes lacking. But they had a different attitude toward life. They had no concept of entitlement or safety nets. Social Security did not exist. Welfare was largely unknown and even if it were available, the poor but proud people of the agrarian Midwest wouldn't think of accepting charity if there was work available. Alas, many times there was no work and no money. Families frequently lived in multi-generational settings because families were viewed as God's and nature's plan for taking care of the young, the old, and the handicapped.

One day, Harold Breech's adopted daughter and grandchildren asked him to tell about his life and experiences. They must be unusual because many of the younger generation just do not care. So Harold sat down and wrote his autobiography in simple homespun language but with the joys, the sadness, the despair, and the hopes of his life and generation. His book should be required reading in our modern schools and history courses. Harold's book tells the real story of the America of the 20th Century.

I was born in Missouri in a rural community on January 18, 1919. I was born at home before the doctor could get there. I always say that I beat the doctor there because I didn't have as far to go as he did! There were five children in my family, but two died at an early age. One died from a lung infection caused by a watermelon seed that he had inhaled. They didn't have x-rays back then so they had no way of knowing which lung it was in. He was nine months old. My other brother died from diphtheria at four years old. They didn't have immunizations back then either. Only two boys and one girl, my younger sister, survived to adulthood. My family were farmers. We grew corn, wheat, and oats to feed the stock and, of course, ourselves.

We also had a garden where we grew our own vegetables, if we had rain. If it didn't rain, the vegetables just withered and died. It was a time when modern conveniences and appliances were unknown. The schools were simple one-room buildings with outhouses. The walk to school was quite a distance, and we would be practically frozen by the time we got there. When I started school, my older brother had to blaze a trail for me so I wouldn't get lost on the way home. I was the first child in our family to go to high school. But it was tough because we had to buy books, and we didn't have any money to buy them. Momma sold young chickens until we raised enough money to buy some used books.

About that time, Dad left the family, so grandfather took charge and kept us going. He was gone about three years, and things were tough. Those rough times taught me to pray. I asked the Lord to show me what to do in order to get out on my own.

35¢ to Saw a Cord of Wood

We lived in a multi-generational family that included my grandparents, parents, and my sister and brother. We were very poor, but we didn't know it because we didn't have anything else to compare ourselves to. Everyone was poor. My Dad was amazing because he could do anything. During the winter when there were no crops, he would hook up a team of horses and would go around and saw wood for people. He charged .35 cents per cord of wood! This was during the great Dust Bowl of the Midwest. I could tell, even in Missouri, which state the winds came from. The color of the dust told the story. There wasn't any rain to water the crops. One day I walked into the barn and found my father sitting on a box, with his head in his hands. He was crying. I remember going over to him and asking him, "Dad, what's the problem, why are you crying?" He straightened up and said, "Son, I'm sorry you found me in this state of mind. You know how hard we've worked each year, planting a crop, seeing it come up only to turn dry and blow away in the wind. After two years of this, and I have you kids to put through school, I have to clothe and feed you, I have the stock to feed… I don't know where to go from here." He was at his wits end. I remember going over to him, putting my hand on his shoulder and saying, "Dad, you'll think of something. You always do."

That was just like a shot in the arm for him because he got up, blew his nose with a big old red kerchief, and went down to the bank the next day. He got a loan for $50.00, and bought an old 1928 Chevy truck. My older brother was a mechanic, so he overhauled it. Instead of pulling the saw with horses, he could use the truck, which meant he could work within a 25 or 30 mile range instead of just two or three. That winter, we had food and clothing. Early that next spring, Dad went back to the bank and paid off his loan.

Times Stayed Tough—Dad Left

One Wednesday night, on Thanksgiving eve, I went to church with Mother. I was 16. When the invitation was given at the close of the service, this dear lady who was sitting on the other side of me, leaned down and said, "Harold, that's for you." I knew it was, so I took that first step towards the altar. In that moment, our Lord changed my heart and life forever.

Prayers Were Answered
—$1 per Day and Room and Board

I graduated from high school in the spring of 1937, and the day before graduation a young kid came to me and told me that his mother wanted him to ask me if I would come and help her put in a crop that summer. His father had passed away that winter. They had a farm with 160 acres, so I went to work plowing and planting and harvesting grain. An answer to my prayers! The lady would come out everyday, about mid-day, and bring me a cold drink and a sandwich. Mid afternoon, same thing again. Later, I found out that her kindness was not so much for me as it was to give the farm animals a rest because I would never stop that team of mules. She needed to do something to give those mules a break! My pay was $1.00 a day and room and board for the week.

The job at that farm was only for the summer, so I knew that I was going to need another job. The lady asked me to go along with her to Kansas City to visit her brother who owned a service station. It was great for me, because I had never seen that part of the country before. I liked what I saw, so I told him, "If you ever have an opening for help, would you consider me?"

I went back and finished up the job at the farm, and then when winter came, I went back home and helped Dad plant potatoes. One day my sister came in with a special delivery letter. It was from Mr. Warner, and it said, "Get a Social Security number, your job is waiting for you." I didn't even know what a Social Security number was because this was 1938, and it had only gone into effect the year before. I went down to the courthouse and got one, then got together what little clothes I had, and took a bus. I worked there just short of three years at $1.00 per day for 14 hours per day, driving a 1936 Chevy pickup truck. I hauled gasoline to all the surrounding farms, and I slept in the back of the service station when I was off duty. Mr. Howard had studied to be a Baptist minister, so he allowed me to attend church every other Sunday. He became like a father to me.

World War II starts—off to Aircraft School

World War II began while I was working at the gas station. A couple of friends stopped by and said that they were going to aircraft school and they suggested that I go too. It was a school in Kansas where they trained mechanics for the air industry. With my meager savings, I paid $165.00 for tuition and a mechanic' box of tools. When we finished school, we set off for California to look for jobs in the aircraft defense industry.

A Good Paying Job at Douglas Aircraft in Santa Monica

It was 1941. For so many people from the Midwest, Southern California was a wonderful place with orange groves, trees, flowers, and birds singing. I thought that we must have died and gone to heaven! The four of us rented a one-bedroom apartment in Santa Monica near the beach. With proof of our schooling, we found employment at Douglas Aircraft Plant in Santa Monica. The starting wage at that time was 50 cents per hour plus 2 cents an hour for a night bonus. When I received my first paycheck for twenty-one dollars, it was a lot better than the nine dollars I was getting at the service station when I left. This of course, was for only an eight-hour day instead of fifteen at the station. Time and a half for overtime, a nickel an hour raise, 10 cents for a large malted milk shake, ice-skating in Westwood – what a wonderful life! I started dating a girl that I had met in our church college group, and six months later we were married.

Pearl Harbor Bombed—I'm 1A

On December 7, 1941, I was leaving church when I heard newsboys screaming, "Pearl Harbor bombed." The Douglas Aircraft plant shifted from making warplanes for the British to making warplanes for the USA. A draft notice came classifying me as 1A. That meant that I was at the top of the list for the military draft. There was a tug-of-war between my employer who needed my skills to build warplanes and the military that needed me to join. So for a while, I received deferments but eventually, my time ran out.

I was drafted and sent to Fort Leavenworth, Kansas to be inducted. I was then sent to Buckley Field in Denver, Colorado for basic training. Every soldier remembers basic training. We would like to forget it, but without it, you're not a soldier. Most familiar would be the manual of arms, weapons qualification, close order drill, military hygiene, gas attack training, long marches, plus the usual in your face screaming belligerent sergeants.

Harold Breech on leave in Missouri in 1944.

Basic Training in the Army then off to the Air Corps as a Sergeant

We were living on base just waiting until one morning at about 4:00 a.m., they came in and instructed us that those whose names were called, needed to fall out and be ready to ship out at 8:00 a.m.. They called every person in the barracks except me and one other fellow. After they were all gone, I went to the orderly room to find out why. On my service record, I had stated that I had asthma as a child; that kept me out. All those soldiers were sent into Patton's army in Italy as foot soldiers.

About a day later I was called into the orderly room, and they said, "We see on your records that you have aircraft experience. If you don't mind, we'll give you a verbal test." As I was leaving the Sergeant at the door said, "Congratulations!" and I said, "What for?" and he said, "You are now a 555, in the Air Force." That meant that I was a sheet metal specialist with a Sergeant's rating.

I was assigned to Lincoln Air Base followed by mechanic's school. I wasn't always impressed with the Army way of doing things as compared to Douglas Aircraft Company. At times, everything seemed backward.

I was finally assigned to Grand Island, Nebraska as part of the 6th Heavy Bombardment Group, and I started training on the B-29s. Unfortunately, our hands-on training had been on the B-17's, which were being used mostly in Europe. The B-29 was a revolutionary aircraft with double bomb bay doors and pressurized cabin for high altitude flying. I learned all the new procedures of this new airplane; then they put us on a troop train headed for Washington State. We had no idea where we were going.

They put us on an old banana boat that had been converted into a troop transporter. We were soaking wet because we had to stand in the Washington rain for four hours waiting for the ship. They instructed us to get into our bunks, with our bag between our legs, and not to move until morning.

Arrival of the 6th Bomb Group on Tinian, 1944.

PHOTO COURTESY OF HAROLD BREECH

From Working on B-17s to B-29s Then to Tinian Island in the Pacific

So, the next morning, we got up and went to the chow line. That morning, the fish were well fed! Everybody was so sick. We pulled into Honolulu Harbor to pick up supplies, then to Pearl Harbor. It was less than two years after they had bombed it, and it was still a horrible mess. There were forklifts going like ants on an anthill, double-time, everywhere. We then joined a naval convoy because we were in enemy waters. We did a zigzag, seven minutes this direction, then seven minutes the other direction. We had destroyers circling us the entire time. I was beginning to wonder how big the Pacific Ocean was because we had been on it for three weeks already.

Finally we woke up one morning and we had dropped anchor at a tiny bombed out Island called Eniwetok. We had to drop anchor there because the Japs were still bombing Saipan. I thought that maybe we were going to Saipan. Two days later was Christmas Day, 1944. On the 29th, we dropped anchor again, off the Island of Tinian.

PHOTO COURTESY OF HAROLD BREECH

Fully loaded B-29 on Tinian ready to go to Japan.

We went down the side of the ship on rope nets, with full packs and rifles onto Ducks. They dropped us off onto a rolled-down sugar cane field, and said, "This is home, boys!" We camped in pup tents and ate rations while the infrastructure of the island was being constructed. Drinking water was limited to one canteen a day plus half a helmet for washing. Seabees were building a runway. Guard duty was a must because there were still Japs on the island, in caves, hiding out. The flight crews and B-29's started to arrive on January 18, 1945. The big bombing raids over Japan began in March, with every B-29 from Tinian, Guam, and Saipan placed into action. Our bombing raids caused mass destruction of Japanese factories and of the city of Tokyo as well. When the tempo of air activity increased, our ground crews were working round the clock. We had to sleep when we could; sometimes we'd even nap on the workbenches. Many of the planes we worked on, didn't come back. They would run out of gas a lot of the time, some crashing into the ocean upon their flight back home.

Then on August 5 and August 11, two lone B-29's took off from Tinian to bomb Hiroshima and Nagasaki. These were the atomic bomb raids that ended the war in the Pacific. I was among the last of the Bomb Groups to go home. But I kept busy acting as camp barber, playing some baseball, and catching up on mail from home. Finally, I boarded the U.S.S Olmstead and headed home. Aboard ship, I was once again the ship barber. I think I cut just about every sailor's hair on that ship before we reached the shores of the US!

Harold in front of one of the planes that never came back from its mission.

PHOTO COURTESY OF HAROLD BREECH

Returning Home

Every wartime service person can tell you, returning home to the US is an indescribable feeling. We had a big family reunion and celebrated Thanksgiving before my wife and I returned to Douglas Aircraft Company to go back to work. My wife and I were not able to have children, so we adopted an adorable little girl. Unfortunately though, our marriage didn't last. I received custody of our daughter and after three years I met my current wife. We both worked at Douglas Aircraft but were eventually transferred to the Huntington Beach facility where I was assigned to the Planning Division.

Time takes its toll and I ended up having a heart attack, which eventually led to my retirement and subsequent move to Ojai where we have lived for more than 20 years now. I am very active in my church, and am a member of the Senior Patrol, assisting the local sheriff's department. I am also assistant manager of the mobile home park where I live.

The thread of my life has been the Lord and His leading. He has directed my steps through everything, with exception of a few detours that I took. I can tell you from experience, that Father knows best! I have so much gratitude that I have been blessed with the love of my wife and family. I thank God each and every day for these blessings.

PHOTO COURTESY OF CHUCK BENNETT

Harold Breech, 2002

John Cal

WWII—Corsair Ground Crewman, Saipan

Japan bombed Pearl Harbor sinking or destroying the main battle arm of the United States Pacific fleet. For years, nations had wrangled over allocations and ratios of battleships for their respective navies. The world view was that whoever had the largest fleet of battleships would dominate world politics and trade. The Washington Naval Conference in 1922 had established the ratio of battleships among nations.

It was very much the same as today when nations wrangle over missile power and numbers. Japanese military warlords felt that they had delivered a crushing blow to American Naval power at Pearl Harbor. The irony of the event was that the battleship was not to be the decisive naval weapon in the war against the Japanese. The decisive naval weapons would be the submarine and the aircraft carriers, which had been spared from annihilation at Pearl Harbor. Most of these ships were out at sea and escaped unscathed.

Aircraft, carriers, and submarines are sophisticated instruments of war. They require vast armies of technicians who are trained to keep these modern weapons in action. At the same time, the technicians are trained to fight at a basic level, especially if their support activities are near the zones of combat. This was the role of John Cal.

Without aircraft, carriers, and submarines, the United States would have lost the war. And without the armies of technicians and ground and naval support crews, the modern weapons of war would not function. The war in the Pacific lasted almost four years.

The most decisive battles that determined the final victory occurred very early in the war. Those actions were the naval air battles at the Coral Sea and at Midway where the Japanese juggernaut was halted. But without the technicians and naval air support crews and staff, these victories would not have been possible. This is the story of John Cal, a sailor/technician that kept Navy Corsairs flying.

Basic—Sampson, New York at Finger Lakes

I was raised in the Albany area of New York. I worked as a machinist at General Electric during the early years of the war. My basic training took place in Sampson, New York. Later, I was shipped to a school in Detroit to learn metal smithing at the Ford River Rouge Plant.

Zig Zagging to New Caldonia in a "Kaiser Coffin"

I was then shipped to the Pacific Theater upon completion of my basic and advanced technical training. As with most personnel in World War II, I was sent overseas by ship. In those days, airplanes didn't have the capability to fly to the far reaches of the Pacific Ocean. Probably the most worrisome experience was sailing zigzag to New Caledonia and then to Espirtu de Santos in a liberty ship. We had to zigzag so that we wouldn't get torpedoed. Our ship was unaffectionately known as a "Kaiser coffin" because of its vulnerability to Japanese submarines and aircraft. They were also poorly made. One of the trades that I knew was welding, and I can tell you that these ships were not welded very well.

Repairing Pratt and Whitneys in Corsair Fighters

For over a year I repaired fighter plane engines from the fleet carriers while I was stationed on the Island of Espiritu de Santos. I worked on the overhaul of the Pratt and Whitney engines. They were part of the gull winged fighter planes, known as Corsairs.

Our repair units were called AROU's or Aviation Repair and Overhaul Units. Our job was to keep the combat operations functioning. As has been said before, no unit in the global war of World War II was immune from the hazards of enemy attack by land, sea, or air. And later, as the Naval forces hopscotched closer to the Japanese mainland. I was transferred to Saipan where I continued in aircraft support services for another six months.

PHOTO COURTESY OF JOHN CAL

A Jungle Souvenir I didn't Want

John Cal in front of a Japanese gun on Saipan, 1943

I'm a curious person, so sometimes I would go out into the jungles of Saipan to find souvenirs. I found spent shells, casings, a Japanese flag, and a good luck head banner from a Japanese soldier who obviously did not have good luck. One day, on my day off, I was out in the jungle with my buddy. I had carried a 45-caliber pistol just in case. As we were nosing around, we heard the click of a rifle bolt slamming a round into the chamber. I whispered to my buddy to see if he had heard the sound. He said, "Let's get out of here." We knew that there were still Japanese survivors out in the jungle, and apparently, we had come close to one of the diehards, and he was ready to kill. Needless to say, we made a quick retreat to the base with our hair standing on end.

PHOTO COURTESY OF JOHN CAL

Buggy Mutton

The food we had was awful. I learned to hate mutton, which was being supplied from Australia to feed the troops. Australian mutton is rank and the bread was full of weevils. Between the weevils and the rank mutton, I was hungry for fresh food where I didn't have to pick out little black bugs before I ate.

Python is Scary Fresh Food!

I turned to the jungle as a source of food. I found wild bananas and papayas, which were so delicious. Things were great until everyone else found my secret. Suddenly all the fruit was gone. In the jungles of Saipan, there were man-eating pythons. At least that's what the stories said, One story told of a 33-foot snake that had swallowed a man whole. I ran into one of these snakes in the jungle one day and I had to beat it to death with a shovel. I dragged that eleven-foot snake back to camp. I think people starting believing those stories after seeing that python! After that, most sailors were afraid to go into the jungle and I had the jungle to myself again. Pretty soon I was able to harvest wild jungle bananas and papayas again.

While all this was going on, the Japanese were flying over the base, bombing us where possible. Our units would disperse and hide under the banyan trees so we made it out alive.

John (left) and friend in San Francisco on the way home in 1945.

PHOTO COURTESY OF JOHN CAL

Home—Selling the New Fangled Television

I came back home to upstate New York and started working in the appliance business. I took a GI Education Bill sponsored course in radio and television and learned to set up TV antennas and hook up the sets. It was a new technology and soon every house had a giant TV antenna mounted on the roof. It was during a time when television was in its infancy and the opportunities were abundant. Appliance sales were good, especially with a pent-up demand from the war years when new consumer appliances were non-existent. Twenty-five years later, I moved to California with my wife.

A Patriotic Volunteer

Over the years, I was involved in a number of different jobs and activities. I worked at Villanova Preparatory School. I became an administrative officer at the Moose Lodge in Oak View. I was the American Legion Commander and later the County Commander of the American Legion. I am also a life member of the American Legion and the Ojai VFW Post 11461. I try to attend when possible. However, like so many comrades of the World War II era, my health is failing and I have moved to Georgia to be with my daughter. I want to stay in contact with the Ojai VFW and the comrades I have known for so many years. I look forward to the completion of the Living Memorial Book of the Ojai Valley Veterans of Foreign Wars. Like all veterans, I feel a kinship with all that served in the great causes of our Nation.

■■■■■■■■■■■■■■■

SEBASTIAN CATARROJA

— FILIPINO GUERRILLA

What would you do and how would you react if you awoke tomorrow morning and went to the market and suddenly discovered foreign soldiers occupying your town? What would you do if they were cruel and vicious and butted you with their rifles and jabbed at you with their bayonets? What would you do if all your civil rights and freedoms under the Bill of Rights and the Constitution were suspended? Current civil rights issues would pale beside the injustices of such a foreign occupation. Suddenly, your property could be confiscated, your liberties would be nonexistent, and your possessions could be commandeered at the pleasure of the enemy. Indeed, your very life was at the disposal of these foreign troops. How would you react if the enemy forced your daughters, wives, and sisters into brothels to serve the carnal pleasures of the soldiers, even sending them to service the needs of the army throughout Asia. You yourself could become forced labor for the conquerors, a virtual slave to the monster masters.

By the grace of God, America has been spared such a grievous calamity. Few Americans understand what defeat of our nation could ultimately mean. Most aggressor nations are not prone to treat the vanquished with generosity and kindness. The ancient Roman dictim still applies, "To the victor belongs the spoils."

But such was the very real experience of Sebastian Catarroja as he experienced life under the heel of the Japanese Army in World War II. It was a savage and cruel experience, mind-boggling in ferocity and unmitigated oppression.

Foreign Soldiers Control My Town

I had just completed high school and like most ambitious young men, I was planning to enroll in college. Planning a future is a normal activity in a normal world, so that morning, I went down to the bakery across the street to buy bread for our morning breakfast. It was January 2, 1942. I noticed that the streets were full of foreign soldiers with rifles and fixed bayonets at every street corner not far from the American Embassy. I remembered hearing the news that Pearl Harbor had been attacked and General Douglas MacArthur had declared Manila an "open city" to spare it from destruction. But the sudden occupation of our capital city by a foreign army, less than a month after Pearl Harbor, was a shock to us.

Our Lives in Turmoil, Our Freedoms Lost

The main door of the bakery was closed as a precaution against rampant looting; only a side window was open. As a result the customers clustered around the window fighting for the small space in their hurry to buy bread. Suddenly, a Japanese soldier posted at the street corner approached us and shouted, "Kurrah!" We didn't understand what he was saying and we continued reaching for the window in a disorderly manner. The grim-faced soldier began slapping us around, and I was hit hard as I was near the front of the line. We realized that all he wanted was for us to fall into line. I never forgot that "baptismal slap." It was probably at the back of my mind when I decided to join the guerrillas two years later in my hometown, which was being occupied by the Japanese garrison.

Under enemy occupation, everything changed. All that we owned or possessed could be commandeered for the use of the Japanese enemy forces including food, livestock, motor vehicles, fuel, sea craft, etc. We had no freedom. The civilians were brutalized daily by the Japanese soldiers. And as the news of Japanese atrocities spread, many of my countrymen fled into the mountains to be able to fight back. But this only endangered the civilians more. During times when the guerrillas ambushed enemy patrols, the Japanese soldiers would round up whole villages, force them into the Catholic Church, and machine-gun them to death. Some villagers were "masked" and forced to inform on other villagers. Many of us young men realized that we had no future and no rights as long as our nation was under Japanese occupation. We realized that freedom was not free, and that compliance with the enemy's demands was no assurance that we would be safe from torture, and our women safe from abuse. With this realization, my elder brother and I joined the guerrillas operating in the countryside. Our father objected because he feared for our safety.

I Join the Guerrilla Forces

Being a guerrilla was a death sentence, if caught. Your friends and family were not safe if the Japanese knew of your activities. In the face of terror, oppression and death, I was designated liaison officer of our military company. My duty was to deal with the civilian population. Primarily, I was responsible for the acquisition of food and other supplies for our unit. Because of my previous Junior Reserve Officer Training Corps experience in high school, I was given the rank of Second Lieutenant, while my brother, who had ROTC training in college, was designated company commander with the rank of Captain.

The guerrilla forces were poorly equipped and lacked logistics to efficiently accomplish their major mission to obtain intelligence for transmission to guerrilla headquarters and eventually to the American forces. Under equipped and outgunned, the major advantage of the guerrillas was the element of complete surprise and quick withdrawal after an ambush. These guerrilla "hit and run" operations were tricky at best. The Japanese who taken prisoner were immediately executed, as brutality begets brutality. Besides, we didn't have any food for them. However, this policy changed when the American Army returned in early 1945. Our unit was ordered to turn over to them every Japanese soldier we captured in compliance with the Geneva Convention.

My unit was the 44th Regiment of Hunters. ROTC Guerrillas on the main island of Luzon were attached for logistics and operations to the First Cavalry Division of the United States Army. I was designated Adjutant of my regiment in charge of the daily morning report, the updating of the roster, and the making of the monthly payroll. My unit was among the first guerrilla units to be paid real Philippine money, which had been printed in Australia. That replaced the Japanese "occupation" money, which was not worth the paper it was printed on due to wartime inflation. With the coming of the Americans, we were able to buy American cigarettes and other PX goods for the first time in three years. The Philippine peso was then worth 50 U.S. cents or two pesos to one U.S. dollar. (As of this writing the exchange rate is about 40 pesos to the dollar.)

Manila's Destruction Second to Warsaw

My regiment was attached to the American forces operating in the Ipo Dam sector in Bulacan Province, which was the source of Metro Manila's water supply. There was heavy fighting, as the Japanese wanted to hold on to the strategic mountain area just north of Manila. The really heavy fighting, however, took place in Manila itself. While it was declared an "open city" at the start of the war, the Japanese engaged the American liberation forces throughout the city, particularly in the Government Center in the middle of the city where some hand-to-hand fighting was reported to have occurred. The fighting was so savage that the destruction of Manila was second only to Warsaw. When the fighting stopped, it was discovered that underground tunnels connected all the city hall, legislative and other major government buildings. The Japanese had dug them in order to make their last ditch stand. All these buildings were heavily damaged by mortar fire, and the Japanese had suffered heavy casualties.

Upon the liberation of the Philippines, the guerrilla units of the Philippine Army were disbanded. I then re-enlisted in the Army of the United States (AUS). After basic training, I took a special course, which qualified me for duty in the Division's Adjutant's office. In response to a "want-ad," I applied for a position on the editorial staff of the Daily Pacifican. It was the U.S. Army newspaper for the Western Pacific, published in Manila by the Troop Information and Education Section of General MacArthur's headquarters. I eventually became news editor.

A young Sebastian at the Daily Pacifican, December 25, 1947

Production – T/Sgt. Sebastian Catarroja, T/4 Lucio Rabago and S/Sgt. Eustacio Sagrada

Filipinos Serving in the US Army Promised American Citizenship

Like all other Filipinos serving in the Far East (USAFFE) under General MacArthur, I was supposed to have qualified for U.S. citizenship after a three-year enlistment. This is especially so because Filipinos were considered U.S. nationals before our nation became politically independent on July 4th, 1946. However, the American and Filipino politicians conspired to deny Filipino veterans U.S. citizenship by discharging us a few days before completing our three-year enlistment. I was mustered out of the U.S. Army with the rank of Master Sergeant.

After the Military—the Manila Daily Bulletin

After the war, I joined the staff of the Manila Daily Bulletin, which was an American owned morning daily. I became editor of the Sunday magazine. In 1975, I retired from the Bulletin after 25 years, and joined the Philippine

Foreign Service as Information Officer in the Philippine Consulate Generals office in Chicago, Illinois.

Los Angeles, then Ojai

In 1983, I moved to Los Angeles. There, I edited several Filipino-American community publications until 1993.

I moved to Ojai in September of 1993 to join the World University of America as Press and Public Relations officer. At the same time, I continued to be active in veterans' causes, while maintaining ties with the Theosophical Society of which I am a lifetime member.

PHOTO COURTESY OF SEBASTIAN CATARROJA

Photo of Sebastian taken 2001 at the World University in Ojai.

When my wife passed away in November, 1999, I moved to Los Angeles to be with my only daughter who is a U.C.L.A. graduate and is employed in the administrative section of a major medical clinic in Los Angeles. I still continue my writing activities. I consider my involvement with my comrades of VFW Post 11461 to be one of the highlights of my experience in Ojai. In closing, I would like to mention that during President Bush Senior's administration, the injustice of denying Filipino veterans United States citizenship was finally rectified.

Interviewing Sebastian is like talking to a philosopher, a man who has lived and experienced life, suffered the vicissitudes of life. He has come out the victor as he sorts out ideas and events in such a way that all that has transpired has given meaning and purpose in life. Sebastian never acknowledged or suffered defeat of his spirit within his inner being.

Betty Culbert

- The Changing Role for Woman During WWII

Historically, the role of women in most any society has been limited. Occasionally, in times of duress, strong women obtain leadership positions and exert great power. But more often than not, women operate in the background exerting their subtle wills through sons and husbands. Boadicea, warrior Queen of the Britons, was one of those great exceptions, along with Elizabeth the First. Catherine the Great was another influential woman of history, but in general, women had limited roles until the advent of World War II. It was then that ordinary women were called to fill the gap in manpower needs necessary for the war effort.

The women of this era were not self-promoting. The women of World War II accepted the challenges of the day because of their deep-seated patriotism and loyalty to the nation. In other words, they stood for something beyond self-promotion and ego. The women survivors of that era still stand for the triune values of faith, family, and country. Betty Culbert was no exception.

Sometimes the restrictions on one group or class of people are broken because of economic and practical necessity. An underclass is frequently established, created, and maintained when there is an insufficiency of goods and services, work and employment, opportunity and attendant benefits.

The economic and political benefits of the women's suffrage movement had little effect upon the status of women and their ability to contribute to society beyond the home and family. Opportunity and employment were limited for men during the late 1920's and 1930's. Families, in general, were struggling to survive the economic and social catastrophe of the Great Depression. Minorities and women were still in the backwater of society, with a few exceptions.

Suddenly, the onset of World War II changed all that. Suddenly, there was a shortage of men and qualified workers as military aged men were pressed into the Armed Forces. Demand for goods and war materials exceeded the manpower needed to feed the hungry maw of the gods of war. In many cases, the only manpower was women power! Planes, ships, munitions, foodstuffs, and all manufactured goods needed to be produced in prodigious quantities.

Past prohibitions and taboos against women in the work place were rapidly lifted. Indeed, what had been prohibited became patriotic as women flocked to fill the employment needs of defense factories and offices, the Women's Army Corps, the Waves, as pilots for ferrying planes, as administrators. The genie was out of the bottle and the genie proved that she could do a man's job even while raising children and caring for a household.

Betty Culbert was one of those Depression girls from whom little was expected other than fulfilling the prescribed role as housewife and mother. The Depression years were limiting years, limiting in opportunities for all people. But World War II changed all that. The skill and talent of every American was needed to ensure victory against a deadly foe. Betty Culbert was one of those old fashioned girls who became a modern woman in the best sense of the word. Her story is included with her husband's story, which follows, because of her special involvement with the famous USO and work in the oil industry during World War II.

I Remember the Sleepy Town of Ventura

I was born and raised in the sleepy little town of Ventura. Ventura was known for two things primarily. It was known for the oil patch with the numerous transplanted communities of Midwesterners who founded the oil business as drillers and roughnecks. It was also known for extensive agriculture with different sections of the county supporting different specialty crops.

I lived on Ocean Avenue. not far from the Pacific Ocean. My mother was a widow and that necessitated growing up and assuming adult responsibilities quickly.

Japanese Shelled Our Shores

At the beginning of World War II, my family discovered that we were ensconced in close proximity to a coastal defense gun position. I reasoned that a gun emplacement was also a prime target if the Japanese decided to shell Ventura as they had just done up the coast with some oil wells in Goleta.

I moved inland to Foothill Road. That created another problem in my young life; gasoline rationing was in full force and my ration coupons were insufficient to provide for my transportation needs. I moved to Poli Street where I could travel to downtown Ventura merely by releasing the brakes thus saving gasoline. I secured employment at the Pacific Naval Air Station but despite my patriotic instincts, I did not want to be working in a zone subject to hostile enemy action. Ventura was a big oil town then, and oil was a vital industry to the war effort. I transferred to an office job in the oil patch where I continued to pull my weight in industry. Certainly, without oil, the nation could not win the war.

No New Autos—Everything Rationed!

Throughout the war there were shortages of everything: food, gasoline, clothing, appliances, and automobiles. No new automobiles were built for civilian use during the war years. Everything was rationed. One day I went to the market to buy a jar of mayonnaise and was challenged by the store clerk because I was too young to buy mayonnaise. I had to go home to get my birth certificate to prove my age.

Constant Air Raid Drills and Blackouts in Ventura

The town and coast were the scene of constant air raid alerts, blackouts, and motorized trucks driving through the streets blaring air raid sirens. Air raid wardens ensured total blackouts checking each house against visible lights during the night alerts. I remember the War Bond drives where people purchased war bonds to help finance the war. This was a particularly significant event in the oil companies. Top firms got to fly a special flag for their achievement and patriotism. I was ambitious and attended night school at Ventura College with studies in Spanish and Accounting. Sometimes the air raid alarms would sound and all the lights would go out. Students would have to walk home in the dark because no vehicles were allowed on the streets during blackout conditions. The next day required an early rising to walk back to college, get my car, and then drive to work.

Dancing with Red Skelton at the USO

Beset with a full schedule of work in the oil patch and night school, I still made time to make a contribution to the USO, United Service Organization, an entity that existed to make life more bearable for homesick G.I.'s stationed in Ojai, Ventura, and Port Hueneme. The main USO center was on Ash Street near Main, not far from the present Post Office. There were Navy dance bands that specialized in the popular dance band music of the 1940s like the Glen Miller Band. At times the girls went as hostesses to Hueneme. During one of these events, I had the opportunity to dance with Red Skelton, the famous comedian who also donated his time and service for the entertainment of the G.I.s.

Many of the enlistees and draftees in the area were from Nebraska and that accounts for the fact that many modern day Venturans have Nebraskan roots. They liked the area and returned after the war. Several other girls and I created a dance band combo specializing in the big dance band tunes of the era. I played the saxophone. One night the Navy band was a "no show" so our dance band combo was pressed into service providing music for the servicemen. Initially, they wanted us to play square dance tunes, but later as we became better known and more sophisticated, we played the big band tunes and developed a uniform of white skirts and red blazers. Eventually, our combo was designated the official USO Dance Band. In addition to the service dances, the band played for service clubs as our fame grew.

The German P.O.W. Camp at Saticoy

One unusual assignment was playing for the German Prisoners-of-War at the detention camp in Saticoy. There were military service outposts dotted in the back country of Ventura County. Occasionally, we would play for these out of the way places. All our military performances were donated as our patriotic contribution to enhancing the morale of the soldiers and sailors.

Canned Pineapple and Ham—a Luxury

Many of the foods of the civilian era were nonexistent. Ham and pineapple were nonexistent luxuries except when the dance band combo played at the Officer's Club in Hueneme. Despite gasoline rationing, the officers went to Ventura to transport the band to Hueneme. There the girls enjoyed those foods that civilians could only remember in their dreams: ham and pineapple. As we all know, rank has its privileges. Eventually, the band members received extra gasoline coupons because of their patriotic activities and efforts.

Patriotic Bracelet From a Japanese Zero

We became acquainted with many service men that sent mementos long after they were deployed overseas. One memento is a bracelet made from a piece of a Japanese Zero shot down. Other mementos include patches from the various units stationed in the area, and occupation currencies sent to us by G.I. acquaintances. Those years seem like yesterday, yet they were so long ago. Americans were a united people then. We worked together in a common cause.

Women of that era fulfilled so many roles in the war effort and war industry. We had been liberated with a purpose and a goal higher than self-interest. We were fired with the zeal and patriotism essential to preserving our democracy and traditions of freedom.

Sweat Equity Ranch in Ojai

After the war, I met and married Phil Culbert. a returning Army Air Force veteran from service on Tinian. We developed, or should I say created, a citrus and avocado ranch on the slopes of Nordhoff Mountain out of the alluvial sage-covered talus and rocks that covered the area. Much of our investment was through sweat equity with my husband clearing the land with a war surplus Caterpillar tractor while I managed the office and business end. As we built the ranch, we raised two children and now a grandchild.

Their marriage was never the prewar master over servant, man over woman, but life partners jointly participating and sharing in all the struggles and pain and blessings each of us experience in life. By working together, pooling resources and talents, they made their common effort a benefit to the common good. The benefits of Betty's lifetime experiences in World War II had given her the tools and confidence to build a successful and satisfying life with her husband, Phil Culbert.

PHIL CULBERT

–B-29'S, TINIAN, BOMBS AND ATOM BOMBS

The story of Phil Culbert is a story of the history of Ventura County as well as some of the events and experiences that molded his life. It tells of the prewar depression years in Ventura and Los Angeles Counties, years that helped mold the character of the patriots of that great generation. Phil's happy and inquisitive nature carried him through the years of military service and into a productive and interesting life as a rancher in the Ojai Valley.

1929 in Oxnard

I was a small child living on a family farm in what is now part of the housing projects and city-park in old Colonia in Oxnard. It was 1929 and The Great Depression had just begun. It seemed that times had always been hard for the farmers, but now, times were hard for everyone. Ventura County and the Santa Clara River Valley were distanced from the center of world events, and life was really quiet. Most farmers like my family, raised specialty crops. Our specialty crops were lima beans and walnuts, which were staples before the days of frozen food and fast food restaurants. In those days, our methods of farming were very similar to Biblical times. Many farmers allowed poor people to glean food after the harvest. The local mountains were remote wilderness areas inhabited by deer, bear, coyotes, and bobcats.

During the intervals between planting, cultivating, and harvesting, my father would take the family for country drives into the mountains. Los Angeles back then, was a relatively small city, and like Ventura, was the urban hub of vast agricultural development. The LAX airport was just fields of beans and row crops. The surrounding hills supported large herds of cattle and sheep. The Whittier Narrows supported walnut orchards, and Bellflower and Chino consisted of miles and miles of dairies. Citrus, walnuts, and vineyards covered much of the land that is now covered with housing, industrial parks, and shopping centers.

More Stable Water Supply was a Must for Los Angeles

The great manufacturing plants and mills had not arrived, but Los Angeles had men of vision, if not perfection. As always in the western states, the people who controlled the water also controlled the land. And William Mulholland, a water engineer for Los Angeles, was one man that understood that. He knew that in order to grow, Los Angeles needed water. In Colorado, the river alternated between floods and total drought. So they started programs to bring some of the water from the Colorado River to the Los Angeles basin—but more water was needed.

The city of Los Angeles trapped and tapped the deepest water resources of the Owens Valley. The settlers of the Owens Valley fought for their ranches and farms, which became desert due to the insatiable thirst of the city of Los Angeles. Gun battles were fought, and dynamite was used to blow up Los Angeles' installations. Men went to jail fighting for their farms and water. Although few people knew it, Los Angeles had built a large dam in an obscure desert canyon in what is now called Canyon Country. On one of our Sunday drives, we drove to the site of the new Los Angeles dam in "San Francisquito Canyon." It was amazing. We marveled at it, then returned home to let the experience slip from our minds.

Before 9/11, One of the Worst Man-made Disasters in America

One night I woke up to the frantic voices of my parents. It was 2:00 am, and my parents were in such a hurry that I couldn't even change out of my pajamas. I just pulled my clothes on over my nightclothes as my parents rushed me out to our 1928 Pontiac sedan. I can still remember the brass hood ornament--Chief Pontiac with his flowing feather war bonnet. All over Colonia and the surrounding areas, cars and people were moving east away from something horrible. The dam had broken—and that night, the Santa Clara River Valley became the scene of the greatest disaster in Southern California's history.

The dam was built in an area where the footings were of weak and decaying sedimentary rock. The cement was of terrible quality. When you would pick it up, it would just crumble. The dam's footings had torn loose and all that water came down on the sleeping valley. It took with it all the farmhouses, labor camps, and isolated buildings. Trees, houses, animals, mud and people were ground to a slush. Five-hundred people died. Afterwards, we saw piles of debris decaying in orchards, and fields stripped bare. Family and friends identified the corpses pulled from tangled debris and smothered in the mud. Los Angeles paid the families a token for their loss, and quickly erased the incident. But as child of Ventura, I will always remember that night. In Ventura County, the Mulholland name was literally mud after that.

Early Schooling in Ojai

The summer before I was supposed to go into first grade, I went to summer school in Ojai. My kindergarten teacher thought that I was allergic to the dust in Oxnard, and my grandmother who lived in Ojai caught wind of that and had me live with her. When school was about to start at San Antonio school, they really wanted me to attend, because they needed more students. There were only about 7 or 8 of us in the entire school. My aunt was on the school board, so she would pack me a lunch and I would walk to school from my grandmother's house on

Grand Avenue. My Grandmother's mother had home steaded that piece of land in 1880. They were the fifth family out here. My grandmother was quite a person. She and my grandfather were farmers. They owned about 60 acres from McNell Road to Carne Road. My grandparents met while they lived in England, and decided that they needed to come to this country. So they did, and they claimed the property out here, hired some Chinese men and got to work clearing the rocks and planting trees. My Grandfather's name was Bill Friend. He was known for having hand dug a water well 90 feet deep! My grandmother would lead the horse that pulled all the rocks out of that well.

A Love for Machinery and Mechanics

My whole life up until this point consisted of machinery, mechanics, and production procedures. So as I continued school, my favorite subject at Ventura Junior College was Industrial Technology, which was taught by a mechanical engineer. I graduated from Ventura College in 1941. There was war talk in the papers. Hitler was conquering Europe and the Japanese were on the march in Asia. My father was a farmer, but he also owned and operated a garage business. I helped my father repair farm equipment and machinery.

Once, when I voiced interest in turning some of the scrap metal into cash, my father warned me that the scrap would go to Japan and that "Some day, Japan will hurl that scrap back at the United States." He was a little different from most people.

A Job at Douglas Aircraft in Long Beach

Most people said, "If the Japs do anything, it will be over in 30 days" Little did we know, how right my Dad was. A lot of the young guys I knew were signing up for the Navy, but I decided that the best thing to do was to get a job in an airplane factory. I wanted to wait and see what was going to happen. One of my friends had the same idea, so we went down to Lockheed in Burbank to see if we could get a job. The man we talked to said, "We're not hiring right now, but why don't you go to Long Beach because I think that Douglas is hiring." So we drove to Long Beach, and gosh, we both got jobs! I got a job in a machine shop, and my friend got a job in final assembly.

We were in a new factory, with new machinery. Douglas had a lot of orders for aircraft for England, including B-17's, C-47's, and A-20's. The interesting thing about it was, that that was the first job I had that paid money—working on the family farm didn't pay anything! I did work for my room and board, and for gasoline for my Jalopy though. I thoroughly enjoyed the job I had at Douglas Aircraft. Douglas began hiring women to work because the wartime draft was taking so many men for military service. That was interesting. At first, most of them couldn't even read blue prints. These women became the famous Rosie The Riveters as their skills were honed and they began producing the fighters and bombers. We worked six days a week. We would get orders called "Red Orders" which meant they needed them immediately. So they would ask us, "Any chance that you could work seven days a week?" I was always a willing person to work overtime because that meant more money! I started out getting paid 60 cents an hour, and then every couple of months it would go up a bit. I think I finally got up to about $1.00 an hour.

The Army Air Corps Needs You...

Then one day in August of 1942, I got my 1A draft notice. I had seen an advertisement in the Long Beach paper, that Santa Ana Army Air Base needed young men to enlist in the Army Air Corps, which was then a branch of the Army. They said that if we were interested, to go directly to the Air Base. The first thing I had to do was to take a three-hour mental exam. The following week I had to go back for the physical. I passed, then they made me raise my right arm, and they swore me in!

But the service had enlisted so many men for pilot training, that they couldn't train them all. So they deferred my enlistment for six months. I didn't know a thing about it though. So I just kept waiting for the mailman to bring a notice for me to report to the Air Base.

A Pilot—or B-17 Mechanics School?

Finally, I got a notice to report to the Federal Building in Los Angeles, so I did, and we went to Santa Ana Air Base. After basic flight training at the Santa Ana Air Base, I was sent to Thunderbird Field in Arizona, where we flew Steerman Airplanes. It was in the middle of summer, 114 degrees! I disliked all the aerial maneuvers we had to make. I thought that the instructor was overdoing it, because we were supposed to be fighter pilots! We had a discussion about it in the barracks one night, and there was one fellow there who had worked for the FAA. He said, "You know, the future is in technology. Look at all these guys who are training to be pilots! After the war, you won't even be able to find a job! But if you have training in technology, you should be okay." And he was right. So three of us made an appointment to talk to the young Army officer in charge. Fortunately, he was one of these pilots who had flown his 25 missions over in Europe and had survived. He was a nervous wreck, but very polite. And he immediately said, "We need a lot of airplane mechanics. I'll send you fellows to a real good school in Amarillo, Texas." So that was the end of that! Off we went to B-17 Mechanic School in Amarillo, Texas.

German Prisoners
Picking Oranges on Grand Avenue in Ojai!

One day during the six months of school, I received an emergency letter from the Red Cross. I was needed at home. Nine hundred sacks of lima beans were sitting in the fields of the family farm with no labor available to load and transport them. My father had hurt his back and wasn't able to hoist the heavy sacks of lima beans. I was given two weeks' leave to go home to complete the harvest. While visiting my grandmother, I remember seeing German Prisoners-of-War wearing their summer uniforms, picking oranges on Grand Avenue. After loading and hauling all 900 bags of food, I returned to the base in Amarillo. I was then sent out on a field test during the worst blizzard in 54 years. All the machinery and equipment froze and quit working in the cold, so we hiked back to the base. Oddly enough, my otherwise useless, standard issue gas mask, saved my life. I used it to prevent my face from freezing as we had to walk directly into the stinging storm!

A Mechanic Assignment with 505th Bomb Group

The school ended up being real easy for me because I had been working on machines my entire life. But they kept trying to get me back into flying. They sent me to further training at the Boeing factory in Seattle, then they had me fly engineer on a brand new B-17 back to Wyoming where they put the guns on the planes. They were trying to entice me into becoming part of an aircrew with a brand new plane. But, no, I wanted to be part of the ground crew. I had to report to Lincoln Army Air Base for processing so I just hopped on a train.

Experimenting with the New B-29

I was all on my own so I could have just kept on going, on down to Mexico, but they trusted me. When I arrived at the base, they called me in to look at my records and I asked the guy who interviewed me, if I qualified to go to a B-29 outfit. It was a new airplane. The details of the plane were still top secret, real "hush-hush." The plane included a pressurized cabin along with many other advanced features. Besides, it was going to take the war to Japan, and I thought we'd be based in the Pacific on a nice tropical island, with coconuts, palm trees, hula girls.

Anyway, I had three good letters of recommendation that I needed to join the service, and they were well written so I qualified. They were forming a B-29 group in Harvard, Nebraska, called the 505th Bomb Group, so they sent me there. I really enjoyed working with ten or eleven young, happy new aircrew members, getting on this new plane.

In May, 40 of us mechanics were sent to the B-29 engine factory in New Jersey. There was a lot of work to get everyone ready to fly this new thing. The inspections were quite lengthy, and the pilots were still training on B-17's. After training, they would fly them down to Bautista, Cuba. They wouldn't give the navigators any help figuring out how to get there. It was training for the real thing.

We had been there in Nebraska from July to November, and it was starting to get real cold when we packed up on the train bound for Seattle, which was our point of embarkation.

We had to climb rope ladders in training for the ships and other stuff to get us ready, then we boarded a Liberty troop transport carrier and set sail for Pearl Harbor, where we sat for 10 days. We could not get off the ship, we could not write home or communicate with anybody. We were one of the first B-29 outfits, and our mission was to take the war to Japan. So everything was real hush-hush. We were told nothing, except that our destination was a small island in the Western Pacific.

Tinian Island—Going 24 Hours a Day

We first dropped anchor on the atoll of Kwajalein in the South Pacific. There was a beautiful swimming beach there with 80-degree water, but the rest of the island was bombed out. That was a nice break from the ship with saltwater showers though. After that, we loaded back up again and went to the island of Tinian, which was to be a major base for bomb runs against Japan. The entire trip lasted 42 days with a destroyer escort.

I remember climbing down the rope ladder on to a strange boat that was bouncing up and down. Right before we got to the shore I saw the driver shift gears, but he just kept going! Now I didn't know it, but we were on an Army Duck, which was an amphibious vehicle. I had no idea that these things even existed! Once we landed, boy, was that island a busy place! These Seabees were building an airfield, hauling one dump truck after another of coral rock, going as fast as they could go. They worked 24 hours a day. At night they would have big searchlights going so that they could work. Anyway, they gave us one-man pup tents and fed us K- Rations. Most of the men complained about the food, but I remember thinking that it was pretty good!

We did that for a couple of weeks, until they gave us five man tents to sleep in--just in time for a major typhoon with winds over 100 miles per hour! After the Seabees were finished building the 8000-foot runway, the planes started coming in. There were five of us mechanics, and we were assigned to one particular airplane. I was the Assistant Crew Chief. The Crew Chief was a 20-year Army man and he was, well, I guess he was tired. I guess that's why they gave me all the tough jobs to do. But I was 21 years old, and in good health, so it was quite a fun experience. While the air crews were doing practice runs it was pretty easy. But once they started flying to Japan, that was tough, because a lot of the airplanes didn't come back. They would run out of gasoline trying to get back. One morning we woke up and there were around 400 ships gathered around the island. They were getting ready to invade Iwo Jima. Once we invaded Iwo Jima we didn't lose as many planes because the planes could stop there, get more gas, and fly back to Tinian.

What to do for a Good Night's Sleep...

I remember a not-so-life-threatening midnight requisition that happened in broad daylight as my buddies drove down the base road. While driving behind a Seabee truck piled high with mattresses that were not tied down, my friend pulled up as close as possible to the leading truck loaded with the mattresses. One of my buddies climbed on the front bumper of our truck and snagged five mattresses. After that, my squad slept quite well in spite of our uneasy consciences.

Horrible and Constant Loss of Planes and Airmen

As good as our ground crews were, I still feel horrible about the loss of so many planes and crews that never returned from Japan. Some were shot down. Some were damaged and later ditched, never to be found again. U.S.

submarines rescued a number of men far out at sea. A few planes ran out of gas and crashed at sea. Other planes limped home to Tinian and crashed on the airstrip. Ever-present reminders of the war. Our hearts really went out to the combat pilots who endured daily dangers.

One terrible event that I remember is when a bomber crew of young men was complaining when the engines on their plane were not running properly. I remember that B-29. We maintained that plane with TLC, and it had a real good record of coming back with all four propellers turning. The plane had made a lot of missions and the nose was decorated with several small Japanese flags and about 35 small bombs representing its bombing raids over Japan. I'm pretty sure that it was a new crew of young men who had been assigned to the plane. They were very nervous and felt strongly that there was some mechanical problem with the plane. They were looking at the airplane, and were kind of suspicious. Most of the air crews didn't take the time to look at the planes. I overheard one of them say, "Well, I wonder if this old airplane is war-weary." Well, they got on board anyway and taxied out, revved up the engines, but they didn't go anywhere. Soon a Jeep drove out there, full of high-ranking brass. They boarded it, and commenced to rev the engines with a series of very high RPM tests. When they finished, the brass told the young pilots and crew that, "nothing was wrong with the plane, and to go ahead and take off." But what the brass failed to mention, was that the plane had consumed much of its fuel, and was intensely overheated due to their "testing." I remember watching the plane taxi down the runway, using the entire length of the runway to get off the ground. The plane was heavily loaded with 10 tons of bombs and 5000 gallons of fuel. It was having an obvious difficult take-off. It never gained altitude. Then it just dropped into the ocean in a huge fireball. Saying nothing, the "brass test-crew" just drove off. An entire flight crew lost. I felt just horrible about it.

I See Atom Bomb Come Through Tinian

I remember sometime around the month of June, a mysterious squadron appeared on base. This group had their area separate from everybody else. They were way off on the side. We wondered what in the world they were up to! I remember telling one of the guys that, "Those guys belong to a goof-off squadron, and they're not flying the regular missions." This new squadron never flew on bombing raids to Japan; they just practiced over and over.

We had to pass their planes to get to ours, so one morning as I was passing; I saw this bomb that was about half way up into the bomb bay. There was an MP standing there with a rifle, and we had never seen that before because everything was very laid back. So finally, one General became suspicious of the squadron, and went to the hanger of the new unit. He was ordered to leave. When he insisted on his rights and authority as a General, the Sentry threatened to shoot him if he didn't back off.

The incident created even greater interest and curiosity, until eventually, the whole world came to know the story of the atom bombs that were loaded at Tinian Island. The targets were Hiroshima and Nagasaki. Well, after the first bomb the Japanese would not surrender, so we had to have what is called an "all out effort" That's where every single airplane had to fly in the next mission. We were quite busy, trying to get all those planes ready to fly. In one day, 800 B-29's dropped bombs on Japan. That lasted about three days then we dropped the second atomic bomb. Boy that was it. It was all over. They had had enough.

Home on an LST to Hawaii

It was November, and I had 36 points. I was allowed to go home. Every morning I would get up and see what ships were going back to the States. And I saw that there was an LST going to Pearl Harbor the next morning, hardly anybody on it either. I remember thinking, "An LST, I wonder what that is?" Well I found out! It was another adventure.

While en route to Hawaii, we ran into a storm. I came to find out that LST's have flat bottoms, so that they can get in close to the shore to unload the tanks and vehicles. That flat bottom made the boat extremely bouncy. It would go up in the air and smack down onto the water. The whole ship would shake, and in my mind, I can still see the ship bending up to three feet between the bow and stern. After having watched "perfectly good planes" drop from the sky, I decided to talk to somebody about it. I asked this officer if he was concerned about the ship bending too much and he said, "No, it was designed to be flexible, because if not, it would break in two." That storm was horrible. There was water coming up over the sides and bow, and you had to go on deck to get to the galley.

I was on the tank deck, which is where they kept all the K-rations and the C-rations. So I had it made! All the food I could ever want. Fifteen days later and still alive, we reached the port at Pearl Harbor, Hawaii.

We were taken up to an Army post, where we waited until the next ship came in that was headed for the Long Beach Harbor. And would you believe, that I got a ride on the battleship U.S.S. Nevada. It was just as steady as can be! Our wake up call was, "Sailors, man your brooms, fore and aft!" In the 1950's the government destroyed that beautiful old battleship in the testing of the atomic bombs. I had quite an adventure during the war, not even one sick day during the entire time I was in the service. Never missed a meal!

Home to Ojai for Christmas

We got into Long Beach on Christmas Eve. I hopped on a streetcar headed for Los Angeles, and then I took a Greyhound bus to Oxnard. I got to Oxnard at about the middle of the night, and I called my Dad. He wanted to come pick me up, but there was a yellow cab right there so I took it home.

14 Hour Days at the Ojai Shell Station

I returned home to Ojai and I needed work. I had some connections though that helped. There was a Shell station on the corner of Ojai Avenue and Fox Street, and I knew that it was going up for lease. So I went in there and started selling gasoline, and working on automobiles for about 14 hours a day. I had to stay open every day in the year except Christmas Day. I met Betty in 1945 and we started dating. She did my billing for me for free. I was so tired after working so much that when I would drive to Ventura to Betty's house, I'd just fall asleep in her big chair. I'd take her to a movie and I'd fall asleep and snore, so she had to punch me to wake me up. I never had time to go shopping, so she went shopping for me. We dated for seven years, so she knew what she was in for! We didn't have the money to do what we wanted to do, so we just dated and worked while she was paying off some property she was buying in Ventura.

We Invest in Rocks, Rattlesnakes and Brush

When we got it all together, we were married in 1952. Then we purchased some land on the east end of Ojai. It was just a bunch of rocks, rattlesnakes, and brush, and the neighbors around here thought I was crazy because the rocks were so big. But I used my GI preferred status to purchase some low cost tractors from the Navy base in Hueneme. A young nurseryman that had too many trees came by, and said, "I'll let you have as many trees as you need, and you can pay me when you get the money." Imagine that! No interest, and an eyeball-to-eyeball agreement. So we got all our trees that way.

The "Hired Man" is My Wife

Things were different then. When the tractors needed work, I was the mechanic and my wife was the go-fer. When it was time to farm the land, I ran the equipment and she was the office crew. Betty was my "hired man" until we could afford to hire help.

When the kids came along, we built our house for $25,000. Betty designed it along with the help of an interior decorator. They took some rope and some stakes and laid it out on the spot! Betty drew up the plans and I and a carpenter friend built it. We have been a team throughout our whole marriage. We went into this marriage thing, not planning on getting out if we didn't like it. It will be 50 years this year, so I think it's going to work!

Phil Culbert, 2002

SANFORD DRUCKER

—*THE FORGOTTEN WAR ON AMERICAN SOIL*

Most Americans know of the Japanese attack on Pearl Harbor, December 7, 1941. But most Americans do not know that the one of the deadliest battles during World War II was fought on American soil. It truly is a forgotten war, but not by those who fought it. The Japanese invaded and occupied the American Islands of Attu and Kiska located in Alaska. The fight against the Japanese invasion of Alaska was a bitter campaign, but there was another enemy every bit as relentless and unforgiving. The second enemy was the weather and climate of the frigid Arctic. The American forces were poorly equipped to survive the blizzards, ice, snow, frigid temperatures, and the Willawalla winds that could create wind chill conditions that froze human flesh. To live and fight in such conditions was a constant and daily struggle to survive. The Aleutian Islands stretched across the Arctic regions of the North Pacific from mainland Alaska almost to Siberia.

From Poor Immigrant Sweat Shop to Entrepreneurs

It has taken me over fifty years to be able to speak about my war experiences in the Aleutians. I was born after World War I on December 20, 1919, to immigrant parents. My parents came to the United States from Russia and Poland when they were eight and ten years old. They worked in "sweat shops"—child labor factories. They lived in Chicago, and learned the language. When my father grew up he built from scratch the largest millinery company outside of New York, the Drake Millinery Company. They made ladies' hats.

Stock Market Crash and Depression Begins

In 1929, the stock market crashed. People could not pay their bills, so no money was coming in to the business. The domino effect...and it was not long before I saw men and women in the alleys of Chicago looking for food in the garbage cans. My father lost his business, then our home, so we had to live in a one-bedroom apartment, all seven of us. As I was the oldest of the four children, I slept on the kitchen floor. I remember selling Liberty Magazines at the elevated train station, working at the A&P market, delivering newspapers, and working in a paper factory to help put food on the table. Eventually, I got a job selling ladies shoes on commission. To escape the turmoil in my life, I used to listen to Buck Rogers on the radio. It inspired me to learn to build and fly rocket ships.

The Chicago Four-Year City College Committee

I decided to attend Wright Junior City College. There, I learned that if I joined the ROTC to be trained to kill people that the government would pay my tuition in a university. But I had more altruistic motives. To attend school to learn warfare was upsetting, little realizing that in a few short months I would be fighting for my life in the bitter Infantry combat in the Aleutians Islands. Instead I felt very strongly that everyone should have the opportunity for food, clothing, shelter, and education. I believed that education was a means whereby I could bring my convictions to fruition. I decided to form the Chicago Four Year City College Committee. I, and a team of like-minded people, worked diligently for several years, to pass legislation allowing this new opportunity in our education system. This team of people that I led attracted a lot of attention. Paul Douglas who was a University of Chicago professor and later the Senator from Illinois; Charlotte Carr of Hull House; the Reverend Bradley Preston; and even Eleanor Roosevelt, our president's wife, joined us!

War in Europe, Isolationism in the U.S.

In 1941, the radio and newspapers led us to believe that the "American First" proponents were strong. They said, "Let them fight in Europe. We need to take care of ourselves." I knew a few students who went over to fight in the Spanish Civil War against the dictator General Franco, who was backed up by Nazi Germany. Have you read For Whom the Bell Tolls by Ernest Hemingway? It's about that war—The Spanish Civil War.

Sanford at Camp Roberts California, 1941

PHOTO COURTESY OF SANFORD DRUCKER

In June 1941, at the age of 20, I volunteered for a one-year draft in the Army. I decided to join during the month of June so that I would get out in June, 1942, so as not to lose any time with my college education. Incidentally, the day that I was drafted, "The Chicago Four Year City College Bill" was passed in Springfield, Illinois! All of our hard work had paid off. That was to be the first of many four-year City Colleges in Chicago that were subsequently formed.

Boot Camp at Camp Roberts, California

When I got on that westbound train in Chicago, I had no idea that war was imminent for the U.S. It was the first time in my life that I traveled more than a hundred miles from my home. I was amazed to see this large wonderful country of ours as the train wheels clicked away mile after mile. Finally I ended up in Camp Roberts, just outside Paso Robles in Central California.

In the hot sun of Camp Roberts we endured basic training for desert warfare. I met a couple of other draftees who became my buddies: Herman A. Erickson and Bill Boscamp. And although we have lost touch, they are dear to my heart even today. So, after we completed basic training, we were lined up and counted off—the first ten were to go to one place, the next ten to another place. And so forth. Herman, Bill and I were in the same group.

Off to War in Alaska

Bingo! We found ourselves in Fort Lewis, Washington where we then boarded an old ship headed for Alaska! What a memorable voyage! I had never been on a ship before. The ocean waves were taller than the ship, and they came crashing over the bow and deck. I remember troops crowded down below in bunks that were eighteen inches apart with hardly enough room to crawl in. Bunks were stacked six high. Everyone was sick and throwing up on each other for days. Finally, we arrived at Anchorage, Alaska.

Abuse and Challenge

The three of us—Bill, Herman, and I—were sent to Fort Richardson and became members of the "Fourth Infantry Regiment Anti-Tank Company." We never saw a tank. We were Infantrymen. Our company was a regular army outfit and we were the first draftees they had even seen. "A bunch of college kids," they thought. I remember walking into the barracks for the first time. Three tall guys grabbed me. Two of them held my arms and legs while the other held my head and poured white lightning down my throat. In that moment, something happened within me. Like a flash, I said to myself, "I would rather die fighting than let anyone treat me this way." So I started fighting back, quickly becoming a bloody mess. But every time they knocked me down, I got back up. It was not long after that day, that I led those men into battle as their squad leader.

PHOTO COURTESY OF SANFORD DRUCKER

Attu island off the tip of Alaska, 1943. Photo procured from a movie newsreel that my parents had seen me in.

The men that I was serving with had come from the Depression, from the Oklahoma dust bowl, from hunger, and with little or no education. But they were great soldiers. I remember one chap from Kentucky. He was about five feet tall; he couldn't read or write. All he could say when you spoke to him was, "Don't know what to tell you. I'm too much losers." It was a rough group.

No Protection—Lungs Froze and He Died

On December 7, 1941, while the Japanese were attacking Pearl Harbor, Dutch Harbor, an Aleutian Island close to the Alaska mainland, was also strafed and attacked by

Japanese planes. That morning, I was sleeping at Fort Richardson near Anchorage when a fighter plane strafed our barracks. The bullets whizzed by on both sides of my cot. And from that moment on, I fought for my life, in the battles of the Aleutian Islands. I was there for over three years without a day off.

It was bitterly cold. I remember one soldier who attempted to cross the landing strip without his parka. He got halfway over when his lungs froze and he died instantly. Somehow though, our pet, Molly the Moose, didn't seem to have that problem. She was about the only thing that made us smile in those days!

My Short Cut to Hell

There we were in Alaska--trained in desert warfare. There were so few soldiers around, that each of us had to patrol five to ten miles of the Cook Inlet, totally alone. We carried 1903 Springfield rifles. I will never forget the day that I was patrolling alone in the forest. Everything was white with snow, and the bitter wind was blowing. Suddenly I saw a short cut, which looked like a five or six-foot jump into the soft snow below. I jumped through the snow and hit the ice of a frozen river below. I landed hard and my lower left leg was jammed out to a 90-degree angle. My kneecap ended up near my crotch. I was in excruciating pain. I don't know how long I lay there, but it seemed like forever. As the pain continued to increase, I finally said to myself, "I can't stand this any longer." I could see my rifle about ten feet away--so I grabbed my left leg and crawled, inch by inch until I reached it. With my finger on the trigger--I blacked out. When my eyes opened, my left leg had two pieces of tree limbs wrapped around it and I was in a medical tent in the forest. To this day, I don't know who saved me. I am so thankful to that person! That injury continued to cause me pain for many, many years. My knee was operated on four times after the war and was completely replaced in 1998. Nevertheless, several months after my wounding, the Army said that I was fit enough to go with our outfit when it took off for the first Aleutian Island to be occupied by US force, the island of Adak.

First American Troops to Reclaim Adak

On the way to our new destination, our ship's engines stopped suddenly and everyone was instructed to be absolutely silent. I remember hearing the Japanese submarine engine. It was so close to us! We waited and waited and waited, huddled together in the bowels of our ship. You could hear everything. You could hear each controlled breath of the men. Time stood still. Eventually, we reached a safe harbor on the big island of Kodiak. And yes, there are huge Kodiak bears on Kodiak Island. They are about ten feet tall when standing! There are also giant crabs crawling on the beach. The natives had huge oil drums filled with boiling water and they threw the live crabs in to cook them. After a day or so on Kodiak, we proceeded to Adak where we were the first American troops ever to land. Adak was a wasteland of frozen tundra—a few blue foxes and no trees whatsoever.

Our task was to lay metal strips on the tundra so that airplanes could land. But an even greater task was just to stay alive! Most of the time it was so foggy that I had to get very close to a person even to see him. The "Willawalla Winds" got up to 120 miles an hour. I remember being so afraid that the wind would carry away one of our buddies who was only about five feet tall and weighed ninety-nine pounds. When the Willawallas would blow, we would put a rope around his waist and connect him to someone on his right and on his left, otherwise he'd blow away just like a kite! He was small all right, but he was tough. His words would give me courage when he'd say, "Don't f---- with me, I'm ninety-nine pounds of dynamite!" He was too. One day Mr. Dynamite and I were on patrol when all of a sudden the ground started shaking. It shook so much that we had to get down as if we were doing push-ups. About twenty feet in front of us, the earth opened up like a crack and widened until it looked like a huge canyon. Just as quickly as it opened, it closed again leaving a sheer cliff in front of us as high as a two-story building.

Men of the Ojai Valley—Freeze to Death

We were told that the Japanese were small, slant eyed yellow people. But we found on Attu that we were fighting the Japanese Imperial guards who were six feet tall, well armed and trained. They were as dedicated to their country as we were to ours, and they fought to the last man. Sometimes, new U.S. troops, fresh from basic training camps with canvas legging desert uniforms, would disembark from landing boats. When they would hit the water, most of them would freeze to death. I can still remember frozen bodies floating on the shores of Massacre Bay as we climbed down a net on the side of our ship. I found out later, those most of those men had gone through a training camp set up at The Ojai Valley Inn. It's strange how life works, as 60 years later, I now live in Ojai.

Sanford Drucker spent over three years on Attu Island in the Aleutians with the 4th Infantry Regiment, Part of the Polar Command.

PHOTO COURTESY OF SANFORD DRUCKER

Drive the Japanese Off Fishhook Mountain

I was sent as a scout to the island of Shemya, where we were sent to watch the Japanese on Attu prior to the invasion. When our company arrived, the Japanese were in the mountains. Our mission was to go up Fish Hook Mountain and drive them to the sea.

Native Alaskan, "Blanket Ass" in My Squad

In my squad there was a guy named "Blanket Ass" (the only name we knew) and his brother. They were native Alaskan Indians with some Irish and you name it mixed in. They were fur trappers who were inducted into the U.S. Army when a snow plane landed near their trap lines in the middle of an Alaskan forest. They could hardly read or write, but they were experienced in surviving in this frozen climate. Great soldiers! As we climbed up Fish Hook Mountain, the enemy had us covered with machine-gun fire almost everywhere. We were lying flat on the ground when Blanket Ass' brother got hit. Blanket Ass rose like a mountain, put his knife between his teeth, and walked toward the machine gun nest. How he never got hit, I'll never know. We covered him as best we could. When he got to the machine gun nest, he grabbed an enemy soldier by his foot, picked him up like a twig of wood, and smashed him to bits on a rock. The others fled in terror.

PHOTO COURTESY OF SANFORD DRUCKER

American soldiers killed in action on Attu-Little Falls Cemetery

Stay Awake or Die

On Attu, the only fuel was hundred pound sacks of coal that were dropped off by aircraft. One day my injured leg was hurting so badly that I could not go up the side of the mountain to retrieve a coal sack. Blanket Ass came over and without a word, just a pat on my back, he went up the mountain instead. He came down with one sack of coal on his left shoulder and another sack of coal on his right shoulder. At night we slept in pup tents, back to back, sitting up. One of us had to stay awake as the other slept. Because if not, the enemy would slit the tent open and knife us as we slept. We had no time off. We were gladiators—forced to kill or be killed. No talk of freedom, liberty or justice for all. Many of my buddies couldn't take it any longer. They killed themselves to escape what seemed like inevitable death.

Friendly Fire Kills

One day, we landed on Kiska, where the Japanese had been entrenched on American soil longer than they had on Attu. Our forces came up on one side of the island and Canadian forces came up on the other side to get the enemy in the center. The Willawallas and fog surrounded us. When we could see figures in front of us we just started shooting. We didn't know it, but we were shooting the Canadians and the Canadians were shooting us. There was not a Japanese on the Island of Kiska! They had escaped undetected under the cover of the Willawallas and fog.

After Three Years of Misery We Return

After spending over three years without a day off, no trees, and no women, we left the Aleutians to go back to the USA to train officers at Fort Benning, Georgia. We lined up on a wharf to board the transport ship, but Blanket Ass was not allowed to come back with our outfit. All of us were devastated. We were brothers. Alaska, at that time, was a territory and for some reason, which I still do not understand, Blanket Ass had to stay. When we lined up to get on board, General Bruckner reviewed us but we turned our backs to him. We did not want to salute him because our petition to allow Blanket Ass to come with us had been turned down.

Kept Like Prisoners, or Animals, in U.S.!

When we got back to Fort Lewis, Washington, we were kept like prisoners, or animals. They said that we were not fit to be with civilized people. We had yellow jaundice because of the water that we had been drinking for years. Our yellowed teeth were falling out, and all of my teeth, except for my front ones, had cavity fillings. I kept pushing them back up so that they would not fall out. After over three years active Arctic service defending Alaska including bitter combat with no time off, having survived the violent and bitter weather, no trees, no women. I was still alive. In October of 1945, four and a half years after I had enlisted for what I assumed was to be a one-year tour of duty, I was discharged.

My Vow to Promote Peace

While I was living in that frozen hell, I swore that if I ever got out of the war alive that I would do all I could to assist in creating peace and harmony within myself first, then in others. I understood that somehow we needed to put an end to the senseless killing. World War I, the war to end wars, didn't do it. Neither did World War II. Has any war since WWII changed anything? The reason I am writing to you, is that after being discharged, I spent years having violent dreams. I would wake up screaming. And if anybody even pointed a finger at me, I wanted to attack him.

Graduation and Investment Banking

I returned home, and under the GI Bill, I went to Stanford University. After graduation, I worked hard and eventually became a Director of Bateman, Eichler, Hill, Richards—Investment Bankers. There, I served for 23 years and I also served on various boards of directors for numerous other firms. I helped sponsor a number of new companies such as the International House of Pancakes, and Scientific Data Systems. Despite those horrible years during the war, I still believe in the power of goodness in people.

In 1993, I founded "Living Treasures" in Ojai. The concept that it was built on has become a tradition in Ojai, and is now becoming a worldwide concept for Rotary International. Living Treasures is a simple grassroots, caring and sharing process. Each year, worthy and deserving citizens are sought out, nominated, and recognized for their contributions to the good of the community and society. It empowers the individuals that participate with vitality and peace within themselves, and hence to the community and the world. In 1999, I co-founded "Vivo-Metrics," the makers of the "Life- Shirt."

Justice and Liberty for All

In closing, we "Veterans of Foreign Wars" are telling our stories, not to say, "Oh look at me I'm so brave." No, it's because we fought for justice and liberty for all. In this way, through this book, for example, we can be the role models for others. If we can do all of this in the name of war, imagine what we can do in the name of peace. Let us use this same energy to live the best lives we can. We can be caring and sharing role models to our loved ones, to the Ojai Valley community, and thus, worldwide. I have started with my family. I started with my wife Christine, three children and their families, including five grandchildren. I pray that you will never have to go to war. I pray that you will never have to kill another person in order to learn what we have learned.

> When Freedom loving people march, when farmers have an
> opportunity, when workers have an opportunity, when children
> of ALL PEOPLE have an opportunity to attend schools which
> teach them the truths of the real world they live in, when
> opportunities are open to everyone—then the world moves
> straight ahead.
> --A letter, quoting Vice-President Wallace, that Sanford sent to
> his family on June 3, 1942.

JOHN MAGILL

— FLYING THE HUMP TO CHINA

John Magill was from that unique generation Tom Brokaw calls "The Greatest Generation." It is a generation whose beginnings were dismal and disheartening. John's roots are in the rural state of Iowa where he grew up during the Great Depression, called great, not because of any salubrious benefit, but because it was so intense, so devastating to the life and well-being of the American people and the global economy. Like most Americans of that era and in spite of poverty and hardships, the Magill family had a patriotic commitment of service to this country. John's father was so concerned about the German threat to the United States that he went to Canada to join the Canadian Infantry in World War I and was subsequently wounded in action. How is that for patriotism? – Just the opposite of the dark days of the Vietnam War when Americans fled to Canada to escape the draft. A well known commentary about the Infantry of World War I was that they were led by donkeys but fought with the hearts of lions. I am sure that John's father had the heart of a lion.

Most military activities are in support roles. It has been said that for every Infantryman on the line, there are 20 support troops behind him including artillery and armor. In recent years, support troops have not had to contend with enemy planes and submarines scouring the planet for likely targets. World War II was different. From the moment that ships or planes left the shores of continental United States, they were vulnerable to enemy attack. John was in a support role as an air controller, but this did not negate the constant hazards of global war. From the day his troop ship sailed out of San Pedro Harbor in California, John was in a war zone. This is his story.

My father was a veterinarian in Iowa when I was born in 1920. Our family of three boys and one girl was typical of the families of those days. My mother did not work outside the home. I grew up in Iowa. In 1940, a friend of mine who had been living in California came through Iowa on his way to Michigan to pick up a new car. He convinced me that California was a land of opportunity for a young man, certainly more so than Iowa so I went with him to Los Angeles.

Before leaving Des Moines, Iowa, I notified my draft board where I could be reached in the even of a military call up. In those days, every adult male of draft age was required to register for the draft into military service. It was a serious offense and considered quite unpatriotic to shirk this responsibility.

Draft Board and Bureaucratic Confusion

Arriving in Los Angeles, I took a job in a storage and moving company in Hollywood where I re-registered with the draft board located at the Pantages Theater in Hollywood. It was in August, so I had some time before I had to go in. After a while my Dad said, "When you get the chance, come on home to Iowa, it would be good to see you again before you go into the service." About a month later, I decided to go back home to Iowa.

I went down to the draft board and told them where I would be, and they shipped everything back to Iowa, thinking I was going to stay there! That wasn't the idea at all. I told them that I was back there on temporary leave, here's where I am if you need me. And all of a sudden I got a call to come back to Des Moines for induction. I went in there with maybe five other guys who had come from the farming area, and they looked healthy to me, but three of them were sent home and only two of us stayed. About two weeks later, I was in the service!

I was drafted for the war on November the 13th, 1941 during the second big draft. I won't ever forget that date or my Army serial number, which was 33110590. They shipped me to Louisiana, where I trained as a Communications Sergeant in the 3rd Armored Division, then we formed the 7th Armor Division, and finally the 11th Armor Division. But my heart was in aviation. I applied for aviation school and qualified as an air cadet.

Wide Open Hatches and Railroad Ties

From there I went to Camp Polk, Louisiana, and after that I was sent to Santa Ana, California with two other men. They put me in a pressure chamber test, equivalent to 18,000 feet of altitude. My lieutenant was a Chinese-American officer. He washed me out because my ears were jammed and I couldn't hear a thing for three days. From there I went to an Air Force corps doing a lot of air traffic control work. We were also teaching the pilots Morse Code, a system of dots and dashes that stood for letters of the alphabet.

We learned to drop cargo out of a plane. For practice, we had to go up in the planes with the doors and supply hatches wide open, and we had to kick railroad ties out. This was merely practice work for kicking supplies out. After being bounced around from base to base all over the U.S., I went to Fort Wayne, Indiana, where we were processed and then sent out to different fields. They split us up so completely that we didn't know where we were! While I was there, I worked from something like base operations. I was assigned to a Jeep and I had to go out and get things like generators and turn them back into the base for them to be rewound and stuff. Everything was accounted for. Everything was by the book, you couldn't make a mistake!

Troop Transport to Calcutta India

In World War II, combat was global and ships entering the open seas were vulnerable to Japanese submarine attack throughout the Pacific Ocean. After all my training, I shipped out of San Pedro Harbor in California. I have a clear memory of the discomfort and fears during the 34-day voyage sailing south of Australia to Calcutta, India. We had no naval escort or protection whatsoever. Nothing! The conditions were horrible, soldiers were crammed into cargo holes. I remember the seasickness and the mess halls that had stand-up tables. Nothing in modern military deployment can compare to the miseries and dangers of the World War II troop transports. In the event of a submarine attack, there were no means of saving us since we were all alone in the vast reaches of the South Pacific and the Indian Ocean.

R and R–Tiger Hunting

India was a totally different world—it was so primitive. When I first got there I noticed a beautiful tiger skin up in the tower of base operations. At that time, you were allowed to check out a rifle and go hunting for Bengal tigers. You had to have a driver and a guy with a spotlight. But wouldn't you know it, someone shot a goat on accident, so we were no longer allowed to hunt tigers. Goats are sacred animals in India! At night, the jackals prowled the compound and between the tents. The living conditions were horrible. We were on atabrine, an anti-malarial drug that made your skin turn yellow. Malaria and venereal diseases were rampant, so I didn't want to have anything to do with anybody! You couldn't drink any of the tea because it transmitted some sort of disease. You never saw the women. They would hide in their adobe houses that were made of straw and mud.

Air Traffic Control and Flying the Hump

My new assignment was as an air traffic controller for a vast array of cargo planes carrying war supplies over the Himalayan Mountains to our ally in China, Chiang Kai-shek. On occasion, I flew the "Hump" and received one battle star for being in the Chinese theater of operations near Luliling.

After watching the Chinese workmen on the runways, I wasn't impressed with their ideas on workmen's safety.

They would even smoke cigarettes while working with gasoline and munitions!

One time when we came back early, we saw a B-24 blow a right tire. It went over to the side, and plowed into a group of Indian workers on our runway. A sergeant had to pick up all the body parts, legs and stuff, and throw them into a "carry-all." He buried the remains in the forest.

The Himalayan Mountains

My principal mission was to direct the air flights over the "Hump"—directing the course of the C-47's and C-104's "Liberator Bombers" at 1000-foot intervals. A lot of the pilots were really inexperienced. Some only had 40 hours of air time and they were unable to gain enough altitude to clear the mountains so they just returned to India or even Burma. I remember one time when a young co-pilot was flying. He clipped all the trees with the wings, and he flew that plane for 90 miles, only 500 feet off the ground.

You could see the natives as clear as day, right outside the windows. The pilot finally took over. Flying the Himalayan Mountains was a dangerous mission in those days and many planes were lost in the remote icy peaks and valleys. One night when flying back from China, we realized that there were no runway lights on the airfield. It was pitch black. Being in a World War II plane low on fuel, circling in total darkness, looking for an air-field, is not a good situation! So we ended up landing at Tezgon. Cremaltola and Tezgon were only three miles apart, and you never knew who was landing where.

Another night, I was all alone in the tower on the midnight shift, and all of a sudden everything got busy! There was a whole flight of planes coming in at one time, fifty of them. I brought them in and without advanced warning! Not one plane was lost during my watch though.

My second cruise
of the Indian and Pacific Ocean

Upon rotation, I was able to experience another "ocean-cruise" on the U.S.S. General Freeman. It took us 28 days to reach the USA landing at Fort MacArthur. I ended up serving overseas for a total of seven months.

When I was released from service, I spent about three days with my friends in Los Angeles, California. From there I took a bus and traveled to my sister's house in Sioux City. Busses were much more available in those days. I started school at the University of Iowa where I took a year and a half worth of work aimed at becoming an orthodontist. I was told that some company was hiring traffic control officers, which was what I was doing in India. But it turns out that we had to use their procedures. We couldn't use the army procedures, and they would have had to retrain us, so that was out.

I decided to come back out here to California where I had lived before the war. There I continued working toward becoming an orthodontist until I ran into a bureaucratic snafu involving the G.I. Bill and transferring school credits. Hearing of opportunities in the United States Postal Service, I took the Postal Exam and became a postman for the next 35 years.

Marrying My Boarding House Acquaintance

Years ago, boarding houses provided food and lodging for many young working people. Where I boarded were four girls, myself, and my buddy. At the breakfast table we met each other. The boarding table was like feeding a thresher crew in Iowa. One young lady tried to introduce me to her friends and fix me up with one of them. But I was interested in another girl, her. Eventually, we dated and after two years, we were married on February 18, 1950.

My wife is from Connecticut. She moved to California because her sister was getting married in Las Vegas, and she was supposed to be the maid-of-honor. Her sister's fiancé lived in Texas. They were corresponding by mail, and were supposed to meet in Las Vegas to get married.

But the wedding was postponed because the groom-to-be had a bad tooth. The delay necessitated that my future wife get a job in Los Angeles. That's why she was at that boarding house where we met. Eventually, the marriage did take place in Las Vegas. The girls were all dolled up in beautiful dresses, but the groom came in a sports-shirt, looking like he had just come off the job!

Sgt. John Magill upon his return from China and India, 1945

PHOTO COURTESY OF JOHN MAGILL

1957, Post Office—Oxnard and Living in Ojai—4200 Population

I worked in the Los Angeles Post Office for a number of years eventually transferring to the Oxnard Post Office. We moved to Ojai in August of 1957. There were only 4200 people in Ojai City at that time. We raised four children, and we now have 10 grandchildren! Between children, grandchildren, and the Veteran's of Foreign Wars, I have a full and active life. I especially enjoy watching my grandchildren play in competitive sports.

John's life and military experience was often dictated by snafu's and bureaucratic confusion. He was drafted, probably prematurely, as the result of bureaucratic

misunderstanding. He trained for the Armored divisions before he became an air cadet, only to be reassigned because of a hearing problem, something that should have been noticed early in the game. Later, lost in the darkness on a flight from China to India, his pilot finally brought the plane down at the wrong airport.

Communications failures resulted in a near impossible task of directing landings for 50 planes that appeared out of nowhere. John wanted to be an orthodontist, but transcript errors and confusion over Veteran's Educational payments derailed that objective. Later, at the boarding house, he met the love of his life who was redirecting him to her girl friends, not herself. In that situation, John lucked out and married the right girl.

In a way, John's life was a serendipitous adventure. Yet, he was always flexible and realistic seizing the opportunities of life as they unfolded. Like so many men of that era, opportunities had to be seized when they presented themselves. John learned to roll with the punches progressing through each challenge living life to its fullest.

Lester Petersen

—FIGHT FOR DUTCH HARBOR IN ALASKA

In the safety of a modern United States and with the end of the Cold War, it is easy for historians to forget that the war against Japan began with an air and sea assault against the Hawaiian Islands and that the territory of Alaska, now a state, was the scene of a Japanese invasion. It was right here in Ojai where troops trained for the Alaskan counteroffensive against the Japanese occupation of several small islands in the Aleutian chain. And further north in Santa Cruz, the 205th Coast Artillery was mobilized for the same mission. The rapid advance of Japanese forces throughout the Pacific Theater created a serious threat to the actual territory of North America. The Aleutian invasion could have led to the conquest of all Alaska with its remote and lightly defended shores and hinterland.

It has been said before that wars are fought in the most God-forsaken and inhospitable terrain imaginable. The Aleutian Islands were no exception. Imagine having to land on a rocky volcanic island with active volcanoes spewing sulfur fumes and ash clouds continuously. Imagine being stationed on high mountain peaks where winds of fifty miles per hour could blow a soldier off the slopes. Try to visualize windstorms so intense that the superstructure of boats could be blown away. Continuous storms, sleet, fog, rain, snow, and willawalla winds conspired to impress on the soldiers' minds that they had two deadly enemies to fight, first the Japanese and secondly the weather. The action of the Aleutians took place on three islands: Attu, Kiska, and Dutch Harbor. The Japanese actually invaded two of the Islands.

Dutch Harbor was defended by heavy artillery and was spared.

From Nebraska to an Active Volcano Rim In the Aleutians

I was born on a farm in Nebraska. Like so many men of that time and age, I joined the war and was activated shortly after. My National Guard unit was Federalized as part of the United States Army and was sent to two remote places. Part of our unit was sent to the Philippines where I later heard that they were overrun and destroyed by the Japanese. My battery was sent to the Aleutian Islands in Alaska. The island had an active volcano that spewed ash, smoke, and sulfur. My buddies and I took several days to climb the mountain and when we reached the top of the volcano, we decided to remain at the crater for several days in the middle of winter because it was nice and warm. We enjoyed the heat from the volcano. What a switch from the flat lands of Nebraska! In the summer, there was another benefit; the smoke from the volcano gave us relief from the swarms of mosquitoes that lived in the tundra. I remember that there was only one tree on the whole island!

Upon our arrival at Dutch Harbor, we dug in our 155mm guns into the mountainsides to prepare for the predicted arrival of the Japanese. The tunnels were dug deep into the mountain with other tunnels connecting to other support facilities. The heavy guns were mounted on tracks so we could position them for firing as the Japanese approached. We were trained as gunners. We learned to set fuzes. We coordinated with the Fire Direction center and prepared the bags of propellant. We loaded projectiles. Shortly afterwards, three Japanese troop ships arrived. But because the Japanese transports had no naval support, we soon drove them off by firing our 155mm coastal defense guns. Later Japanese bombers tried to locate and destroy our coastal defense guns, but damage was light and ineffective since the pilots were unable to locate our gun positions and other defensive installations. I served on the gun crews in any position assigned since all artillerymen were cross-trained and capable of performing any duty. Each gun throughout the mountain complex was pre-registered for any eventual invasion or attack. A base station or fire direction center was located in another section of the mountain.

Four Years in Quonset Huts Under Tundra

For four years, I lived in Quonset huts buried deep in the ground. Each Quonset hut had Sibley stoves that burned presto type logs. Despite the frozen tundra above, when we were buried in the ground, our dwellings stayed quite comfortable. Sometimes I was assigned to the 90 mm guns located on the shoreline. To avoid boredom, we were issued a special parka and a boat that we used for fishing. The halibut fishing in the coves around Dutch Harbor was great! We would take the fish back to the base where the mess sergeants would prepare them for meals to supplement the canned food stores.

PHOTO COURTESY OF LESTER PETERSEN

Aleut Indians

About 35 native Aleut Indians lived at Dutch Harbor. But after awhile the Indians were removed to Anchorage and

Lester Petersen above his encampment with Dutch Harbor Alaska in the background, 1942

hospitalized. Some of the women had gone into prostitution to earn extra cash and the result was an outbreak of social diseases affecting some of the GIs.

Lester Petersen before his death in March 2002.

After the Service

After four and one half years, the Alaskan contingent of the 264th Coast Artillery was repatriated. I returned to my civilian occupation as an upholsterer and moved to San Fernando Valley. In 1972, I moved to Ojai where I was in business for myself for a number of years. I married and had three daughters and six grandchildren.

Lester's health had been failing at the time of the interview. His hearing was greatly impaired, a rather common problem of former artillerymen. Unfortunately, Lester died before the interviews were completed.

Once the Japanese were repulsed, his unit remained on duty in the cold, desolate, lonely, and inhospitable Arctic with the subzero temperatures and wicked willawalla winds. Military service often means enduring loneliness, isolation, and boredom. It takes a special mind-set to overcome such an existence. In World War II, this could go on for years, yet, the defense of Alaska was so essential that the military planners could take no chance that the Japanese Imperial Army would strike again.

Six months of darkness and summers of perpetual light can create mental depression and mental unbalance. Hardy souls learn to survive. Some soldiers went berserk, a malady in Arctic climes. Lester survived , but those best years of his youthful life were lost forever as he served his country in that miserable forgotten episode of World War II.

Elton Perkey

WWII– "JUNGLEER"

America was a very different country sixty or seventy years ago. Today's standard of living is far above the poverty that existed throughout the nation then. Nowhere was poverty as intense as in the rural heartland of America. Modern day support programs of welfare, food stamps, SSI, Unemployment insurance, government guarantees in banking, and government oversight commissions did not exist. The Great Depression was global in scope and affected almost every locality; however, the American Midwest was hit with a double catastrophe caused by the Dust Bowl and drought of the 1930's. Elton's story begins in Nebraska. Yet like so many Midwesterners, his family migrated to Oregon in search of a better life in the Willamette Valley. Even there, there was little work for the men coming of age, but when the various New Deal programs of the Roosevelt Era came on stream, many men seized the opportunities provided. In the Northwest, the Civilian Conservation Corps provided work and a living in forest camps. For many men, it was their only opportunity available for meaningful work.

Elton was a descendent of the early German colonists with roots in New England and the South. One of his immediate ancestors was a Cherokee Indian. He had sufficient Indian blood that he would be entitled to government recognition in this modern age. He was related to the great plant scientist, Luther Burbank, on his mother's side. Elton, like Luther Burbank, had a passion for growing plants.

The economic insecurity of the age developed men and women more security conscious than men and women of today. They did not trust banks because many banks had failed in the Great Depression. They tended to be frugal. They saved money for a rainy day. They distrusted the stock market like they distrusted banks. They paid their bills promptly and seldom used credit in any form. They were not investors or entrepreneurs for the most part. They accepted discipline as a trade-off for security. Once employed, they clung to the job tenaciously. For all their poverty and lack of opportunity and despite their horrific economic struggles, they were totally patriotic. The story of Elton Perkey is a study of the formative factors that molded his life and existence.

Stoop Labor in Oregon

I was raised in the rural heartland of the nation, where hard work and daily chores trained me for my future vocation. Like so many people of the pre 1940s era, I experienced economic hardships and scarce opportunities. Even farm work was difficult to obtain and wages were low. I recall doing stoop labor picking strawberries in Oregon. The farmers didn't want to waste a minute's worth of labor. When the field workers had a call of nature, we were not even allowed the decency of going in the bushes. We had to go out in the middle of the field so we wouldn't waste any time! The labor was so difficult, and the wages so low, that thinking of marriage and family was out of the question. Frequently families lived in multi-generational units simply because families were often the only social support system.

I Joined the Civilian Conservation Corps

For many of us farm boys, the ticket to getting out on our own was to join the newly formed Civilian Conservation Corps. For me, this was my opportunity to leave home. I was assigned to forest camps in the Northwest, mostly in Washington and Oregon. The pay was low. The training was militaristic except we didn't have weapons. The camps were run like the Army. An occasional dance in one of the local towns provided limited recreation on some Saturday nights. Not all the local townsmen welcomed us because they didn't want the CCC boys involved with their daughters.

For extra money and opportunities, many young men joined the 41st Infantry Division of the National Guard. I joined the artillery where I became a mess sergeant because I had learned the culinary arts in the Civilian Conservation Corps. In some ways the National Guard encampments were little different than the CCC, except that the National Guard trained with weapons.

The 41st Infantry Division Heads to Australia

When the Japanese bombed Pearl Harbor, General MacArthur had only four infantry divisions to defend the whole Pacific Theater. Few historians are aware of the fact that this lack of military ground forces forced the United States government to augment the Army by federalizing sixteen Reserve and National Guard divisions from the States. Within a short time, the 41st Infantry Division was mobilized and shipped to defend Australia.

Private Elton Perkey, 41st Infantry Division, at home on leave.

PHOTO COURTESY OF ELTON PERKEY

One of the great ironies of the war is that while Australia was in immediate danger of Japanese invasion, the British government had sent the Aussie and New Zealand soldiers to North Africa to defend Britain's oil supply through the Suez Canal! Australia needed more manpower desperately. On the map, Australia looks like a huge country. But in reality, it is small in population, yet rich in mineral resources. The mission of the 41st Infantry

Division was to complete our training, and at the same time, defend Australia.

New Guinea – The Site of Our First Combat

New Guinea was next door to Australia and was a remote jungle-clad island. It was here that the Japanese established their staging area for the invasion of Australia. It was here that we, the 41st Infantry Division, entered combat.

Fermented Coconut Juice Makes Great Doughnuts

My role was to keep the troops fed. The rations were very limited. Some of them had been sent from Australia, mostly mutton, which all of the soldiers came to loathe. Australians ate mutton but the Americans preferred lamb. They taste very different from one another. Mutton is strong and rank and tastes of oily sheep's wool, whereas the flavor of lamb is very delicate. There isn't much an army mess sergeant can do with mutton! But at least it was protein and it kept our soldiers fed. Another ration we had was canned sockeye salmon and Spam. Very few of my compatriots can stand sheep, lamb, Spam, or salmon even to this day. Baked goods were nonexistent because we didn't have yeast. But I remember figuring out one day, that coconut juice fermented. So I began experimenting with it. Somehow, I managed to make a credible batch of doughnuts from my jungle juice concoction. The artillerymen were delighted and raved about real doughnuts. But high-ranking officers from headquarters got wind of my doughnuts and descended on our mess facility ready to court martial me for pilfering yeast from some nonexistent supply source. I had quite a time explaining the ingredients. Fifty years later at some of our reunions, the survivors still rave about some of those doughnuts and other improvised dishes. They tell me that I was a good cook, despite the conditions.

Japanese Infiltrators

Jungle fighting is uncertain and unpredictable. The Japanese had built coconut log emplacements that were almost impervious to medium artillery fire. Sometimes the Japanese would infiltrate into our artillery positions or break through our infantry. I remember one time during an emergency withdrawal; I was so excited that my adrenaline was pumping big time. The war in the Pacific was not one where surrender was an option. We knew the fate of any soldier that fell into Japanese hands. The Bataan Death March was still on our minds. My mission was to take care of the kitchen. And without thinking, I threw the field stove on to a two and one half-ton truck by myself. Not realizing or feeling it, I had wrenched my back severely.

Often the field kitchens were fairly close to the firing batteries and sometimes Aussie units were attached to our Division. One day I saw an Aussie field piece explode, killing all the cannoneers. It was a bad scene. Handling artillery shells and propellant can be very dangerous. Any breach of procedure or failure to swab out the artillery tubes properly can result in a premature explosion.

Cannibals & Crocodiles

When we first landed near Hollandia, I witnessed considerable air action with the Japanese planes causing a lot of damage to our ships, planes, and troops. The Japanese planes seemed to have the advantage. We were not sure of victory or our fate if we were defeated in the God-awful island and subsequent battles. There was no assurance, but we were trained to follow orders and do our duty. Our release from our jungle hell was death, disabling sickness, wounds, or victory. We waded ashore hoping for life and victory. Many soldiers, sailors, and airmen did not escape from that jungle hell. They died and were buried there. Many bore the diseases and injuries for the rest of their days. What should be a carefree and happy youth was denied them. Few people can comprehend our suffering and loss of youth.

While we were there, I saw fellow soldiers feed live grenades to salt water crocodiles. Some of them were over 20 feet long! Needless to say, the grenades were not good for the crocodiles' digestive systems. Local aborigines would pull the dead crocodiles from the water and then they would sing and chant for the souls of the reptiles for the rest of the day. Later in the evening, the natives would devour the crocodiles. Apparently, they thought that they were some kind of relative to the beast. In general the natives were friendly to the American and Australian forces. But they hated the Japanese. They carried many injured Americans to safety and they helped build the roads and airfields for us. They were very primitive people though, barely out of the Stone Age. In some of the more remote areas, the natives were cannibals. We used to hear tales of wounded Japanese who provided a meal or two for the natives. I'm not sure if that is true or not, but that's what I heard.

The Best National Guard Unit in the Pacific

The 41st Infantry Division was a close-knit group. We all came from the same region of the Pacific Northwest and we served together for years. We were praised as being the best National Guard Division in the Pacific with a combat effectiveness unmatched by any other division. But the climate and terrain of New Guinea steadily took its toll on the men and our machines.

Between the inhospitable climate with high heat and humidity, the impassable swamps, malaria, dengue fever, jungle rot, trench foot, venomous snakes, and salt-water crocodiles—I had had enough! But I lasted through the campaigns from Hollandia to Biak before I was sent Stateside with malaria and dengue fever. I came home a physical wreck and ended up needing extensive medical treatment.

The Butchers of Biak

The men of the 41st "Jungleers" had been the first division deployed overseas, and ended up serving overseas longer than any other division. We fought more campaigns than any other division, and killed and captured more Japanese than any other comparable unit. Tokyo Rose labeled us "The Butchers of Biak" because when we found that the Japanese troops had butchered and eaten American prisoners, The Jungleers destroyed the Japanese defenders of Biak with a fury. Little is said in politically correct history books of today, but there were several incidences of such behavior by the Japanese during World War II. Even former President Bush barely escaped from such a fate. A Japanese commander, who was ultimately tried for war crimes, had executed and devoured one of Bush's fellow aviators.

A native village in New Guinea.

Civilian Life and the Post Office

I returned to the United States in horrible health. But in time, with treatments at the VA hospital, while being supported by a disability pension, I got back on my feet. I married late in life and eventually was employed by the United States Post Office at the Terminal Annex, where I worked in the registry until my retirement. The Post Office was a government entity like the Army and the CCC's. There was a system, regulations, and job security. I was assured of a decent pension and fringe benefits.

As an employee in the postal registry, I handled large amounts of money and securities. Frequently, I carried a 45-caliber Army regulation pistol when transporting securities and money. The Terminal Annex was in Central Los Angeles at the train station.

Bureaucracy Creates Stress

Over time, the stress and strain of responsible work combined with Los Angeles smog and traffic began to affect my health. Though I enjoyed the economic benefits of a secure government job, the U.S. Postal system had a political system where frequently, management was drawn from personnel less qualified than many of the worker/employees.

The resulting confusion caused the competent workers unnecessary stress and anxiety. The Postal system has been over managed throughout my career with more than a fair share of incompetent micro-managers. I suffered a paralyzing stroke and when I recovered, I decided that I would retire to the quiet little town of Ojai in 1981.

Perkey's Place Names for Nebraska

In retirement, I wrote historical sketches about my youth in Nebraska and the Pacific Northwest. Drawing on my knowledge of place names from work in the Post Office, I wrote a research book called Perkey's Place Names for Nebraska. It was published by the Nebraska Historical Society and is now a reference book in many libraries throughout the country.

I continued my cooking interests from the old CCC and Army days providing meals for the family at each special holiday season. Compared to the poverty of my youth, I feel very content with the outcome of my life. I have a modest pension and if I am careful, my wife and I never have to worry about our economic future again.

Elton died in 1995 and is buried at Ivy Lawn Cemetery. A notation of his rank and military service marks his gravestone, like all veterans' gravestones.

Elton was a child of the 20th Century; he knew poverty, backbreaking farm labor, camp life in the CCC, and eventual service in the 41st "Jungleer" Division. Working for the Post Office was like completing the circle. He followed up by continuing to serve his country and government.

LARRY PRINCE

–THE LAST BATTLE OF THE BUNKER HILL

The novel, All Quiet on the Western Front, tells the story of a German soldier who fought all through World War I escaping all the hell and destruction of the nightmare of trench warfare. As the Armistice is negotiated and the time set for the end of the conflict, the hero of the story reaches out of his foxhole for a flower that has just bloomed only to be shot dead as the hour of the Armistice commenced. In Korea and Vietnam with the system of rotation of troops after a year of fighting, soldiers became increasingly anxious as their day of release from war approached. The fear existed that as they approached rotation day, they would be killed or wounded. And that happened to many combatants.

What'll it be Recruit, Army or Navy?

I was the only child in my family, although I had three half siblings because my mother had been married before. I was raised in Wichita, Kansas by my grandparents. I graduated from high school in May of 1944, when I was seventeen years old. I knew that I was going to be drafted when I turned eighteen, on July the 2nd. It was no surprise when I received my notice. They sent me down to Ft. Leavenworth for my first physical. They told me that the Armed Forces were short of manpower. There was an urgent need for more soldiers and sailors. When we were finished with our physicals, we were told to walk out the doors where there was an Army NCO and a Navy chief. They said that it was our choice where we went. I chose the Navy because I didn't want all that dirt and foxholes that was part of soldiering. Some men didn't like the thought of being on the water, so they chose the Army instead. But I knew how to swim because I used to go to the river all the time with my friends when we were kids. Anyway, I joined the Navy.

Saboteurs in Needles, California!

I was shipped to the Great Lakes Naval Station for boot camp with all the usual abuse and demands inflicted on new recruits. There were shortages of manpower in the late stages of the war, so the Railway Express service impressed the Naval recruits into moving mail in downtown Chicago over the Christmas holidays. But the war took priority and I was soon aboard a troop train headed for Bremerton, Washington. There were 550 sailors on board. We celebrated Christmas of 1944 on the train with a steak sandwich and an apple for dinner. Just outside of Needles, California the people outside were screaming and yelling at us to stop the train. What had happened was, some Japanese had taken out some of the track, trying to derail us. We stopped in time and the tracks were repaired.

The Bad, Bad, U.S.S. Bunker Hill

We landed at Bremerton, Washington at 3:30 in the morning. They fed us all breakfast; there were about 5000 of us. Then they had us march down the city street to the docks, twelve to fifteen of us abreast. You had never seen so many white hats! When we came to each ship, we were paired off to fill the quota for each ship in dry dock. My ship was an aircraft carrier, the U.S.S. Bunker Hill. When I first saw it, I thought she was in a terrible state of repair. She had been to sea for eighteen months. She was all rusty and in major need of an overhaul. Civilian crews, including the proverbial Rosie the Riveter, were hard at work returning her to ship shape.

Before we were allowed to go to sea, we had to take a swimming test in the Puget Sound. They said, "You see that raft out there?" "That's 150 yards. If you can swim out there, then you pass you naval test." Well, when we got out there, there were sailors stomping on our hands, so we couldn't stop. We had to turn around and come back. I almost drowned. We had to swim 300 yards, that was the swimming test. One hundred fifty yards was easy, but 300 was tough! I swallowed a lot of water before I made it back.

Larry Prince, first time home on leave getting the mandatory handsome military man photo out in the back yard.

When the ship was ready, she looked great! We set sail at 28 knots to Alameda to pick up our planes. We got about 100 planes including Corsairs and Avengers, which were the Navy bombers. We then sailed to Pearl Harbor. We were not allowed to go ashore and they told us, "Don't you men dare fall over the sides, there's nothing but barracuda here, and they'll eat you alive!" With that in mind, we headed out into the Pacific.

Once we were under way everybody was so sick. You couldn't go to the latrine without slipping and sliding on all the vomit. It was something else. By February of 1945, we were we bombing the coast of Tokyo Bay, and that was my first indication that we were really in some kind of a wild war. After that we sailed south and regrouped. You could always tell when we were going to Japan, because they would issue us foul weather gear. Initially, I was assigned to an air group, but after a cursory review of my high school mathematics and clerical training, they reassigned me to the office and supply division of the ship. I was paid $54.00 a month and I was given the responsibility of working with the payroll. The sailors drew pay twice a month. They would have everyone line up, and then two guards with 45 caliber pistols would stand at each end of the pay line.

An Aircraft Carrier is a Floating Bomb.

The decks were loaded with a hundred planes including TBF Avengers, fighter-bombers, and Corsairs. Below deck were thousands of tons of bombs, gasoline, torpedoes and other volatile substances and munitions. The conditions of Navy life are the envy of the soldiers in the field who have to deal with the physical hardship of terrain and weather. But we had our own horrors to deal with. Ulithe was a main base for aircraft carriers. It was in the South Pacific, right next to Yap Island, which was controlled by the Japanese. Sometimes at night Japanese planes would come over and attack our carriers. I saw seven big carriers hit there. The Randolph, The Bonhomme Richard, The Essex, on and on. It was horrible. Thousands of men on each ship drowned.

A Second Battle Star

We went to the Marianas, then we were involved in the Battle for Iwo Jima where I earned a second battle star. Every member on our ship received a Presidential Unit Citation, signed by President Harry Truman. I used to watch the planes fly off the deck and strike the islands that I could see in the distance. Except for the pilots and accidents of carrier duty, we were at the apex of naval action in the Western Pacific, but we were relatively unscathed. The Japanese had invaded the Philippines, so we had to go up to Luzon to get it back. On our way, we went right up to the equator. While we were near the equator, for training, we had to wear our dress blues, winter wool uniforms. We had to stand there on deck at attention all day. You would hear "thuds" and it was the sound of guys hitting the deck. They were dropping like flies. Insane. It was so hot!

After Two Years, One Day of Liberty

The only time in that whole two years on that ship that we went ashore, was for one day of liberty. They sent us to an Island called Mog Mog. It was in the Ulithe chain. All that was on that island was sand and palm trees! I remember they gave us two beers and a sandwich, and we got to watch the ball game. A couple of big league players were there, like Johnny Mize, first baseman for the St. Louis Cardinals. It was a whole day out in the hot sun, no shade at all! That was our only time off.

PHOTO COURTESY OF U.S. NAVY

U.S.S. Bunker Hill after being attacked off Okinawa, 1945

The Battle of Okinawa

The war in Europe was almost over and I had a good job on a fine ship. We were off the coast of Japan and our planes were flying missions against the cities around

Tokyo Bay. From the ship, I could see the Japanese people on the shore, we were that close. The war was supposed to be over in a couple of months and everyone would be free to go home. Then we were sent as support for the battle of Okinawa, the first and the last of the Japanese home islands to be invaded.

On May 11, 1945 at 10:17, I was having a late breakfast in the galley. I had just sat down when I heard a "thud" The IFF, "Identify Friend or Foe." system had failed. The observers had incorrectly identified an incoming fleet of planes. They thought that they were our planes coming back from some mission. But they were Japanese. Depleted of trained pilots, young Japanese trainees were told to crash their bomb-laden planes into the ships of the U.S. Naval Armada. These suicide pilots were called kamikazes, named after the divine winds that had once saved the Japanese from a Mongol invasion fleet back in ancient history.

Two Kamikaze Planes with 500 lb Bombs Hits Us

The "thud" that I had heard was a plane that struck the 3rd deck bakery station with a 500 pound bomb. It killed twelve out of seventeen men, including two twin brothers. Several other hits knocked out all of the elevators. The flight deck was 8" thick steel filled with wooden planks, and the fire was so intense that it melted clear through it. I felt something on my leg, a burning. I didn't pay any attention to it though. I found out later that it was shrapnel. I heard the call to general quarters and to our assigned battle stations, but being a kid, I wanted to see what was going on. I was on the same deck as the flight deck, so I went out there. There was just solid fire and gasoline everywhere and many of the planes on deck were damaged.

Flaming Ship Saved with a Hard 90°

The hangers were flowing with burning gasoline, which ignited munitions. Bodies and body parts were strewn everywhere. We had so much fire on the ship that the Captain made the decision to throw the ship into a hard 90-degree turn in the water. He saved the ship by doing this because it allowed much of the burning gasoline, bombs and munitions to flow over the side. Three of our planes were badly damaged and were just pushed over the side of the ship. Joe White, a friend of mine, who took care of my laundry was so terrified that he jumped overboard. The sharks ate him, just like that. Some sailors caught in the infernos jumped overboard to escape and were eaten by sharks too.

My Battle Station
—Down in the Magazine Compartment

I ran down to the magazine compartment, which was my battle station on the 2nd deck. And I started hoisting five inch, 48-pound projectiles to the gun turrets up above us. We put on our gas masks, but we could barely breath. I put my back against the bulkhead and I could just watch the smoke filling the room. Pretty soon, it was so thick that we couldn't see a thing. It was pitch black in that compartment. We just waited. We weren't given any instructions or information as to what was going on because everybody was busy.

Finally, at 4:00 in the afternoon, a message came over the PA system. We were told to grab the back of the shirt of the guy sitting next to us, so that we wouldn't lose each other, and that someone would lead us out. They led us to the back of the ship, which was called the fan-tail, and we stayed there all night. We didn't want to go to our bunks, even though we could have, because there was fresh air on deck. That night they fed us boxes of apples and oranges for dinner and we coughed up black soot all that night and for the next two days as well.

Afterwards, the Horrible Clean-up

When it was all over, we had lost 395 men and we had 365 wounded. Many guys suffered horrible burns, and a lot of guys died of smoke inhalation. Burial details commenced almost immediately. They laid all the dead out on the hanger deck. Four of us had to go through the personal effects and the pockets of each dead sailor before burial at sea. Their wallets, watches, dog tags, etc. were kept for identification and for their relatives back at home. The dead were then wrapped in canvas and tied with rope with a 48-pound artillery shell between their knees for weight. As the chaplain said the words, we dropped them into the sea, five at a time. We had never seen so many bodies. We had to do that all day long. It was horrible.

Vice Admiral—Three Ships, Three Hits

Three other ships were hit that morning as well. I think that the Japs were trying to hit Vice Admiral Marc Mitchner, because Mitchner was on the U.S.S. Essex that morning, and it was hit. He was then transferred to the U.S.S. Enterprise. Thirty minutes later, it was hit. Then he came over to the Bunker Hill. And we were hit.

PHOTO COURTESY OF U.S. NAVY

The USS Bunker Hill had the second heaviest carrier casualties of WWII

Battle Stars from One of the Worst Battles of the War

Throughout the battle for Okinawa, the kamikaze attacks continued destroying dozens of ships and killing thousands of sailors. It was one of the most horrific naval conflicts of the entire war. Those of us who survived were given battle stars.

Eventually damage control restored the essential functions of the ship, and we limped back to Guam. When we were at Guam we found a guy on the ship that had been dead for two weeks. They didn't even know he was there. We spent another few months transporting people home to the US from the war. When we had enough points to go home, we went to Hawaii and then back to Bremerton, Washington.

Home to Kansas, Crazy Guys, Cars, and Girls

I returned home to Kansas in June of 1946. I had saved up enough money to buy a car, but I could hardly find one because they had stopped making them during the war. They were making tanks instead. So my grandfather took me to Wichita and we found a black 1940 Ford. It was a beauty! A friend of mine had a 1941 Plymouth. We were out driving around one night and pulled into an alley, which was about half a block from a nurses' dormitory. My friend said, "Wouldn't it be fun to floor it, then at the end, do a u-turn?" I never will forget it! He was crazy. Anyway, it was almost 8:30 and there was this group of nurses there that needed to be in at 8:30. So, we picked them up and drove them about half a block. My wife to be thought I was obnoxious!

Those nurses and my Navy buddies eventually became friends once we ended the attention getting stage of our relationship. My future wife later decided that I was okay after all. She was a U.S. Army Cadet Nurse at a good hospital in Kansas where she had to register for three years in order to get her license. There was such a shortage of nurses during the war that the government had decided to start the cadet nurses program again. We had to wait until she completed her course to become a registered nurse before we could get married.

So What'll it Be, Coke or a Doughnut?

I got a job selling Coca-Cola, but my wife's father kept bugging me to go down to the police department. He knew the Chief of Police. Finally, I took the test, and became the City Investigator then I was appointed as Under Sheriff for the next two Sheriffs.

Then I ran, and became Sheriff of Barton County twice, before term limits forced me to seek other employment. We lived in a brand new jail facility. My wife cooked for the inmates, and we had two kids with us too! We had a lot of scary things happen in law enforcement, but I never had to pull my gun. I always treated people how I wanted to be treated.

FBI Helps Us Send "Shakey" Back to the Pokey

I remember one time when one of our officers stopped some guy for a traffic violation. The officer radioed in and said, "I don't know what it is, but this guy is really shaky." I said, "Well the only thing I can think of is asking him to come down to the Sheriff's department. Let him know that he is not arrested, but that we just want to talk to him."

We brought him into my office, and sat him down. He said, "I've never been arrested Sheriff, I've never done anything." We fingerprinted him, and I called the FBI. They said, "Sure Sheriff, why don't you look down on his ankles. Does he have marks? If so, he is an escapee from a chain-gang in Atlanta, Georgia." Sure enough, it was him! Weird stuff happened.

A Sheriffs Job in Ventura
Until They Started Shooting at Us

In 1957 I was offered a job in Visalia. We waited for one snowstorm to pass, then loaded everything and came out to California. When we got to Visalia, we were told that we had to be residents to work in that county. There went my job out the window! We stayed in Visalia for about six months until some guy said, "Why don't you go to Ventura? It's really a beautiful city." One day we drove to Ventura, and I walked in the Sheriff's office. I told them that I had been the Sheriff back in Kansas and they wanted me to go to work that day!

We rented a house in Ventura, sight unseen, and I went to work two days later. I worked with the Sheriff's Department until people got crazy and started shooting at us. This was at a time when the sheriff's department had only one deputy per patrol car on the night shifts. This was a money saving measure. However, a lone deputy was sent to set up a road block on Highway 150 near the present entrance to Lake Casitas. The deputy stopped a car looking for some bandits from Santa Barbara. When he turned away for a moment, the bandits shot him to death. There were several other police issues that created special hazards for law enforcement officers at that time which resulted in injuries.

So What'll it be, Cigar or Candy?

When all that started I left police work because I didn't want my wife to have to raise two kids by herself. I took a job selling tobacco products and later worked for a candy company until I retired. I can't believe how much candy people eat!

Larry Prince, 2002

Avid Lions Club Volunteer

I am very involved with the Lion's Club and have held offices such as District Governor in 1997-1998. I also started a new club in Summerland and Montecito and I helped in the formation of five Leo's Clubs as well. The Leo's Club is the youth branch of the

Lion's Club. I am also a charter member of the Ojai Valley Veteran's of Foreign Wars Post 11461.

Larry survived that last great battle of World War II. He survived the last Kamikaze plane, bomb, shot, and shell that hit the U.S.S. Bunker Hill. Each day is a precious gift of life to him as he remembers his hundreds of comrades that didn't return.

THE KOREAN ERA

*T*he seeds of the Korean War were sown at Yalta and Potsdam where the Allied powers parlayed with the Soviet Union in the mistaken notion that Russia was a friendly power. In reality, the brutal Communist regime was just another form of Fascism with a different name. The conquest and extermination of peoples and dissidents claimed more lives than the vaunted Third Reich. Not only did the Soviet system claim many lives; it would continue its march of aggression and national self-aggrandizement well into the future resulting in numerous wars in Africa, Asia, and China.

The Western Democracies and Allies demilitarized. The Soviet Union continued its military and economic conquests through subversion, intimidation, and unbridled force. While posturing as a system for economic justice and equality, the Soviet Union was a super state where the party leaders were more equal. The NKVD, deportation to the Gulags of Siberia, or outright execution, met any challenge to their supremacy.

With the fall of Red China, a billion people came under communist control. Immediately after the United States had dropped the two atomic bombs, the Soviet Union declared war on Japan and struck at Manchuria, North Korea, and annexed a number of Japanese Islands. A puppet client state was established in North Korea under the Soviet citizen Kim Il Sung. South Korea was under the influence and protection of the United States. Minor border clashes occurred between 1946 and 1950 when a massive, highly trained North Korean Army attacked South Korea in force.

The poorly equipped and trained South Korean forces were quickly overrun. An emergency session of the United Nations condemned North Korea aggression and authorized U.N. nations to take military action. From the end of World War II to 1950, the U.S. had demilitarized to the point that the country had relatively limited resources in men and *materials. Yet, President Truman ordered poorly trained and inadequately equipped units of the 24th Infantry Division, the 25th Infantry Division, and eventually the 1st Cavalry Division to South Korea.*

Under-strength and poorly-equipped units were unable to stop the highly-trained and superbly-equipped North Korean Army. American forces traded lives for time as America geared up for war. However, the American people were not told the truth about the conflict. It was euphemistically referred to as a police action, not a war. The American Army was driven back to a small corner of Korea known as the Pusan Perimeter. They were given orders to "stand or die."

With time the U.S. Forces staged a rapid build up and a strategic amphibious landing at Inchon. The North Korean Army was defeated and rolled back to the Manchurian border. It was at this time that China had secretly deployed hundreds of thousands of troops in the mountain spine of North Korea. When the Chinese attacked, the U.N., American, and ROK Forces were defeated once again.

The U.S. Marines gained fame and notoriety for remaining a cohesive unit throughout the long retreat from the Chosin Reservoir to the coast where the survivors were eventually rescued and redeployed far to the south. The advanced units of the 8th Army were shattered with the loss of tens of thousands of men killed, captured, or wounded.

Far to the south, reserve units of the 8th Army dug in across the width of Korea eventually being reinforced by the battered remnants of the 8th Army who had survived the retreat from north of Pongyang. For months the battle lines seesawed around the 38th Parallel. When peace negotiations began, the war became a war of patrols, small unit actions, continuous artillery and mortar bombardments, and constant air assault against the massive Chinese and North Korean forces. After three years, an armistice was signed. The war never officially ended and periodic small unit actions by the aggressor North Korean units continued to take So. Korea and American lives.

North Korea remains a rogue state feeding the hungry and impoverished North Koreans a steady diet of hate and fear.

GENE CARPER

Men and women join the military service for many different reasons. Some join out of a sense of pride and patriotism. Some join for the challenge. Some join because jobs are scarce and they have no other options. Some are dragged kicking and screaming, so to speak. Once in service with the dawn of reality, new attitudes and emotions surface. The service can be a form of involuntary servitude and even the most zealous enlistee can have second thoughts when the shooting starts or when the system fails to respect individualism. Some enlistees are very comfortable in the service as they make it a career. There is a security in the system if you learn the ropes and can accept some of the pain.

Some men never adjust and as soon as they have served, they turn their back on the whole experience. Those that have seen heavy combat may be traumatized and avoid anything that reminds them of the painful past. Other men go through the same experience and are able to relate to their military service. Often, for a draftee, the service can be an unwelcomed intrusion in their young life causing them to put marriage, family, and career on hold until the ordeal is over. But over all, the military service helps build character and responsibility. Many young people drifting through their young life have been resurrected by the military experience.

Though frequently unpleasant, the experiences are never forgotten and are often translated into a source of pride in later years, pride in having answered their country's call and pride in having done their duty with fidelity and honor. Unfortunately, many that have borne the battle, did not return or were grievously wounded limiting their ability to achieve their goals in life. That is the saddest part of service. As has been mentioned in other articles, long separation of spouses works a hardship on any marriage. Divorce and Dear John letters are par for the course.

Depression, Drought and Raising Horses

I was born in Arkansas on December the 18th, 1928, but my family was from Oklahoma. I had one full brother and one full sister and four half-brothers and two half-sisters. My mother had two girls from a previous marriage and my father had four boys. They had both lost their previous spouse. I was the oldest of the three kids from the second marriage, although I had an older sister that had died at birth. My father was a rancher and a farmer. During the depression it was difficult, and I remember many years of drought. We used to keep water in a cistern, and since there wasn't any refrigeration, we would put the milk and butter in a bucket down in the cistern to keep it cool.

I got into horses at a young age because my Dad raised horses and sold them to the government for the Cavalry. We raised wheat, barley, oats, corn, and other stuff, so we used horses for farming as well. I was a drifter type person, so I ran away when I was a youngster and came out here to California. I ran away because I wanted to see what was on the other side of the next hill! I worked in a Cannery up in Sunnyvale, California, just outside of San Jose, picking cherries.

Things got slow there, so I hitchhiked and rode freight trains out to Denver, Colorado in 1947. One of my family members had a construction business there, so I went to work for him as an apprentice contractor. Then I got into rodeoing, riding broncos. I did all sorts of ranch work on horses, so between that and being a contractor, I always had some money in my wallet. In 1948, Colonel Zack

Miller, who was a well-known and colorful character of that part of the Middle America, hired me He bought and sold livestock and he hired me to drive him to various purchasing sites and help him with the livestock and horses. Col. Miller bought horses for Ringling and Barnum Circus. Once we went to Argentina to purchase polo ponies.

Series of photos from 1st Battalion, 4th Marines on maneuvers at Rainbow Canyon. Here, cleaning weapons.

PHOTO COURTESY OF MARINE CORPS YEARBOOK, 4TH MARINES, 1952

"A Few Good Men"— and Then There's Me

My brother in law, who owned the construction company, was a Lt. Commander in the Seabees during WWII, so he got me to join. I was in the Seabee Reserves when the Korean War broke out. In 1952, I volunteered to go into active duty, but they turned me down because I had had a bad knee accident while riding broncos. It used to pop out all the time. They discharged me from the Seabees and drafted me into the Marine Corps! As Korea progressed and the battle casualties continued to soar, even the Marines were failing to attract "A few good men." I was assigned a carpenters MOS (Military Occupation Specialty) number. My MOS was as a construction carpenter. But one thing about the Marine Corps is that every man is a rifleman, first and foremost. As I started basic training, I caught the mumps, very serious. I had one of those real bad cases that men don't like to talk about. But I was cured and fully recovered, eventually raising four children. Sixteen weeks later, I completed basic training and was assigned to a floating bridge building company.

Fourth Marine Regiment Formed—1952

In September of 1952 the Marine Corps formed the 4th Marine Regiment of the 3rd Marine Division. It was organized with the usual rifle fire teams, squads, platoons, and companies. Integral to the units depending on level were flame-throwers, heavy water cooled machine guns, tanks, engineers, and recoilless rifle teams. The new unit was sent on maneuvers at Twenty-Nine Palms out in the California desert. In March of 1953, we were in "cold weather" training in the High Sierra Mountains above Bishop, California. Back at San Onofre near Camp Pendleton, we practiced amphibious landings where I was part of the aggressor force opposing the attacking Marines. The unit moved back to Twenty-Nine Palms where we lived in pup tents. By then I was involved in training new troops on the rifle range, taking them through dry fire, familiarization, and live fire. We were constantly getting replacements though, so unfortunately we got Master Sergeants who couldn't even muster men out! Apparently, their rank was formed from years of stateside service working in the office or something! Being a field Marine, I was shocked!

Company "A" Positions

PHOTO COURTESY OF MARINE CORPS YEARBOOK, 4TH MARINES, 1952

Dysentery and Salt Water Showers to Japan

Eventually, we boarded an old WWI troop ship in San Diego. The U.S.S. Black. She was in bad shape! And the living conditions on board her were horrible. There were 1300 people crammed into that old beat up rusty ship. We all got dysentery, and we had to take salt water showers. We didn't know where we were going, although we had heard talk that the war was supposed to break out with Indochina. Twenty-three days later, we landed in Kobe, Japan, which was quite distant from Indochina. That was about the time that helicopters became famous in the Marine Corps.

We set up our tents, and we had to sleep with our packs on our backs. It was September, and typhoon season had started. It was hot and muggy, and the wind would blow, and the rain…it was miserable. First thing off, they called my platoon for MP duty. I had a rifleman spec number, which qualified me to be an MP and our platoon had done real well in aggressor training, so they picked us. We were "squared away Marines." That meant that we were experienced in all facets of Marine training and experience—field soldiers, trained in weaponry, knowing how to command troops and do close order drills.

Battery "C" Readies their Guns in Garrison.

PHOTO COURTESY OF MARINE CORPS YEARBOOK, 4TH MARINES, 1952

Because a Marine Doesn't Like a Soldier Telling Him What to Do...

We were sent to Nara, which was the old capital of Japan. The Army was set up there, and so were the Marines, so they needed MP's to keep the peace between the soldiers and the Marines, because a Marine doesn't like a soldier telling him what to do! Marines were expected to be ready to fight anywhere at any time, so in mid-winter they sent us to Mt. Fuji and it was cold! We slept in tents with blanket-lined sleeping bags until finally we got some down ones. The old sleeping bags had been stored after WW II and we all got body lice. We lived on C-rations.

The Only General Captured in Korea

We were then sent to Korea to assist with the prisoner exchange that was taking place. I had the opportunity to see the newly freed Americans who had been Prisoners of War, as well as General Dean who had been captured in the early days of the war when the 24th Infantry Division had been overrun. He was the only General who had been captured in Korea. Most of the prisoners appeared to be okay. The Chinese were not as brutal to their prisoners as the North Koreans were, who generally executed their prisoners in the early days of the war.

We Get the Short Timers Treatment

Always training and always preparing, we were soon back in Japan on amphibious operations when my enlistment came to an end. They sent us back on the U.S.S. General Walker. The Marine Corps kept trying to recruit us to stay in, but guys like myself, who didn't want to stay in, got the treatment. The entire trip back, I was given mess duty. We knew that if we joined the regulars though, that they were going to send us right back over there.

Capturing and Interrogating CIA Spies

They sent me back home to Treasure Island where they gave me shore patrol for three weeks. Another job I had was capturing CIA spies who were in training. If we saw them out in the field, we had to capture them, take them out to some deserted barracks in Alameda airfield, and interrogate them. We had to toughen them up, just in case they were captured for real in enemy territory.

Getting Bronko Riding Fever Back Home

Finally, in 1954 they released me, and I came to Carpinteria and got a job with the Edison Company until the rodeo started creeping back into me again.

It was getting close to the time when the Cheyenne, Wyoming rodeo was going to start, so I loaded up and came back to Colorado. I was single so I could just take off and go when the rodeo started up—until I met my wife in Colorado Springs at a dance hall that they had on Saturday nights. She had moved out from New Mexico. I went to the dance with this girl I was dating from Braniff Airlines. But she used to drink too much and she was kind of crazy.

So, I was there, and my friend had a date with some new girl because his girlfriend and he had just broken up. Well, my friend saw his girlfriend out on the dance floor with some other guy, so he left the girl he had come with all alone. I ended up marrying that girl in 1956 and having three girls and a boy!

Roads, Missiles, Bomb Shelters, Tunnels, Towers, Dams...

I spent the rest of my career working in construction on different projects. For instance, from 1956 to 1960, I helped build a road at Fort Carson at the Air Force Academy. In 1961 I went to Wyoming and worked on missile sites, then worked on the road from NORAD to Fort Carson, then I worked for NORAD for four years. They were building a tunnel and a bomb shelter in case of an atomic bomb. Then I worked for them on microwave towers that we built to send information back to the intelligence center. During this whole time I worked on a few dams in Colorado and Utah. This was during the Cold War. In 1957, I was taking metal working classes and shoeing horses.

Finally a Horse Fingered Me Out

One day I was shoeing a friend's horses and I had just gotten through shoeing a mare, but she looked funny from behind, so I went to tie her up and she took off with the ends of two of my fingers! Between that and getting married and all, I had my last rodeo competition in 1958. Besides that, my horse was worn out!

Gene Carper, 2002

PHOTO COURTESY OF CHUCK BENNETT

Ojai Since 1969

In 1969 I heard that there was work out here in California, so we moved out here to Ojai, mostly to get away from that cold weather! All four kids graduated from Nordhoff. For most of my 51 years of active employment, I was a card-carrying member of the carpenter's union. Among the construction jobs I worked on out here were with the Los Angeles Department of Water and Power, Diablo Nuclear Power Plant, various oil refineries, and Point Mugu. I've worked as a rancher, a Marine, a bronco rider, a laborer, a foreman, a construction superintendent, a husband, father and now great-grandfather. I have a grandson who is a West Pointer, and two of my daughters are into horses! Must be in the blood.

HARRY HUNT

WWI (FATHER) AND KOREA
– THE MYSTIQUE OF BEING A MARINE

There is a mystique to being a Marine. It is a sacred brother-hood. It is a band of military brothers with few equals in the history of human warfare. Being a Marine is a uniquely American thing. While submitting to the most rigorous training and exposed to the most life threatening missions in a total military environment, the Marine lives, trains, fights, and dies for the ultimate cause of Constitutional government and the freedoms derived from a government based on the consent of the governed.

Once a Marine, always a Marine. It is a justly proud institution based upon a common tradition purchased with the blood of thousands of valiant Americans from the fights with the Barbary pirates of North Africa to the current fight against the aberrations of Islam and unmitigated terrorism exported from Afghanistan.

As long as there is a United States of America, there will be a United States Marine Corps, a Corps ready willing and able to defend this Nation against all foes.

Each person's experience and background varies ones view of military service. My experience and background was first formed by my father, a veteran of the U.S. – Mexican Border Skirmish of 1912, and World War I. He had been decorated with the Bronze Star for bravery in the trenches of Northern France and received the Purple Heart for war wounds. He also had the usual service ribbons typical of the overseas veterans of World War I. Being committed to veterans and veterans' causes, my father was a lifetime member of the American Legion and the Veterans of Foreign Wars. After World War I, Dad worked in the oil fields for Shell Oil Company on the Ventura Avenue. In an industrial accident in 1924, he lost his right arm.

Dad was the Constable for Ojai with One Arm

Because of his outstanding war record, Tom Clark, who was sheriff at the time, appointed Dad as Constable of Ojai in 1933. They had served in WWI together, and Clark knew what kind of man Dad was, so he got the job. The appointment of a one armed constable would have been unthinkable for a lesser man. I was born on March 27, 1933, right about the time my family moved to Ojai because of Dad's new job. I was the oldest of three kids.

Even though Dad was right handed, he learned to shoot and drive a stick shift patrol car with his left hand. Dad played the horn and bugle and sounded taps for many Ojai veterans buried in the Ojai cemetery. He became a law enforcement legend, protecting the people of Ojai in this capacity until 1943. I practically grew up in the back seat of his patrol car. We were always tagging along with my dad on calls.

Dad Killed the Man That Killed Him

But one day my Dad went out without us, leading a posse in search of an asylum escapee that had tried to rape a woman who lived on a ranch in upper Ojai. Dad caught up with the escapee near Steckel Park, and the crazy guy tried to ditch my Dad by jumping down an embankment, but my Dad jumped over after him. The escapee hailed my Dad with bullets, and even though Dad had been shot, he managed to shoot the guy, killing him on the spot. Dad was rushed to the hospital in critical condition. He was tough though. He convinced the doctors to release him.

They let him go, and a few days later he died. They never really could determine what had caused his death though. Some kind of complications from the gunshot wound. I was nine years old at the time.

Nordhoff buddies;
Harold Bangs, Harry Hunt,
and Bill Luttrell
—Class of '51

PHOTO COURTESY OF HARRY HUNT

Dad's early death caused things to get really tight. Our family had to work together to make ends meet. Mother went to work for Doug Jordan's Grocery Store in the Ojai Arcade. I took a paper route, and so did my brother and sister to help support our family during our teenage years. I also got a job working at Phil Culbert's Shell station. He was real nice to work for. In fact, everybody in town was very helpful. I think they knew what had happened and wanted to help take care of us.

Nordhoff Class of '51, Some Were Graduated Early for the Korean War

But we made it, and in 1950, I was a junior at Nordhoff High School, when the Korean War broke out. So in 1951 my Nordhoff High School class was greeted by the draft. We had the choice of whether we were drafted, or whether we enlisted. The Navy and the Air Force had shut their doors to enlistments because when the draft is on, they don't take people for a while. Mr. Drews, who was the Principal of Nordhoff at the time, called several of us into his office. He said, "You guys are slated to graduate in June. You already have your credits to graduate, so if you want to go into the service a few months early, that's okay." So we did. Two classmates, Harold Banks and Bill Lattrell, and I went down to Ventura and enlisted in the Marine Corps. We left in February, but we got leave to come home during graduation, so that we could graduate with our class at Nordhoff. We ended up being pretty close together the entire time we were in the military.

Like all recruiting officers, the Marine recruiter highlighted all of the benefits of enlisting in the United States Marine Corps. He was so encouraging—but the reality of the Marine Corps didn't fit his description. The supposed joy of the experience was quickly gone when we arrived at the Marine Corps Recruit Depot in San Diego. We were greeted by two screaming drill instructors yelling, " Get off that bus. Move! Move it, you shit birds, ##!!!#!!" Needless to say, it didn't take long before reality set in. Boot camp was a grueling experience, far worse than what was depicted in the movies. We were up and jogging at 5:00 am until 7:00 am. Then we had breakfast, followed by close order drill, firing on the rifle range, etc. When my family visited me at boot camp, they didn't recognize me! We had been turned into lean, mean fighting machines.

A Marine in a Machine Gun Platoon

After boot camp, they offered me Sea School, which would have probably put me on a carrier, serving the Captains. For whatever reason, this didn't sound good to me. Being a kid, I kind of wanted to stick with my buddies, so I turned it down, and I wound up in infantry in a machine gun platoon. We had advanced infantry training at Camp Pendleton's Tent Camp #3. A lot of the guys, upon completion of training, were flown to Korea as replacements.

Anyway, I was assigned to an Infantry Fire Team. We did a lot of mock landings, helicopter landings, and live fire maneuvers with close air support. They had just started using helicopters instead of those big boats where the front would open, and everybody would get killed.

We were the first to start training with helicopters, where they would land the troops way behind the line, so they didn't have to take the beachhead to get in there and fight. It was exciting, participating in defensive exercises, learning about defensive tactics, and seeing the effects of interlocking bands of fire. Night maneuvers were especially spectacular with the tracer fire. One major hazard of training at Camp Pendleton was the rattlesnakes. They were everywhere!

20 Year old Harry in Japan

PHOTO COURTESY OF HARRY HUNT

Assigned to the 3rd Marine Brigade

After advanced training, half of the company was assigned to Korea as replacements, and my company was assigned to the newly formed 3rd Marines, which was a regimental-sized unit known as the 3rd Marine Brigade. Marine General "Chesty" Puller was known throughout the Corps as "one tough Marine leader." He commanded our Brigade. During a "pass-in-review" ceremony, Puller was assigned as the Brigade Commander, so he reviewed some of his accomplishments and he said, "I've won every medal except the Congressional Medal of Honor, and I'll win it too on this tour, even if it takes every one of you!"

Training Under "Chesty" Puller

Training under Puller was extremely demanding. One exercise he ordered was a 100-mile forced march over the mountains of Pendleton carrying full field transport packs. I made it, but many guys fell out and had to be transported to the hospital back at base. Training included crawling on your belly under live machine gun fire, battling aggressor forces in situations as close to the reality of combat as possible. Our training was then extended to desert warfare at Twenty-Nine Palms, where we lived in foxholes day and night and moved in concert with tank forces, learning infantry maneuvers.

In 1952, we had a break from the intensive training, thanks to Hollywood! My regiment was asked to participate in the making of a Korean War movie named, "Retreat, Hell." My company became the Chinese Communist forces dressed in gunnysack uniforms. We charged down at Marine positions portraying the Marine fight and withdrawal from the frozen Yalu River. A classmate of mine who I had enlisted with, named Harold Bangs, was shown in the film as a Marine rifleman walking with the column.

After training for two years, in June of 1952, my unit was assigned to the Marine Air Station at Kanoye Bay, Hawaii. Originally, it was a Marine Air Station used in World War II, where Marine Sergeants were assigned as pilots, flying fighter cover and air reconnaissance missions from Hawaii. This activity continued through World War II following the attack on Pearl Harbor. I was reassigned from the machine gun platoon to the battalion operations section. And in August of 1953, the Third Marine Division boarded ship, for assignment to Korea.

The trip over there was really rough! You would look out the portholes and you'd see sky, then a second later you'd see water. Up and down. Most of the guys were sick all the way over. It was a huge brigade that we sailed over with, and we had submarine and destroyer escorts the whole way. We were supposed to land at Inchon, but prior to our landing, the Armistice was signed. I always wondered if seeing this huge task force coming, prompted the North Koreans to sign the Armistice. Anyway, because of it, my division was reassigned to the 7th Army Command in Japan as reserves.

"Dogfaces" Climb Mount Fuji

We were stationed on Mount Fujiyama, in the Gotemba/ Yamanaka area where we continued our training for about eight months. The training was intense. Live fire exercises.

While I was there, three Marines were killed when a short round landed in their foxhole. A group of us decided to climb Mt. Fuji when we had a few days off. That was quite an experience.

It wasn't too difficult though, because we were in such good shape after all that training. I remember, a Marine "barked" at some soldiers passing by. I guess it was in reference to the soldiers frequently being called "dogfaces," The soldiers answered back, "You ought to bark. You live like dogs!" I laughed because the soldier was right—we did live like dogs.

Lieutenant Harry Hunt with the California Highway Patrol.

When our enlistments came up, they tried their best to get us to re-enlist. They offered us some pretty good deals to entice us. For instance, in September, I was selected for Officer's Candidate School at Quantico, Virginia. But I was more than ready to become a civilian, so I declined the offer and was honorably discharged at Treasure Island,

San Francisco in February of 1954. I came back home and got a job, working for the Edison Company where I worked for five years.

Dogface Duty
—Great Preparation for Thirty Years in CHP

Then in 1958, I decided to go into the California Highway Patrol. The old saying, "Once a Marine, always a Marine," is true. The discipline and training of the Corps prepared me for the 30 years I spent in law enforcement, where I rose to the rank of Lieutenant. It was a great career. My wife, Vesta, and I raised three kids together. She deserves all the credit though. She has always been there for all of us. She and my father are the true heroes.

ED MARSHALL

–THE LONG WEEKEND DRILL

In 1950, North Korea invaded South Korea with a first class aggressive army. By this time, the U.S. Army and Navy were woefully unprepared. The skeleton army in Japan was unprepared for action in Korea: yet, Harry S. Truman ordered this force to halt the North Korean communists based on the most fragmentary intelligence. Little did Truman realize what he was doing and the impossible odds against the tiny American force. The American army was beaten back to the Naktong Bulge of the Pusan Perimeter

It soon became apparent that this was a real war and would require extensive mobilization. As is true of all our wars except Vietnam, the active military looked to the Army and Air National Guard to quickly flesh out the armed force. Concurrent with the activation of eight National Guard Divisions, the draft was kicked into gear to provide the fillers for rapidly depleted forces in Korea. The politicians tried to hide the severe magnitude of the war by euphemistically referring to it as a police action long after it became evident that this was a brutal war by every definition of war. The public had little realization of the seriousness of the situation. Only the active participants in the war knew the full story. The National Guardsmen were motivated by very different reasons to serve.

Many joined the Guard for the drill pay, which supplemented their civilian employment. Some of the young high school age soldiers joined out of a sense of adventure. It was a step up from the Boy Scouts. Many of the Officers and ranking NCO's had joined after World War II because it afforded them opportunities for military advancement and a continuation of military service. The 2nd Battalion had an unusually high number of ex-combat Marines WWII.

The attitude of the body politic and the army planners was that World War II was the last of the old fashioned wars. After all, the United States had the atomic and hydrogen bomb. Old fashioned armies and navies were a thing of the past. Most of the military hardware of WW II had been dumped in the ocean or in the case of naval ships, they were simply used as target ships for atomic testing in the far Pacific.

Cash + Car + Blind Date = Marriage and a Daughter

I was born in Colton, California on December the 18th, 1929, and the minute I turned 17, I joined the National Guard. The reason I joined was because my mother said to! I had started working for Mayfair Market when I was fifteen, and I was making good money, $69.00 a week. That was the highest non-union pay in the State of California at that time. I wanted to buy a car, so I worked hard until I had the money. When I had saved up 1,962.00 dollars, I took the money up in a sack to the dealer. The guy there said, "You're too young, I can't sell you a car." I opened up the bag and said, "I got cash." He took one look at it and said, "I guess I can!" I bought a brand new Chevy, square back, four-door.

Then I got married when I was 19, I married a girl from my high school. I didn't know her while I was in school; we met afterwards through my best friend. His girlfriend was a classmate of Dawn's. He called me up and said that his girlfriend Carol had someone she wanted me to go out with. So we went on a blind date, and we never dated anyone else again! I was 18 at the time, and I was making real good money and going to college at Los Angeles City College. We dated for a year, and then she said, "We need to get married." Her parents didn't want us to get married. They said we were too young and that it wouldn't last. We did it anyway. Eleven months later, we had a daughter!

My 40th Division Gets Activated

In September of 1950, Harry Truman activated the 40th Division. I had just signed up in January for my second hitch in the National Guard. I was a machine gun section Sergeant, in charge of two sections of machine gunners.

Every summer I went up to Camp San Luis Obispo for training, and we trained on the weekends as well throughout the year with the 160th Infantry Regiment at the Exposition Park Armory in Central Los Angeles. Every Monday I attended a two-hour drill that usually lasted for three hours.

One day when I was coming home from work at Mayfield Market, the Daily News had a headline that said, "40Th Division Activated!" So I stopped and bought a paper and it said that all Guardsmen have to report to the Army tomorrow! So I had to call my work and tell them that I was leaving!

The Very Long Weekend

One history book called this activation, "A Very Long Weekend,' a reference to the normal back-to-back weekend drills. It was a very long weekend! For the first week of activation on September 1, 1950, we drilled at the armory while we packed up all of the Army's stuff. After a week, I said goodbye to my wife and daughter, and a train pulled up on Exposition Blvd. loading the 160th Regiment for shipment to Camp Cooke in Northern Santa Barbara County. It is now called Vandenberg Air Force Base. Camp Cooke was a relic of World War II. The whole camp had been deserted for five or six years, and it was in sorry shape! Doors were off the hinges. Windows were broken. Tumbleweeds rolled through the camp. Dust and decay permeated the barracks. So, we went to work restoring some semblance of order to the camp. We cleaned and repaired right along with our heavy physical training.

The combat experienced NCO's and officers became the core leadership cadres for the unit. Higher-ranking officers from WW II combat developed the training programs to make the 40th Division a first class fighting unit. Unfortunately, some of the Guardsmen were underage or physically unfit, so they were discharged and sent home which strengthened the core of the division. I had been in the Guard long enough to have picked up elemental military skills. I had enough experience to fill the need for sergeants at the squad and platoon level, so I was assigned to H Company heavy weapons. My specialty was the heavy water cooled 30-caliber machine gun.

"Get serious! You are going to fight on the field of battle."

I studied really hard all the time, so I did real well on all of the tests they gave us. I did so well that they made me a Sergeant in December. I was put ahead of all the Sergeants who at one time had been over me, and boy they weren't happy! General Hudelson stood up in front of a massed formation of 20,000 men and said, "I want you to take your training seriously, because you are going to fight on the field of battle. I guarantee it, so you guys get serious!" I took him seriously.

The politicians and newspapers kept saying that the California National Guard would not be allowed to leave California; it wasn't considered good politics. In the meantime, my unit was brought up to full strength with draftees and regular army enlistees. Most of the draftees were considerably older than the enlisted Guardsmen. They were the men that had just missed induction at the end of WW II. They were twenty-four to twenty-five years old. Some of them really resented having to take orders from younger, more qualified men.

Some of the Regular Army leadership was determined to make the division merely a training division. This was a repeat of the history of the Division in WW I when the Division was sent to France and then split up as fillers for regular army units. So as the division trained new recruits, the recruits were pulled out and sent to Korea as fillers.

PHOTO COURTESY OF DAVE PRESSEY

But General Daniel Hudelson was determined that the 40th Division would fight as a trained unit. We trained from September of 1950 until March of 1951 when they rounded us up to go to Japan. The reason I knew we were leaving for Japan was, I was on my way back from a weekend pass at home, and I saw another newspaper headline that said, "40th Division Ordered Overseas!" I said, "Here we go!"

Navy Ships Across the Horizon

The mission was to defend Japan against any possible Soviet invasion, a real threat in the age of Stalin. A sister National Guard division, the 45th from Oklahoma, was sent to Hokkaido with the same mission. The 160th Infantry Regiment was sent to the northern part of the island near Hachinoe where they started their amphibious training. After that, we got on board and did all of our amphibious training. When I got up in the morning, there were large numbers of naval ships anchored off the coast of Chigasaki, Japan. The troops climbed down the rope nets to the platoon sized landing craft which were bouncing around in the ocean surge. Each wave of the assault boats rendezvoused in a large circular pattern while awaiting the signal to hit the beach. We were prepared for the landing and each soldier knew the specific objectives of the attack when we landed. Unfortunately, the ocean current had caused the naval flotilla to drift south and we landed on the wrong beach. The beach was filled with Japanese bathers, many were sans clothes and the attractive young women created such a diversion for the young troops that the officers hurried us inland before any confusion ensued.

We assumed that our amphibious exercises were purely for training purposes. Years later, we found out that our operations were part of carefully planned strategies to make the Chinese and North Koreans think that another Inchon type invasion was about to take place. This relieved some of the pressure on the Eighth Army in Korea as the Communist withdrew troops to defend potential landing sites.

Drinking Whiskers and Water

We trained at Mt. Fuji for eight months, day after day after day. Our training intensified to live fire exercises coordinated with tanks, artillery, and air support. The training was so intense that some of the guys were killed in the field. We had to sleep in foxholes. They had tanks come over the hill, right over on top of us. You had better be in your hole, or they'd run you right over! We were in those holes rain or shine. I'd always find a spot right near a tree trunk. If it was raining, I could pull my poncho tight and lean against that tree trunk to sleep, so I wouldn't be in the hole that was all filled with water. It was blistering hot in the summer and we were only given one quart of water per day. They wanted us to shave out of that too. I was so thirsty that first night. I poured what was left of my water into my helmet, I shaved, and then I drank the water. What's a few whiskers!

Buying Our Own Uniforms!

Our clothes were worn out and the Army wouldn't give us clothes. So we had to write home to our families to buy clothes and boots! The Regular Army Command treated us terribly, even though most of the troops were not National Guardmen! There were very few actual Army National Guard troops.

While we were there, they sent me by train to critique a training exercise near Sendai. When we were at the train station, there was Governor Earl Warren, the Governor of California, and the Secretary of the Army, which was a woman. They were investigating reports that we weren't getting supplies. So I talked to him. He said, "Your clothes look good!" I said, "Yes Sir, that's because my mother went down to the WW II surplus store and bought me some and sent them to me. My men did the same. We had cardboard in our boots because the soles were worn out. We were in desperate shape and the Army just wouldn't supply us!" The Secretary of the Army was sitting right there, and her mouth fell open! And wouldn't you know it, within a month, we were sent all new clothing!

Ed Marshal at Camp McNair, Mt. Fujiyama.

PHOTO COURTESY OF ED MARSHALL

No Frostbite —That's an Order!

We were then moved to Camp Zama near Tokyo, for air transport training. We trained how to load in C-119's, how to land as if we were going to attack. Unfortunately, a massive fire swept through the barracks destroying all the weapons and gear of one battalion. We celebrated Christmas and then the day after New Year, we were given orders for the whole regiment to load ship in Yokohama Harbor for deployment to Inchon, Korea. We had all new equipment, new guns, new trucks and all this stuff. But the Army did their old trick again. We loaded everything in the snow. When we got there the Army had taken all of our new equipment and sent it back and we had nothing! We practically froze to death that first day in Korea. They said, "If anyone here has frost-bite, we're going to court martial you!"

Marshall on A-Deck, on the way to Inchon.

PHOTO COURTESY OF ED MARSHALL

We Relieve the 24th Division

Our division was ordered to relieve the 24th Infantry Division on the line. Day and night, artillery and mortar fire was pouring into the positions occupied by the Red Army. Each side shelled each other continuously. If we hadn't been in well-dug emplacements, the casualty rates would have been horrendous. That outfit we were replacing was barely capable of military action and the morale of their unit was terrible. They had some real attitude problems about their duties.

We got really concerned when we realized the sad state of the weapons we were about to acquire from the 24th. I turned to one of the guys and said, "Your equipment is in pretty bad shape, what are you going to do if you get attacked?" He looked at me and said, "We're runnin! All I've got is a 45-cal pistol." The other guy said, "I've got an M-1, but it don't work!" That's how bad the morale was when we showed up. They were not going to stand and fight, but we were eager to fight because we had been training all this time. I don't know how they let it get so bad up there.

All our new guns were gone so we had to fight with this old worn out equipment and our ammunition came from WW II. A lot of the ammunition that we were fighting with was old or damaged and it didn't fire.

We spent quite a while rebuilding the weapons as fast as we could. When we were finished, an officer told me to walk back down the trail and to stay by this giant rock until someone came to pick me up and take me back to the camp.

So I was standing there and I could see our First Aid Station about 50-75 yards up. There were tents, Jeeps, big red crosses on everything. I noticed this guy sitting in a Jeep, then all of a sudden, there was this huge explosion. It hit the Jeep that the guy was sitting in, and his body went flying. The next explosion hit the tents, and three or four shells later; the entire First Aid Station was gone! There was nothing left. I had just gotten there the day before. I looked at that, and I can remember clearly what I thought. I said, "Ed, get used to it, because this is the way it's going to be from now on." I wasn't afraid, just amazed. Pretty soon my Jeep came and took me back to camp.

Chinese Attack to Test Us

The next day, I took my men up and put them in those holes and immediately, we sent patrols out to provide screening against infiltration and attack. Apparently, the Chinese army decided to test us, because they launched a battalion size attack against the most forward units. The Chinese had captured some American soldiers; they killed them and strung one of them up in a tree. They hung him upside down. He was frozen stiff. He was there for some days. Bait to try and get us to come out. They had an ambush all set up, waiting for us.

As the Chinese battalion advanced, our entire battalion became involved. Cooks, clerks, truck drivers and anyone who could handle a rifle were sent up to the line to meet the attack. That was the first time that I saw close air support and what it can do. The Chinese were coming over the hill and they looked like ants, there were so many of them. Probably 400 to 500 guys coming straight at us.

The 30 caliber water cooled heavy machine gun.

I didn't know what we were going to do to stop them. Then the airplanes came. Two P-51 Mustangs, WW II vintage. They made a pass, one after another, firing their machine guns, cutting a path through those enemy soldiers. They made several passes, then they fired their rockets. They had one under each wing. They really had these troops shook up. They were turning and starting to run when they dropped napalm on them. Right in front of our eyes, they burned them all up. I mean, when they got through, there was nobody left! It looked like almost 500 men had been killed there in a matter of no time. I was told later that the pilots who flew those planes, were National Guard pilots.

Getting to Our Hilltop Assignments

As if it wasn't hell already, the conditions were miserable. We would leave the semi comfort of the tents in the rear area after five days of rest. We traveled by truck to our assigned hill, which was usually an ordeal because the Chinese had a view of some of the roads and they fired their artillery, making it hazardous. When we would arrive, we would always look to see how far it was to the top. Sometimes it was so far that the men at the top looked like ants. It was a tough climb in the snow and ice. On the way up, we would sweat as if it were summer, and when we would stop; we could feel the sweat freeze on our backs.

Focused on Water and Warmth

Once everyone was in position on the hill and all the men we were relieving had left, we had to settle into a routine that no one had ever even dreamed of in their worst nightmare. First of all, it was bitter cold. We were told that it was between 20 and 30 degrees below zero! We tied our gloves to our jackets because without them our hands would freeze. When we had to do things that required us to take them off, we had to light a can of "canned heat," so we would have fire to warm our hands by. Our water froze in our canteens, so we were thirsty a lot of the time.

To try and keep warm I wore long johns, wool pants, waterproof pants, a wool shirt, a pile coat, a field jacket, and a full-length parka. And I was still cold! We ate C-rations, frozen solid. We tried to use our small cans of "canned heat" to warm it up. When the rations came, we turned them all upside down so that the guys didn't fight over them. What you picked is what you ate. Beans and franks was the favorite. We also had pork and beans, corned beef hash, and ham and lima beans.

We had mountain sleeping bags, which were also on the buddy system—one bag per two men. That meant if it was your turn to sleep and your partner was already in the bag and not due to go on duty, you had to curl up on a piece of cardboard or on a pile of duffel bags. When we slept, someone in the bunker had to be awake at all times. In the machine gun bunkers, one man had to be awake on the gun and one man had to be awake outside, at all times.

Many times, my wire man and I would take the outside duty along with help from the rest of the squad, because we were responsible for operating the 50-caliber machine gun in the open, right outside the 30-caliber machine gun in the bunker. These two guns guarded the trail up from the valley below. We all wore shoe packs on our feet with three pairs of wool socks to keep our feet from freezing. But they would still freeze unless we were able to dry our socks out every day. During the day we would burn cardboard from ration boxes.

We soon ran out of cardboard though, and that's when "choggi bearers" came into our life. Before long, you could see five or six of them climbing up the steep hill with a bundle of dry sticks, slung over their shoulders. When they reached us, we would give them some C-rations in exchange for their wood, so that we could dry our socks out and warm our feet. They told us that they fed their families with the rations we gave them.

The Every Night and Day Struggle

At night, there was always something going on. Sometimes the incoming artillery fire was so severe that I wondered how anyone could survive it. I once had three direct hits on the roof of my bunker. It held though. Searchlights shone on the clouds to give us some light at night. We never really went to sleep until after 4:00 to 5:00 am because our patrols were out there. I would listen to the chatter on the sound power telephone to see how everyone was doing.

Sometimes we would fire at pre-selected targets several times during the night, to keep our patrols from being ambushed. When we saw scurrying around our targets, we knew we were successful. Around midnight, the bugles would blow, and we wouldn't know what was going to happen. The enemy used them, and it was a real eerie sound. Sometimes after blowing their bugles, the enemy would try to cross a wire that we had strung with cans, so we would open fire, sweeping the wire. Then we would stop, wait, and listen for more rattles. Sometimes they just blew their bugles and did nothing.

After 4:00 or 5:00 am, we would crawl into our sleeping bag, boots and all. We never zipped them up though, because we had heard stories of how the quick released hadn't worked. Then we'd wake up and do it all over again. During the day, we had to keep our movements out in the open to a minimum because, if not, you would draw mortar fire.

Marshall crossing under a C-119 air troop transport.

During the day, we would clean our weapons, write letters, shave every three days, eat, and rest up for the night. Just before dark we would get the order to test fire our weapons to be sure that they operated right. While in one position, we would always fire into a small grove of trees where we suspected that a sniper was hiding. Finally, after 30 days, the order would come to move down the road and load on the trucks. On the way back, we would dream about taking a shower, clean clothes, warm fresh cooked food, and maybe even a beer to drink in front of the hot stove in the tent. That was heaven! We had body lice so bad while we were over there that I ended up using DDT powder in my hair, under my arm pits, in my shorts and in my shoes We were allowed five days off, but we always had a job to do. I was assigned to laundry duty which was no fun. It always passed way too quickly, and then we'd load back up into trucks to a new hill for another month. twenty-five days on, five days off.

ROK Capital Division Arrives

One time we were in our rear area on our five day rest when the ROK (Republic of Korea) Capital Division came on the scene. You could hear them coming for miles. Their kitchen kettles were clanging together like wind chimes. Their trucks loaded with troops also had comfort girls on board. When we went back on the hill, my section was assigned to Fox Company and one of my machine gun bunkers was the last bunker before joining the ROKS. There was a rocky knob between the enemy and us. You couldn't see their bunkers unless you crawled up the knob and looked over. On the hill behind us, about 1/4 mile was a battalion to back us up in case of a breakthrough. Behind them was a complete ROK Division. The whole month we were there, the Chinese kept trying to break through. If it wasn't heavy artillery blasting us, then it was a probe of our defense at night. The artillery caused a lot of casualties in the bunkers of the troops backing us up. The shells would go over us and right into their bunkers.

A Few Chinese Get by Us

My bunker was just over the crest of the hill and right behind my left side was a machine-gun bunker. Greenwood was the squad leader. In my bunker were our wireman and the platoon medic. I would sit outside the entrance till around 4:00 am and then wake up the wireman to watch so I could get some sleep. I always had the sound power telephone stuck in my ear so I could hear what was happening in the machine-gun bunkers. One night about midnight, the machine guns opened fire. I crawled over the ridge and dropped into Greenwood's machine-gun bunker. The gun was firing at shadows around the wire in front of us. We kept firing until we could see no more movement in front. Over the knob the ROKS were engaged in a firefight. The next morning one of the guys crawled up the knob for a look. He said there were a few dead Chinese in front of their wire and one was just hanging there, stuck to the wire.

Finally A Hot Meal
Complete with Hot Shrapnel

In the second month on line, someone in charge decided, that what we needed was fresh cooked food to boost our morale. So one day I was informed that if I climbed straight down 200 yards to the road that a truck would be there with a freshly cooked chicken meal A bunch of us took off down the steep icy trail. At one point the lead person grabbed the muzzle of the rifle of the guy behind and he would lower you down a few feet to solid ground. The kid whose rifle I grabbed had a round in the chamber and the safety was off, as I found out as I got to solid ground! Escaped again. I didn't know how long my luck would hold. A Fox Company sergeant and I, after getting our food off the truck, leaned against a tree to eat when a mortar round hit close. We dove into a bunker, and I managed to keep my mess gear level, but he dumped all his chicken dinner in the dirt. So I shared what I had with him.

While we ate, we watched several pieces of equipment get destroyed. The Chinese had part of our access road under observation and whenever trucks arrived so did the mortar rounds. I never went back for hot, fresh cooked chow again!

Ambushes and firefights broke out in patrol action in the valleys below us, but casualties remained light. I remember this motor pool Captain and Sergeant who wanted to see the war on the front lines. They came with cameras to take pictures! As they came into our machine gun positions, I told them that their actions were dangerous, and that they might get us all killed. The Captain ignored me until enemy artillery and mortar fire blanketed the area. The Captain dove for shelter in the bunker but started to leave as soon as the shelling stopped. Once again, I warned him that this was just a lull. Once again, the Captain ignored me. But the second time shrapnel tore through the captain's chest creating a sucking chest wound. I patched him up with a poncho before we evacuated him.

Daytime Bulls-eyes for Nighttime Bulls-eyes

I remember one time in January of 1952, my two squads with 30-caliber, water cooled, heavy machine-guns were assigned to support Fox Company. After diagramming my fields of fire, I was asked to give fire support to their night patrols with one gun. The Captain pointed out a finger on the hill opposite us and said that the Chinese had a listening post there and he was afraid of an ambush. It was out there about 800 yards. We fired until we hit the target, then we marked and locked the position of the gun. If the tripod wasn't moved we could go back any time and hit the target.

We took the tracers out of two belts, and put a burlap screen in front of the gun to hide the muzzle flash. We usually fired between the hours of midnight and 2:00 am. I always did the first firing, Pete Cruz my gunner, fired next. Heck of a noise at that time of night. Four to six rounds of rapid fire. We used two degrees of traverse and elevation. The next morning there was debris everywhere and the snow had turned from white to dirty brown. No doubt we had inflicted some casualties. The area around the heavy machine guns was littered with hundreds of Chinese corpses. At times, it was quite gruesome as the rats and crows gnawed away on frozen human flesh.

Fireworks Tricks

One day, I believe in February of 1952, I saw the heavy mortars being set up on the reverse side of our hill. The position we were in had a ridge running across to the Chinese positions on the hill across from us. This was just to the left of my heavy machine-gun positions. There was a forward outpost, then No Man's Land, then the Chinese on the ridge. I can't remember the number or name of the ridge and the hill it ran into. All I know is, it got a lot of attention. After dark the mortars commenced firing phosphorus onto the edge of the ridge and the hill across from us. It was the greatest fireworks display I ever saw. It went on for a long time, then there was complete darkness, followed by the noise of mortar shell explosions all over that hill. This shelling went on for a very long time. The phosphorus was used to drive the Chinese into the open and then we used shrapnel to inflict casualties. It was a tremendous display of mortar power. Five months I was over there, day in and day out of battle. We had to sleep to the sound of firing because it was pretty much around the clock.

My enlistment came up while I was over there. They offered me an opportunity to go to OCS, then they offered me to be a platoon sergeant of the platoon I had trained with. I told them that I would think about it.

The next day they called me and said that I was going home! I decided to take them up on it, but it was so difficult, going around to all my men, leaving them there. We had been together for almost two years.

Horrible is as Horrible Does—So, Say no

When I finally got on board ship to come home, this regular Army officer came up to me and said, " I see that you're in the 40th Division" I said, "Yes Sir" and he said, "You're on KP every day!" I said, "No Sir, I'm not, because I get sick." He said, "Then you're going be in charge of this compartment, and if I find one speck of dust, or a scrap of paper anywhere in this compartment, you're going be confined to it all the time!" And I was too, because someone always parked a scrap of paper somewhere.

When I came back home from Korea, we were treated like dirt, and the National Guard wanted me to re-enlist and be a squad leader! I said, "I just got back from fighting the Chinese for five months, and you want to make me a squad leader?"

The records show today, in the 8th Army reports, that the National Guard Troops of the 40th and the 45th Division, were the best Army troops that they had in Korea and many of the National Guard Artillery Units were better than any that were in WWII! But we were treated badly by the Regular Army while in combat, and we were treated badly when we got home. So after eight years in the National Guard, I decided to get out and go home to my wife and daughter.

The G.I. Bill and Mobil Oil

I found a job with Mobil Oil Company in Vernon, California. With the benefits from the G.I. Education Bill, I was able to train as an automotive and diesel mechanic at National Schools. With diploma in hand I launched a twenty-seven year career with the same oil company where my commanding general, General Hudelson, worked. I was able to talk to him about our mutual war experiences. I served as mechanic, dispatcher, superintendent, truck driver, driver trainer, and father of four.

After that I worked at a chemical company until retirement. When I retired, we moved to Washington State for three years where my son lived. Unfortunately, my wife's health hasn't been good for a few years, so we moved to Ojai where one of our daughters lives. I spend much of my time caring for my wife and writing articles for the National Guard about my experiences during the war.

PHOTO COURTESY OF CHUCK BENNETT

Ed Marshall, 2002

I also have a monster garden that I started from seed. One of the first things I did when we moved to Ojai was to transfer my Life Membership in the VFW to the Ojai Valley Veteran's of Foreign Wars – Post 11461 where I met Dave Pressey. It is so strange how life works, because Dave was right there with me in Korea! We didn't know each other, but Dave jokes with me, he says, "So you were the one firing those guns all night that made us jump out of our skin!" I feel really welcome here in Ojai, California; those guys at the VFW Post 11461 are just like brothers.

GENE PETERSON

—*TRAINED VERY EARLY TO SERVE*

Boy Scouts were created to train young city boys for the rigors of the outdoor life and the field with quasi-military organization. The British Army sorely felt the deficiencies of young conscripts in the Boer War in South Africa. In the United States, the National Rifle Association was created and supported with similar objectives: to acquaint people with the correct use of firearms. Later the CCC was organized during the Depression with paramilitary organization and regimentation. When World War II began, the United States had a large number of men ready for military service. But Gene Peterson was prepared and trained for the military life in an orphanage in Montana. It was a sad experience, but the discipline, order, and regimentation prepared him for the military life despite the emotional trauma of being an orphan.

A Third Generation Miner From Butte

I was born in Butte, Montana on August 2nd, 1937. All the copper mines were there in Butte. That was the hundredth anniversary of that company. But as ironic as it seems, my grandfather owned a mine in Butte, and he sold it to Marcus Daley, who worked for the Queen of Holland. She bought all the mines in Butte. That was the start of the Anaconda Company. After that my grandfather, who was a prospector, moved out to Nevada. He was something else. He didn't pass away until he was ninety-six! So I'm a third generation miner.

Off to the Orphanage at Two

Both of my parents were alcoholics, my whole family was. My parents had eight children I was the fifth in line. All of us were taken away by the state, and five of us ended up in an orphanage. I had only a fifteen minute acquaintance with my father. When I met him, he was in a drunken state. The only words I remember from my father was when I heard him tell my older brother to get the little SOB out of here. I was two years old when I went into the orphanage, so I didn't even know that I had any brothers or sisters until I was about five or six because they wouldn't allow us to associate. Your association was one hour a week on Sunday. But like I said, it was about four years before I realized that I had brothers and sisters, and we were all in the same orphanage! They didn't want us to have any family bonds with other people. I have two brothers who I have never been able to locate. I know that one brother spent twenty years in the Navy, and the other one was a mentally unbalanced street person, but it is little wonder considering the nature of our childhood and institutional upbringing. Not all children can survive parental rejection and the absence of normal family relationships. And there's a sister in Roxbury, Wyoming. In fact, she came back here just this past week, and I just met with her again.

I learned three things in that orphanage: work, ethics, and self-sufficiency. They used to tell us that no one loves us except for God. For many years, I wasn't even sure of the love of God. When I look back on it, if you really think about it, God's love never fails us! But I didn't understand that when I was a child.

Meals Regulated by Five Bells

The regimentation of the orphanage is best described by how we ate our meals. Meals were regulated by five bells. The first bell was to go to the mess hall. The second bell was to take our seat at the table. The third bell was to say grace. The fourth bell was to eat. And the fifth bell was to leave the table. It was almost like the eating regime during "hell week" at West Point except we didn't have to eat "square meals."

Anyway, luckily, I was adopted when I was eleven, a few days after my birthday. My adopted mother was from Bozeman, Montana. Her family had homesteaded there. The people who adopted me were good people. But my new mother got a divorce about a year after I was adopted. My mother raised another boy, who is my adopted brother, and me.

Into Military Police at the End of Korea

On January 21st, 1954, when I was seventeen, I went into the service. I ended up putting in eight years in the military. I had my basic training at Fort Ord, California, and then I was assigned to Military Police training at Fort Gordon, Georgia. I was fortunate in that I had gone into the service right as the Korean War was ending. My company was supposed to go over to Korea, but the war ended right before the end of basic training.

Peterson, setting up tents at MASH hospital in Germany near the Saar border.

PHOTO COURTESY OF GENE PETERSON

98ᵗʰ General Hospital, Germany

We took a troop transport over to Germany. It took thirteen days with 5,000 of us on that ship. We left December 2nd and we hit a storm out of New York the second day. As we were coming into Bremerhaven, Germany, at about 4:00 in the morning, a Dutch freighter was coming out. We collided! Luckily, we stayed above water because most of the damage was above the water line. But the Dutch freighter had to be pulled back to port, We were out there for about five or six hours on top deck with thousands of troops just waiting. But we finally got off. In Europe they travel by train, so they put us on a train and it was about a two or three hour ride to where I was stationed at the hospital. It was so cold when we got there. It was January.

I was a Military Policeman and stationed at the 98th General Hospital, which specialized in broken bones and orthopedics. It was right on the Saar border, which is a province in Germany. We went up in the field, set up the hospital and patrolled through all the perimeters and stuff. We were stationed there in order to set up an MP company because we were the government in Germany at the time.

We Were Still "Occupation Troops"

That was before the Germans got their government back. We had control over the civilian and military government. The Germans still had their civilian police force, but they were subject to our rules and regulations. The Germans didn't get their government back until something like 1957. We were called "occupation troops." The only occupation in my sector was that of Americans, nobody else was there. Berlin, that was the capital, was still divided in four sections. So you had Russia, France, England, and the United States each governing a part of Germany.

The Berlin Airlift

It was during the early fifties and the Russians blocked all transportation into Berlin except for airplanes. Our Air Force flew all supplies into Berlin including food, fuel, and as well as any other necessity of life. It was the famous Berlin Airlift. Our military was over there just in case war started with Russia. Our MP Company would have had the duty of escorting all the citizens out of the country through Saarland. One of our main organizational duties was to patrol the border. We had drills where we used a lot of hospital personnel out in the field, and marked out which road we would take to get everything back to the border. But thank God it never happened. I was there for three-and-a-half years. Most of the guys stayed there for about two-and-a-half years.

Mass grave markers of the Jewish dead, Auschwitz Germany.

PHOTO COURTESY OF GENE PETERSON

The Horror of Auschwitz

My ancestors were from Germany. And I did a lot of traveling. Our shift in Germany was three days, three nights, and two days off. So on my days off, I used to just hop the trains. I went to all the big cities including Copenhagen,

Amsterdam, and Paris. The countries are small and close to each other, so you can get anywhere by train. While I was over there, I visited Dachau and Auschwitz Concentration Camps. There were rooms filled with ovens, and I never realized, until years later, the implications of that visit. I went through it and as a young kid, you don't really think about stuff like that. Photographing everything that I saw over in Europe was my hobby at that time, so I am able to look back at myself through the eyes of an adult, and see the horrors of war.

PHOTO COURTESY OF GENE PETERSON

Gene Peterson (r) at Auschwitz Concentration Camp witnessing the incinerators.

A major traffic incident occurred during my tour of duty in Germany when an atomic canon crashed on the highway. That caused an anxious moment because of the nature of the material, security, and Soviet interest in our atomic assets.

Fort Huachucha, Proving Ground

In 1979, I left Germany and I was stationed at Fort Huachucha, Arizona. At this time I was in the 512th Military Lease Company in the Army Proving Ground. Fort Huachucha was my only stateside duty.

The interesting thing about that post is that it used to be the Colored post; Buffalo Soldiers, as the Indians referred to Black soldiers in the Old West. The Buffalo Soldiers were famous for chasing Poncho Villa across the border and fighting in many of the Indian wars. Poncho Villa and his army used to come in and raid Arizona, so the Buffalo Soldiers would chase him back to Mexico.

Fort Huachucha was used as the Signal Corps-proofing route, where they take electronics and test them. I was in the military police at that time, and we had three border-lines that we used to border check. As the GI's came across the border, we'd make sure they had all their papers, and that they didn't get into any trouble or anything. Sometimes they went over to Mexico, and when they got over there and got into trouble, we had to go and pick them up. I didn't speak Spanish. But it was kind of ironic because most of the border patrol people spoke perfect Spanish, so we didn't have to worry about that. That assignment lasted for about a year-and-a-half and then from there, I put in for an overseas assignment and I had to get a top-secret clearance.

Henry Barracks, Puerto Rico

I was shipped to Puerto Rico. I don't know if you remember the history of the Puerto Ricans who went in and shot our U.S. Congressmen while Congress was in session? I think it was in the early fifties. It just so happened that I was stationed at Henry Barracks, which was an old Air Force base, right in the middle of the island. The island is made up of two mountains, and Cayey sits right in the valley between the two mountains. It was kind of ironic because one of our MP's married the daughter of the main leader of that rebellion that had gone in and shot up Congress! And at that time we had orders not to associate with the people because of that.

But he knew he was getting out of service, so he married her anyway.

The Cuban Missile Crisis

Another interesting fact surrounding that incident was that the last year before Clinton got out of office, he paroled some Puerto Ricans. Well, it was that group of Puerto Ricans that he paroled! Anyway, I was there in 1960 to 1961 when the Cuban Crisis came up. And that was the closest I ever came to combat, during the Cuban Crisis. We were all prepared to jump off north Cuba, so everybody was ready at that time. But of course we didn't realize at that time that we were also targets. But we were, because the Air Force/Army base was there in Puerto Rico. One of the largest Naval bases outside of Pearl Harbor is in San Juan. I also got married to my first wife while in Puerto Rico. She came from the states to live with me.

1962— "No, I've had enough."

While I was over in Germany, I had re-upped for six more years, so I ended up having an eight-year obligation. When I got out of the military, I didn't have to keep a sea-bag or stay in the reserves. I got out in 1962 right after the Cuban Crisis. They almost sent me to Vietnam in 1962 when we had hardly anybody there. We weren't supposed to have anybody there either, but we did. They said that they were going to give me another stripe, and send me over there, but I said, "No, I've had enough." I had two children at that time, so I didn't want to go. My marriage with the mother of my children lasted thirteen years, then it fell apart and we got a divorce.

While I was in the military, I had made the conscious decision to become an MP, so that when I got out, I could go into the police field. But at that time when I applied to the Highway Patrol, they wouldn't let me in because of discrimination. You had to be 5' 9" and weigh 160 pounds or over and stuff like that. Today they can't do that, but at those times, they could and they wanted really big guys. The thing that got to me was, all those eight years that I put into training - accident reports, patrols and everything—all wasted as far as I was concerned.

Montana State Prison Guard

But I'm happy how it turned out, because I might not be here otherwise. I did do two stints as a guard in the Montana State Prison.

Law enforcement can a dangerous job, especially today, so maybe it wasn't meant for me to be that way. It just worked out the way it did. I really enjoyed the military service though. I think one thing I had over most of the guys was that I had lived in the orphanage. I was already accustomed to the regimentation because of the way it was in the orphanage. I fell right into it. It didn't bother me like it did a lot of people. I think that that's why I enjoyed the service, it was familiar living with hundreds of guys, working really hard, losing your individuality and all that.

Anaconda Copper Mining

In 1977 I went to work for the Anaconda Copper Mining Company, working in the copper mines, miles below the earth. There were hundreds of miles of tunnels already tunneled and then they started what they called the open pit, which took over five little suburbs of Butte. The pit is a mile wide and a mile deep. But the Anaconda Company went belly-up, so today it's just filled with water because they closed it down. They shut the pumps off so it's just a big lake with copper water, just acid. Because acid doesn't deteriorate wool, I had to wear all wool when I was working underground, and it was usually hot. But it differs; we had some tunnels that were five degrees, we had some that were 98 degrees, it depends. At that time they had six mines running. I also worked on the stack for a while. I had to remove the material that accumulated inside the stacks. Breathing that material was a hazard to my health, but I did not realize it then.

Building 185 Foot Coal Silos in Wyoming

Later, I went into construction building silos. Wyoming has a lot of coal, so we were building a coal silo. In fact, it was one of the first coal silos ever built there. It was 185 feet high. And the hopper floor is 75 feet off the ground. They can run a three hundred-car train through these silos without stopping! There was a conveyor belt that went up and dumped the coal into the hoppers and then into the silos. It was all computerized. They could empty three hundred coal cars quickly.

It was in Wyoming that my current wife and I met while I was working construction. She had five kids from a previous marriage, and I had three. Needless to say, we didn't have any together!

I'm a "prayer warrior."

Still working in construction, I moved out to California to work on the Ventura Government Center, then I went to work on the oil platforms near Channel Islands until I had a heart attack in 1991 and subsequent bouts of emphysema. It was another very difficult transition for me. Working hard all of my life, to nothing overnight. But now that I have time to burn, I'm a "prayer warrior," offering prayers to Christ on the behalf of orphans. I have never forgotten where I came from—It's pretty hard to forget. You know though, it has all worked out, because the orphanage prepared me for what was ahead, and it gave me a place to grow up so that I could prepare for life.

DAVE PRESSEY

—*INSPIRED TO BE A NATIONAL GUARDSMAN*

According to Gibbon, the Roman Republic began its slow downward decline when free citizens ceased to be willing to bear arms in times of threat and crisis. As time progressed and the Roman citizen became richer and more powerful with each new foreign conquest, military service fell in disfavor.

Instead Rome looked to the underclass and to the conquered peoples to fill the ranks to defend what became an empire. Gibbon describes how the wealthy and powerful gained in wealth and power while the poor became poorer and dispossessed. As booty from conquest flowed into Rome, the Empire provided the poor with bread, olive oil, and eventually wine.

When booty ran out, the increasing tax burden became so great that the farmers found that they lived better by joining the ranks of the institutionalized poor until government edicts forbad them to leave the land.

But the poor were bored so the government provided them with the violent and debased entertainment of the

Coliseum. Human slaughter in the arena replaced philoso-
phy, poetry, literature, and honest labor.

The ranks of the army were filled with Teutonic Germans
and Gallic people who learned to hate their Roman masters.
In the end Rome fell from within from greed, political
corruption, and the perversion of values.

The story of Dave Pressey is the story of an individual
whose father taught his sons that military service was
honorable and that rational patriotism was essential to the
preservation of the Republic, the Constitution, and the Bill
of Rights. His sons learned that loyalty to faith, family, and
country was what made America great.

I was raised to be a California National Guardsman. My earliest recollection of any military service in my youngest and most impressionable youth was seeing my father prepare for Monday night drills at the National Guard Armory in Exposition Park in Central Los Angeles. In the 1930's, we lived within walking distance of Exposition Park with its massive armory and two Civil War Era canons mounted on the front steps leading up to the drill floor. Periodically during the summer, a passenger train would stop and load the men of the 160th Infantry Regiment for shipment to Camp San Luis Obispo.

In Awe of Dad's Spit, Polish and Yearly Marching Tradition at Camp San Luis Obispo

As my father dressed for drill, he wore the World War I type uniform with the wide campaign hat and old-fashioned leggings that required careful winding and pinning. My dad wore two division insignias, one for the 1st Infantry Division, The Big Red One and the second for the 40th Infantry Division of the California National Guard. He wore three stripes as a sergeant along with the usual brass, which he polished to a high luster. He looked soldierly and quite manly as he left for drill. He was proud to be a soldier and proud to be a Guardsman.

His Captain was a local school administrator named Captain Homer O. Eaton. We missed my father during the annual two weeks of summer drill but he always came home with his tales of fighting range fires at the Hearst Castle and the antics of his First Sergeant.

Fox Company on the march in 1938. Sgt John Pressey Sr. is circled

Left, Sgt. John Pressey Sr., 1938

Right, Anti- aircraft defense at Camp San Luis Obispo, 1939

One humorous story was how the First Sergeant would come back to Camp early on Sunday morning. He would still be half drunk as he staggered to the encampment. Then he would "fall out" the troops from their Sunday sleep and rest. He would march Fox Company to the chapel for religious services. Then the First Sergeant would stagger back to his tent and collapse on his bunk to sleep off his drunk. He was a strange man, a funnyman, but a good man in a perverse way.

Dad Easily Foresaw WW II —and Said So on Radio

Dad shared pictures of the training and other activities with the family, pictures we treasured and pictures that instilled in us a desire to imitate our father. My father was sure that the Nazi's and the Japanese were preparing for war. With other Non Commissioned Officers, he and his fellow Guardsmen gave talks on the radio station up on Vermont Avenue warning of the need for military preparedness. Friends and neighbors called him a warmonger and thought the National Guard was an anachronism of the past.

But war came and the 40th Infantry Division was activated for service in the South Pacific and the Philippines. My father was raring to go. He believed in the cause. This was a great patriotic war and he was a patriot ready to fight and die for America. But he was not activated because he was deemed too old and had four children to support. It was one of his greatest disappointments in life that he could not fight in World War II. He had to content himself with peacetime service in the Big Red One and his National Guard service.

My brother and I shared his love of the National Guard and as soon as my older brother hit age 17, he became a member of the 3rd Battalion of the 160th Infantry Regiment in Maywood, California. At age 18, he transferred to the Regular Army where he served on Japanese occupation duty until the Korean War. Most of his 18th year was spent as a combat medic for the 25th Infantry Division and the 27th Infantry Wolfhounds. After 13 months of heavy combat, he was decorated for bravery and carried out with shrapnel wounds. Upon return to the United States, he recovered and rejoined the Medical

Company of the 160th Infantry Regiment of the California National Guard at the Exposition Armory in Central Los Angeles. I, as the younger brother, was anxious to continue the family tradition; after all, the first Presseys had fought in their Nation's service as Militiamen at Lexington and Concord and prior to that, they had been Indian fighters in the French and Indian Wars.

John Pressey Jr. and David Pressey at Dad's National Guard's Armory at Exposition Park, in Los Angeles, 1938.

PHOTO COURTESY OF DAVE PRESSEY

Joined the Guard without permission and under age

I joined Fox Company of the 160th Infantry Regiment one day before I was 17. I did not have my father's permission, but I had joined his old company and under the command of his old Captain who was now a Brigadier General. I enlisted as a rifleman. This had been my boyhood dream. To me I was following in the manly tradition and footsteps of my father.

Suddenly; My Brothers Wolfhound Regiment Thrown into the Teeth of a Korean Maelstrom

I was completing high school when, as I turned seventeen, the Korean War broke out. The politicians tried to down play the seriousness of the conflict merely calling it a police action. My brother's unit, the 27th Infantry Wolfhounds, was thrown into the maelstrom unprepared for the pending fight against a world class army. As is common, the leadership, political and militarily, made many decisions and judgments totally out of sync with reality. The Wolfhounds were told that there was a disturbance in Korea and that they would return in a few weeks to the easy occupation duty in Japan. They were told that they might encounter some lightly armored North Korea Jeeps.

Unsuspecting Tropic Lightning Wolfhounds Easily Trammeled by T-34 Soviet Tanks

As the 27th Infantry Regiment approached the conflict, the North Korean Juggernaut slashed down the main highway between Taegu and Taejon. They ran into squadrons of massive T-34 Soviet battle tanks. Rocket launcher crews approached the tanks on foot and fired a few rounds. Most bounced off harmlessly. The Soviet tanks destroyed several rocket crews and began to overrun the hapless American GIs who, seeing that they had no weapons capable of stopping these Soviet behemoths fled for the hills.

They were saved by radiomen who made contact with Aussie planes in the vicinity. Fortunately, the planes were loaded with napalm bombs and soon turned the Soviet North Koreans into "crispy critters."

While the fight raged in Korea, our National Guard Armories were being stripped of "crew-served " weapons and spare parts. The shortage of equipment in Korea was so severe that the Regular Army took mortars, machine guns, and recoilless rifles from whatever source was available.

Truman Believed the "Bomb" Ended War

President Harry S. Truman believed in the myth of the Atom bomb. Where he had been courageous and decisive in ending World War II by bombing Hiroshima and Nagasaki, he assumed falsely, as did most Americans that the "bomb" was the all encompassing and all pervasive ultimate weapon of war. Truman destroyed vast fleets of ships in A-bomb tests in the Pacific. He dumped our weapons and other military hardware in the depth of the sea. He scrapped our mighty bomber and fighter squadrons.

He demobilized. America was totally and absolutely a third rate military power. Truman did all this in the face of rising Soviet aggression and the fall of much of the world's population to global communism. Our National Guard Units became virtual foot soldiers in the absolute sense of the word.

My New Issue "Camouflage" Uniform; Frayed holes and You Do'em Patches

When I enlisted, I did not receive a nice new uniform and shinny boots; I received used boots and used clothing, which had to be disinfected before I could wear them. Larger size men had to wear civilian shoes for months before the Army could supply footgear. Shorts and socks and T-shirts were civilian and provided by the enlistees at their own expense. When a uniform wore out, a replacement could be purchased by the soldiers at one of the local war surplus stores that dotted the nation.

Eight National Guard Divisions mobilized

Eight National Guard divisions were activated for the Korean War with two eventually seeing combat service in North Korea. But with titles and descriptions, the real story is masked in political fluff and chicanery. I speak from experience when I say that few military units were properly equipped, trained, or supplied whether Regular Army divisions or National Guard.

At the time the California National Guard was activated, we had about 77 soldiers in our rifle company. Normal strength is about 170, give or take. Of those that were activated, a number were under-age boys who were enlisted without question and without parent's consent as was my case.

If you were 17 at the time of activation and you secured your parents consent, you were allowed to stay in the unit. If you were under 17, you were discharged. In my case, I was 17 but had never received permission to join. Somehow, some one must have forged some paper work because I was allowed to stay on active duty. I had appealed to the First Sergeant to let me continue active service.

Camp Cooke—Northern Santa Barbara

On September 1, 1950 we began to train daily at the armory in Los Angeles commuting from home on the bus each morning and evening. It was fun playing soldier and wearing a uniform. When school started in the fall, several other high school kids and I merely dropped out of school as we played soldier. I had the rank of recruit and I must confess that I enjoyed the drills and dry run practice firing of the M-1 rifle. But about a week later, a troop train pulled up between the University of South California campus and the armory. We loaded the train for a 200-mile trip to Camp Cooke in Northern Santa Barbara County. Today, the same base is Vandenberg Air Force Base and is the center of numerous missile silos.

We traveled slowly and it took a full day to reach the camp, which had been used in World War II but now was in a sad shape and in woeful disrepair. The area was windswept with tumbleweeds, dust, dirt, rattlesnakes in the barrack areas, and spiderwebs throughout the barracks. Some how, bunks and bedding were obtained, and immediately, we set out to make the camp military and livable.

Taught Correct Choice on How to Properly Incinerate Bad Guys

We worked constantly day and night with military procedures now firmly in place. Classes and training commenced in all facets of Infantry instruction. You name it and we did it. We learned the bayonet. We fired M-1's, carbines, pistols, and finally we began to acquire mortars and machine guns. Specialized classes included flame-throwers, which I avoided like the plague. They were scary even in training. I opted to go through demolitions training receiving instruction in shaped charges, mines, booby traps, cratering charges, and composition C-2 and C-3. We learned the difference between high explosives, low explosives, sensitive explosives and insensitive explosives. We learned to improvise booby traps with hand grenades and in one case an unexploded canister of napalm. But I remained fearful of any explosive substance that could incinerate a human being. Napalm is great when being used on the enemy but scary if you have to work around it.

Later when the Division hit combat in Korea, one of our supply convoys was totally destroyed by Marine aircraft using napalm. By then, we had seen its effect on Communist troops. It was horrifying to think that your own troops had perished in such a frightful mistake.

Back at Camp Cooke, we began to receive draftees and regular army fillers to flesh out the Division. Most of the Officers and higher-ranking NCO's were combat veterans of World War II. In our company, we had a number of ex-Marines from the war in the Pacific as well as an assortment of Combat Infantrymen from the same period.

Army Literally Pushed to a Corner in Korea

Korea was going badly; first the North Koreans had driven the American forces to the southern most tip of Korea and had boasted that it was an American Dunkirk. Ironically, the most powerful nation in the world was turning out to be an ill equipped and under-trained third-rate army. The Communist world was elated and home grown Communists in America were absolutely gleeful about an American defeat. While on parade down Spring Street in Los Angeles, we were followed on the sidewalk by placard-waving Commies denouncing American militarism.

As fast as we trained replacement troops at Camp Cooke, they were assembled and shipped to Korea to replace the thousands and thousands being killed and wounded in this "police action." And the politicians chortled this falsehood long after the war ended. It is said that fifty thousand troops were trained in the 40th Infantry Division of the California National Guard during the Korean War. Because of a misconception and political pressure, the Division was told that we would never serve on foreign soil in this so-called police action.

Our General Daniel H. Hudelson called together 20,000 members of the Division on the parade field formed by rank and units. He stated that the 40th Division would fight on the field of battle. He advised every soldier to make the most of the lessons we were learning because in the near future, our life would depend on the quality of our training and our attention to detail. Hudelson knew combat from his experiences with armored forces in Europe during World War II. He was not just a weekend warrior and neither were most of the officers and NCO's of the Guard.

The men of the 40th Division had been told over and over again that they were not going to be shipped overseas. We were federalized for a short time only, filling the need for home defense while the Regular Army fought in Korea. Despite the political statements, our general assured us that we would fight in Korea.

40th and 45th Guard Deployed to Japan to Defend Against the Soviet Threat

In the spring of 1951, the 40th Division along with the 45th Oklahoma National Guard was deployed to Japan to counteract a growing Soviet Union threat to the Japanese homeland. This was our first mission followed by a continuation of occupation duties. A third activity was to train as an amphibious force for a second Inchon type invasion of North Korea. Subsequent reports of U.S. intelligence operations indicated that the North Koreans and Chinese would pull troops from the front line areas whenever the 40th National Guard Division was out at sea in a giant Naval flotilla. They would beef up possible coastal landing sites as they prepared for any eventuality.

Training in Japan intensified with long marches; constant maneuvers with live fire utilizing the air force, tanks, artillery, and all other weapons of an infantry division. In addition, the whole unit took air transport training and specialized units took ski trooper training.

As training intensified and progressed to all live fire regimental sized maneuvers, the Geisha girls began telling the GI's, "You go Korea real soon GI-san." Most the GI's laughed and kidded about the rumors. It was well known that the California politicians would not approve because of the political climate. Most politicians were more sensitive to National Guardmen and state politicians, much to the chagrin and embarrassment of the active duty Guardsmen.

To Korea
—the Damned Get Practice and Religion

Suddenly, all leaves were canceled and all the detached special units were returned to the regiment. After Christmas of 1951, the Division was alerted for movement to Korea. We boarded troop ships in Yokohama during a snowstorm, a precursor to winter weather yet to come. Shipboard activities were occupied with what all the soldiers thought we should be doing based on old WW II war movies. We cleaned weapons, we sharpened bayonets, and attended chapel and mass.

I remember a resurgence of religion as many soldiers had a ton of sins to resolve before combat. I know that our thoughts were centered around what was going to happen. Would we be killed or wounded? Would we be captured and tortured? Would we manfully do our duty? Would we be able to deal with fear and how would our buddies behave? During the time on board, the usual service rivalry between the Army and the Navy subsided. The sailors treated us with kindness and respect. Some wished us well. The Navy cook served us chow fit for a king with fresh baked bread, pies, and cakes. It worried us some because we could sense that they realized what we would soon face in the days ahead.

Leaving Skin on the Ships Railing at Inchon

After about five days, the fleet arrived at Inchon where the 40th Division landed. In the early gray dawn at Inchon, we were awakened with excited soldiers exclaiming that we were there. I dressed quickly and ran up to the deck sans mittens and gloves. I didn't give it a second thought as I grabbed the rails of the ship peering out toward the faint outline of the distant shore. Immediately, my hands began to freeze. As I pulled them away from the rail, bits of frozen skin were peeled from my hands.

"Lose a glove, lose your fingers."

I then remembered the lectures on winter warfare and the admonitions of the instructors, "Lose a glove, lose your fingers." Offloading, we walked on planks across the muddy frozen flats of the bay to a little ridge on the shoreline where a giant bonfire was blazing. The mess facilities were set up to prepare hot coffee for us. I stood close to the fire drinking the coffee which was freezing as fast as I could finish a leisurely morning coffee. I heard a crack and turned to see what had happened. Apparently, I had filled my canteen too full and while I stood in front of the bonfire, the water in the canteen had frozen and cracked the canteen cap.

The snow in Yokohama Harbor had been cold but gentle, almost peaceful, but as we were trucked to the battlefield up in the snowy Taebek Mountains, we suddenly realized that our concept of cold was just being formulated. Korean winter is bitterly cold. We soon realized that living out in the open would be a continuous battle to keep from freezing to death or losing extremities to frostbite. We huddled in the back of the trucks trying to keep warm with body heat and attempting to avoid the awful Siberian wind and attendant wind chill. The road from Inchon to Seoul was a dreary sight. Everything was gray or white. All surface water was frozen solid. The Korean people were a pitiful sight dressed in rags, hungry, and cold. It was obvious that some were sick or injured but there was no support system for the civilians like for the army. The most pitiful were the wretches deformed by what appeared to be leprosy.

Every river and every stream was frozen solid. Tanks used this opportunity to cross various rivers on the ice as the bridges had been destroyed by retreating armies months earlier. The level of the land began to change as we left Seoul. The level valleys folded into higher and steeper hills and eventually mountains.

Counting Artillery Rounds Instead of Sheep

By evening our convoy entered a narrow little valley where artillery and tanks became numerous. The sounds of war were audible for the first time. Off in the distance, it sounded as distant thunder. Every conceivable type gun was emplaced in the narrow valleys pounding the enemy lines incessantly. The guns were steeply elevated so the shells would clear the ridge in front of them less the friendly troops receive short rounds. The necessity of the situation required that the tents for the new troops be placed in front of the guns with the shells passing overhead.

The valleys shook with the reverberations and sounds of the outgoing shells. With each firing, the night sky lit up for a few seconds in what appeared like a nightmarish scene from hell, a frozen Dantesque hell. I remember why Santa Barbara is the patron saint of artillerymen, for artillery has a habit of premature explosions and short rounds injuring or killing the friendly forces.

The Fight to Keep from Freezing to Death

When we arrived in the Valley of the shadow of death, we were assigned to tents to rest and condition ourselves to this new environment. We learned to appreciate a gentle snowstorm. We learned it was never as bad as the clear nights with the horrific Arctic winds and wind chill factors that guaranteed frost bite to the careless or unwary. Body heat became the only heat. Body heat was retained by layered clothing, so much so that movements became uncomfortable and awkward. Typically, each soldier had the usual pair of shorts and T-shirt. Over that, he wore a wool shirt and pants. Over that he wore a fake fur lined coat and snow pants and a sweater and field jacket. He wore mittens as well as gloves. On his feet, he wore a pair of cotton socks and two pairs of woolen socks. Shoe packs were the standard issued foot gear. Head covering consisted of a fur lined cap with a visor and ear flaps. Over this, he wore a helmet. Even then, we were always cold.

Incoming Chinese artillery destroying our Army trucks in the Taebek Mountains in North Korea.

PHOTO COURTESY OF DAVE PRESSEY

Welcome to the "Finished" Army

Our Korean Mission was to relieve the 24th Regular Army Division on line. We had been given the impression that being National Guardsmen that, some how, some way, we were not on a par with the regular army. I guess we had the impression that the grizzled ground pounders of the 24th Infantry Division were GI Joes or super men. Initially, platoon and squad leaders were assigned to units of the 24th. What a shock to discover that it was a shell of an army. The crew-served weapons were destroyed or frozen and inoperable. Most of the troops carried light weapons like carbines and pistols. Obviously, the Chinese Army was just across the valley from us. I asked what they would do if the Chinese attacked. They answered, "Run."

The bunkers were dirty and filled with lice and rat droppings. There was no attempt at order, neatness, cleanliness, or basic maintenance of equipment. It was a "finished" army if the rest of the 24th was in the same state of mind and proficiency. Immediately, I began to clean and organize the position. I was met by comments of derision and contempt assuring me that I would be just like them in a few weeks. They lived like primitive beasts barely surviving until rotation. But we never were like the division we replaced. As long as the 40th remained in tact with the original troops, the Division performed the mission with a soldierliness that remains inherent in the character and training with most of the original National Guardsmen to this day.

Who Needs Working Weapons When Guardsman Have Esprit de Corps?

The Army, for some God awful reasoning, made us trade our crew serviced weapons with the destroyed or damaged equipment of the 24th Infantry Division. As we drew ammo for our trek up to the front (MLR), we received one cartridge belt of ammo, two bandoliers, two grenades, and of course, a ten inch bayonet. We had machine gun ammo but no operable machine guns. The rationale of the Army was that the 24th Division needed good equipment for training. Later, I learned that this stupid scenario was played out wherever the National Guard units replaced Regular Army units. It was true of trucks or artillery pieces. But the National Guard Divisions were highly trained and motivated with a high level of soldierly discipline. Most Guardsmen improvised, cannibalized, or surreptitiously obtained the weapons and accouterments of war.

Barrages Thunder On Us, Upon Arrival

We were welcomed to the war on our very first position which was the northernmost point on the frontlines. The enemy was to our front and on both sides. Only a narrow draw connected us with the rear. A thunderous barrage greeted us.   Unfortunately, our Korean human pack animals or Chogee boys as they were called were caught in the open. We were in our holes and trenches and left the medics to attend to their screams for help.

At times, all firing would cease. Troops would become careless and expose themselves without adequate cover and concealment. Eventually, such carelessness was brought to an end by heavy mortar and artillery fire.

One night, one of our own quad 50 half track vehicles had moved behind us during the day while I was sleeping. No one told me. When the quad 50 calibre machine guns started firing, I was half scared to death before I realized that they were friendly and firing overhead. Most of us thought that the firing was from Chinese who had gotten to the rear of us and were attacking from our backside.

During the nights, Chinese soldiers dug bunkers into the hillsides under our positions. During the day, patrols were sent out to destroy them. Usually there was a covering patrol with a BAR or LMG and a moving patrol. One morning the maneuvering patrol was ambushed and the point man was shot in the ankle unable to get out. Fortunately, the maneuvering patrol was able to rescue him and carry him back to the lines safely. As he came over the hill, he was in a jubilant mood since he felt he had that million dollar wound and would never have to return to combat. However, he may have been permanently disabled. On the reverse slope, a small helicopter with stretchers hanging on the outside airlifted him to a MASH Hospital in the rear. I thought that if the enemy didn't kill him, the blast of frigid air from the rotor blades might put him in shock.

Hot Chow Peppered with Enemy Artillery

The draw behind our position that linked us to the rest of the 8th Army became the scene of several actions. One of the Quad 50 halftracks set up a position for indirect fire. In short order Chinese artillery and mortar fire put the vehicle out of commission. Next, some rear area officer decided to send hot chow to the frontlines periodically. They chose the "halftrack draw." Troops began scuttling across the ridge to eat, and then scuttled back to their positions. A bunker was built in the event that enemy fire should occur. And it did! Mess kits and eating utensils flew in all directions as soldiers raced to the lone bunker for cover. Most of us had slung our rifles crosswise on our back, but some soldiers were in a panic about being caught in the open. They ran headlong into other soldiers as they were pulling their rifles over their heads to get into the bunker. Some were jammed against the entry unable to move for the press of the throng and hamper by the rifle over their backs.

Two soldiers view dead Chinese soldiers where they fell in the hills above Kumsong.

PHOTO COURTESY OF DAVE PRESSEY

Softest Parts of Corpses are Tastiest

On the front, the CCF positions were clearly visible and a short distance down the ridgeline. Chinese snipers tried to hit us but they must have been lousy shots because I knew of only one person injured and that by a fragment of rock that splintered from a poorly aimed shot. During sniping, we crawled around the trenches keeping low and under cover as much as possible. Everywhere were bodies of Chinese soldier frozen in grotesque positions and half buried in the snow. Because of the filth and garbage debris, rats overran the positions. The dead

Chinese were eaten by these rodents. We noticed that the rats ate the softer body parts first including the guts, lungs, and scrotum. It was a sickening sight, more so realizing that it could happen to us.

Uniform and Ammo Miseries —Worse for Our Aggressors

Most of the dead Chinese were young teenage boys, probably younger than me. I was eighteen at that time. They were dressed in khaki quilted uniforms with wrap around legging and cheap tennis shoes. They had been armed with bolt action rifles and burp guns. Each soldier carried two potato masher grenades made in the cottage industries of China. They had a "wine bottle" screw cap on the wooden handle end. When it was unscrewed, a string was found inside with a circular wire attached. By holding the wire in two fingers when it was thrown, it activated the powder train fuse. They were very unreliable and could explode in the thrower's face or never. They wore a field cap but never helmets. For their assault rations, they had a khaki sock held in their belt. In the sock was a gray porcelain bowl filled with white rice, nothing else.

How to Thaw Rations Enough to Eat?

Eating was a problem for the American soldiers. With no heat or fires, C-rations were frozen solid. We were given naphtha pills designed to heat one can of rations, but in the extreme cold, it was possible to use up a week's supply burning the bottom of the can while the top was still frozen. Carrying a can of food under the arm pits would thaw them out in several hours. All the rations were from WW II and had been in storage for seven or eight years.

A box of C-rations contained three meals for cooking like pork and beans, hamburger patties, corned beef hash, etc. Three other cans had four round crackers, a round can of jam or jelly, and either an oval of chocolate or jellied candy. One can of fruit was in each box. There were paper packets of toilet paper, dried milk, dried coffee, sugar, salt, cans openers, and matches. Some soldiers could consume an entire box a day. I could eat one or two cans a day. Sometimes, supply problems created shortages. We were short of ammo much of the time but we were never short of cigarettes. No matter what happened, cigarettes were in plentiful supply, and I did not smoke.

PHOTO COURTESY OF DAVE PRESSEY

Trading Favors

The Machine Gun Crew of the 4th Squadron, 2nd Platoon, Fox Company, 160th Infantry Regiment. Left to right; Kirby, Corbin, Merslich, and Pressey.

Usually, one can of biscuits contained a round of powdered chocolate. That was a favorite. Who ever received the chocolate would make a canteen cup of hot chocolate. That cup of chocolate was always shared with all the buddies in the bunker there being up to four men in a bunker. It was almost a sacred ritual to share the nectar of the C-rations with each buddy.

Usually, once a month, we were rotated off the front at which time we were issued two cans of beer. Since I didn't drink, I gave my beer to one of my machine gunners who would promptly chug-a-lug producing a mild state of inebriation. One time, he became inebriated and dragged me out of my sleeping bag through the frozen snow covered rice paddy. After that I was reluctant to do him favors. But he got his comeuppance that evening when he was preparing to go to sleep in his pup tent. The Chinese must have had some forward observers hidden in the hills above the rice paddies in the rear areas. We began receiving high air burst from artillery fire. It was so high that the fragments were widely disperse except for one fragment the tore through my gunners pup tent striking his boots and jacket that he had rolled up for a pillow seconds before he lay down to sleep.

Chinese Probes—Shooting Scary Shadows

Tensions remained high, especially at night when we could hear Chinese probing our barbed wire. We would throw grenades if we felt sure they were there. Other times we called for flares. Firing at night was rare. Firing a machine gun at night gives away your position. Unfortunately, the magnesium flares gave off an eerie light that caused the shadows of the trees and bushes to dance and move creating the illusion that the forests were full of enemy troops.

The penetrating cold and bleakness of the terrain along with the awful living conditions created a psychological depression at times. The routine seldom varied as we hunkered down on those lonely mountain-tops waiting for the night. The constant shelling and mortar fire on both sides was occasionally punctuated by the chatter of a machine gun or the burst of a burp gun. Constant patrols kept the enemy from becoming overly aggressive, but patrol action is a harrowing experience at best with the awful sensation that a burst of a burp gun might end your existence in a second.

Other times, listening patrols would go out beyond the lines lying in the snow all night long fighting the frost and cold. Toes and fingers had to be moved constantly in the dark to prevent frostbite. One time, upon returning from an night ambush patrol, my feet and toes began to freeze. When I returned to the lines in the morning I had no sensation in my toes. My buddy opened his jacket and coat and placed my feet against his stomach and chest wrapping my them until they thawed and warmed.

Often the nights exploded with bunker piercing shells to keep the Chinese off guard.

No Place for Tanks

The mountains of Korea form a spine that runs north and south along the peninsula. In my sector the mountains were very steep and almost vertical in some places. Armor (tanks) was virtually useless. However, some officer decided a solitary tank would be brought to the front for direct fire into the Chinese bunkers. A bull dozer was used to scrape a road from the floor of the draw to the crest of the ridge. A short time later, a lone tank clattered and rumbled into place and commenced firing. It fired two or three rounds before return fire damaged the engine compartment and blew off a tread. The tankers came flying out of the tank so fast that one damaged his ankle, but no one was seriously injured.

The Rear Area Under the Muzzle Blasts

After almost a month on line, we were rotated to the rear area which was a tent city built under the muzzle blast of massed artillery, a situation not permitted in normal military operations. But the valleys were so narrow and the hills so steep that the artillery had to back up into the other side of the valley. There we were directed to a shower tent for our first shower in almost a month. We were black with filth and infested with lice. The showers were in a tent large enough for about 15 to 20 troops. The floor was covered with wooden slats over the bare ground. As fast as the tepid water hit the slats, it began to freeze building up a layer of ice. Our shower was fast and furious but it felt good to be clean again.

Our anticipated rest of three to five days was cut short by an assignment to man a fifty- caliber machine gun on the ridge above the valley to protect against a lone propeller-driven plane that usually harassed the troops and artillery below. We called him "Bedcheck Charlie." His modus operandi was to cut his engines just before entering the valley. Hand dropped mortars were thrown over the side and the tents were sprayed with burp gun fire before the engines were started and he flew to safety pending the next night.

In reality, the 50 caliber machine guns were some what useless because Bedcheck Charlie was flying below the ridge and our machine gun would be firing into our own troops. By the time it was safe to fire, Bedcheck was exiting the valley.

Sgt. Dave Pressey (r) loading magazines for an M-2 carbine at the squad outpost in Kumsong, May 1952.

PHOTO COURTESY OF DAVE PRESSEY

We found that the latrines were open air events in a circle around a bonfire. The loathsome indignity of doing your business in public view along with twenty or thirty other soldiers was unpleasant enough, but one deranged first sergeant threw handfuls of machine gun ammo into the fire when he thought he could most discomfit the soldiers. As the rounds began to explode, troops were hopping in a panic in all directions much to the sergeant's amusement. One soldier was injured in this strange demented game.

Bad Attitude Toward Unfit Leadership

I think that the front line soldiers developed an attitude toward leadership and command that has followed us all our lives. We resented the pilfering of the rear area supply personnel that commandeered the best of supplies and rations for themselves leaving the less desirable items for the front line troops. We saw this as a repeated and unjustified pattern of behavior. Generally, the front line troops had a strong bond where they cared for their buddies and looked after each other. One obnoxious army directive generated much anger. During the three to five day "rest period" from the frontlines, the troops would be awakened at 4:30 AM and marched out on the frozen roads to fill potholes and dig out rocks in the bitter cold of the Korean morning. This went on every day until we were returned to the front. We hated the rear echelon. They were warm, well fed, and relatively safe as long as we held back the Chinese Army. We developed an attitude where we were wont to scrounge any supplies, ammo, or equipment that we could pilfer for our next month on line. One day we snagged a large can of powdered split pea soup and a large can of margarine. Oh, how wonderful that was when we got back to the trenches. My month still waters for that hot cup of soup made in a C-ration can with hot melted margarine floating on top. It really hit the spot when the temperature dropped below zero.

On one three-day rest period off the line, a regimental officer had decided to build a massive regimental command post deep underground. The nitwit Warrant Officer had calculated the man hours required for the enterprise. Included was a bunker to house the colonel's small house trailer. It was the only house trailer I had ever seen in the Orient. The Warrant Officer figured that each soldier would dig so many square feet of soil per day. It was the first time I ever heard the expression, "bean counter." And what better resource for construction than two hundred tired and battle weary GI's who had nothing to do except lie around for a couple of days.

Being the youngest and lowest ranking sergeant at age eighteen, I was given the task of directing these weary troops in this stupid project. Excuse my harsh language, but the ignoramus of a Warrant Officer failed to calculate for rock hard frozen dirt that refused to be dug. The process of digging was like chipping chunks of cement with each swing of the entrenching tool shattering the teeth of the poor infantryman. The troops rebelled and refused to work. The Warrant Officer was screaming at me to make them work and I was not about to. I had to live with those men at the front and that could result in accidents and unhealthy experiences. He threatened to order them all back to the front lines for their insubordination. They yelled back that the front line was a better choice than having to work for the "chicken s—t" weasels in the rear area.

Truman Makes Our Tactical Decisions From the White House

Returning to the front, we got our first taste of tactical decisions made from Washington D.C. Our President Truman was experimenting with micromanagement of the tactical situation. The order was given that no shot or shell would be fired unless we were in immediate danger of being overrun. All firing ceased. We had to stay hidden all day coming out at night under cover of darkness for resupply. During the day, if a soldier had a call of nature, he had to do his business in a box or can and empty it at night. In the crowded and cramped machine gun pits or bunkers, this was unpleasant to say the least.

One day I thought that I would peer out the machine gun aperture assuming that it would not be visible to the Chinese. As I finished, I felt the slightest tug of my boot buckle which hit the machine gun trigger. The machine gun was cocked and ready to fire. Before I could react, one shot was fired. I knew I was in for real trouble since we were forbidden to shoot under pain of court martial. After all, the directives came from the highest and most stupid level of command. Each day as we peered out, we could see the Chinese using every opportunity to dig in deep, in depth, and bring in supplies and all we could do was watch and wait.

That night I was sleeping when the anticipated investigation commenced. They came directly to my bunker. I was awakened by the conversation outside. My buddies were lying for me magnificently. They directed the officers to the bunker on our far right. The far right bunker directed them to us. The bunker on the left directed them to us. The baffled and confused officers insisted that the shot came from my bunker until my wonderful lying buddies said, "That can't be because this is a machine gun nest. It is almost impossible to fire a machine gun with one shot." The officers left satisfied that we were not the culprits.

After five days, the whole front line in Korea was ordered to open fire on every target across the whole front. Such a display of smoke and flame I have not seen since in my life time. It must have frightened the Chinese because we took two prisoners, one with a bolt action rifle and the other with a burp gun. We had just received a new officer from some college in the Northwest. He seemed to have little or no military experience except for six weeks or so of ROTC. He was young and grew a mustache to make himself look older. One day the Colonel came on line. When he spotted the young officer, he started a conversation. He said, "Lieutenant, you like to smile?" The Lieutenant said, "Yes Sir." The Colonel commented, "It gets awfully cold in North Korea." The Lieutenant answered, "Yes sir." The Colonel commented, "If I came up to the front again and it was very cold, your mustache would freeze and then you couldn't smile at me. You do like to smile at me, don't you?" The Lieutenant answered, "Sir, I get the point I will shave it off."

When the Lieutenant went to interrogate the new prisoners, they snapped to attention and gave a most military salute. The Lieutenant returned the salute with his left hand which held his carbine. He nearly knocked his helmet off his head before returning a right handed salute. The prisoners looked at each other astonished at such unsoldierly actions. Oh well, ROTC Second Lieutenants have to learn some time or die in their clumsiness.

An order was given that in the morning we would have to send one of our squad as an advanced party to move to a new position. That night while on guard duty with a Corporal Wiklanski, a Polish Catholic soldier, he began to talk to me about his faith and religion. He was the man designated for the advanced party in the morning. He wanted to impart his faith before he left. I assured him that we were both Christians of similar beliefs. In the cold darkness with the wintry snow blowing up in our faces in semi-blizzard conditions, he handed me his rosary and insisted that I take it. As I write this story from my notes 50 years later, I still have his rosary draping over the picture of my wife and me on our wedding day.

Though I'm not a Roman Catholic, that Rosary holds a lot of meaning and memories. The next day John Wiklanski left down the back side of the hill. We heard explosions when shortly after, a man came running up the hill for a medic. John Wiklanski had been injured in an explosion and had rolled to the bottom of the hill. He was evacuated to a MASH hospital down in the lowlands, injured but not critical. He sent us a letter and asked that we save some Commies for him to shoot. Before moving out of that position, our demented 1st sergeant saw my squad gathering fire wood on the reverse slope down in a draw. He had the captured burp gun confiscated from the Chinese prisoners. He saw us and commenced spraying us with burp gun fire as he laughed and giggled. He was a strange sick man much given to drink and womanizing. That night we pulled off the front in darkness along frozen trails that were steep and slippery causing many men to plummet head first in the snow covered bushes in the ravine.

The new rest area was similar to the first rest area. Our rest was a continuation of more road building, a cold shower in freezing tents and replacements for injured or rotated soldiers. Everything was white from the recent snow. It continued to be bitter cold at night. The

Lieutenant told me that I could choose a new gunner to replace Wiklanski.

The Integration of Black Soldiers

At this point I need to explain what may seem inexplicable to a modern generation. Up to this point, the Division and much of the Armed Forces had been rigidly segregated by race. If you had a thimble full of Black blood, you served in all Black units. Ironically, Mexicans, Indians, and Asiatics were automatically classified as white troops. We had heard some talk about integration and Black protests back in the states, but for the average soldier, that was a non-issue.

Pressey Top; Below Cpl. Paul Kirby, light machine gunner and Sgt. Pressey.

PHOTO COURTESY OF DAVE PRESSEY

There had been Black regiments in the early days of the Korean War and they had more than their fair share of criticism as soldiers even though most were good soldiers. Generally, they were led by white officers. The Army's decision to integrate had more to do with practicality than political correctness. Integration gave Blacks opportunities that never existed in the civilian world as many became leaders and acquired skills in areas closed to them at home. However, on that frosty wintry snow white day in February, three Black soldiers filed out of the command bunker. I was told to choose one as a replacement. I chose a young Black from South Carolina who appeared to be physically fit. The other soldiers were on the heavy side and seemed to lumber out rather than walk. When the expected order came to saddle up, draw ammo and grenades for the return to the front, I began to assign the squad in the two man buddy system, but no one, but no one would accept the new Black as a comrade. I was reluctant to force the issue, so I took the new soldier as my foxhole buddy. I could tell that he was afraid –afraid of the artillery booming around us, afraid of all the white faces staring at him, a Black against the new white snow, and afraid of the war that was to greet him up at the much discussed front line.

A Dead Hand Appears in Our Bunker

At the front, we took over a bunker that had been hastily built in warmer weather. Unfortunately, a Chinese soldier had been buried right next to the bunker. As the walls of the bunker thawed from the heat in the hole, the corpse was revealed with a withered hand sticking out. It was disgusting and we tried to cover it with a poncho so we didn't have to look at it when we ate or upon awakening. Corpses were a reminder that we were at war and that we could be like our unwelcomed Chinese visitor.

It is like the old medieval tale where a frolicking young couple came upon a corpse leaning against a tree in the forest. They stared in fascinated horror when the corpse began to speak. It said, "As you are now, I once was; as I am now, you shall be." Such thoughts crossed our minds when we observed the dead Chinaman. One of my other gunners became so agitated that he decided to tear apart the bunker and bury the body.

That day, I had scurried to the reverse slope to find some dry firewood. Apparently, Chinese forward observers were in the area and tree bursts began to occur all around me. I spotted an old shallow Chinese bunker and dove in without consideration of booby traps or possible occupants. It was occupied by one very dead Chinese soldier whose stomach had been blown apart and I was on top of him staring through where his stomach had been and seeing his rat eaten spine. I started to vomit and crawled out and ran through shell fire back to the machine gun bunker where the gunner had been dismantling our machine gun nest to remove the corpse. That was a bad move because it resulted in very heavy mortar and/or artillery fire into our positions.

When All Else Fails—Pray

Being in a pine forest, tree bursts were particularly hazardous. Four of us were cramped into the remaining hole until the shelling stop. One comrade was our new Black soldier, the son of a Protestant minister. He began praying earnestly and out loud. He said, "O Lord Gawd, I aint gonna drink no mo. I aint gonna smoke them dirty cigarettes no mo. I aint gonna cuss no mo." And lastly he said, "O Lord Gawd, I aint gonna messa round wid dem Japanese women no mo." We couldn't help but laugh even in our dire circumstances. Unfortunately, our chaplain was killed in that area about that time. We didn't see it but we all grieved for him because he was a real man of God and a real soldier's chaplain. He was my Episcopalian chaplain. He stood for Christ and right conduct, setting a fine example for the young soldiers. His services were not heavily attended but he was highly respected because he was a true and faithful Christian.

Outposts two Miles From the Front

The last half of my service in Korea was on outposts in front of the MLR. At one point, we were on platoon sized outposts approximately two or more miles beyond the front. Fortunately, we met no resistance as we moved to the top of steep hills overlooking Kumsong Valley and what had been the town below. A second platoon took over another hill about one mile to the east. When we arrived, the knoll was so steep and rocky that we rapped ourselves around trees and bushes to keep from rolling off the hill at night. Every day thereafter, we dug deeper and deeper into the hill creating connecting trenches and sturdy bunkers. The entire hill was surrounded by barbed wire with tin cans tied to the wire so if there were Chinese infiltrators they would rattle the cans at night. As the Platoon Mine and Booby Trap NCO, it was my duty to activate the trip flares and booby traps outside the perimeter about dusk. One machine gun section of my squad was detached to reinforce the platoon to our east. They were sitting right on top of Kumsong and immediately, their position was probed each night. The usual method of defense was to throw grenades rather than reveal your exact position. Chinese bodies were found in the morning on the barbed wire. The pressure became too great considering it was an isolated platoon so they were ordered to withdraw. Unfortunately, the withdrawal was hasty and no provision was made to destroy or remove the considerable amount of ammunition on that outpost.

To this day, I do not understand. Not wanting to lose a good machine gun, especially to the Commies, I tagged along with a reinforced rifle squad to make sure that the machine gun wasn't left behind. When I got to the hill outpost, the troops were just pulling out. I found my machine gun and carried it out while my machine gun crew brought back some of the machine gun ammunition. Unfortunately, mortar rounds, grenades, and much ammunition was abandoned at the site. I am sure that some of it was used against us in the days ahead.

Giant Sledge Hammers Beating the Hill

The Infantry in the foxholes and trenches rarely knows what is going on around them. We were told only what we needed to know and nothing more. If we were ever captured, the enemy would be surprised how little we knew about the tactical situation. We could hear explosions and small arms fire day and night never knowing if it was a jumpy trigger happy soldier or if there was a fire fight or ambush. Years later when comparing experiences, much more was going on than I realized and our positions were in exposed positions that posed a great hazard to us if we had known the details. Certainly, there is no retreat from an outpost under assault. Shortly after the withdrawal episode, I was awakened about midnight by a noise like giant sledge hammers beating the hill side all around me.

We were under attack and white phosphorus was lighting up the sky around us. We had received some white phosphorus early in the day and hadn't given it much thought. Apparently, the Chinese were adjusting fire for the night assault. The unit next to us was being assaulted with small arms and automatic weapons fire. We could see the ring of fire close almost to the top of the hill all the while we were being raked by machine gun fire. We assumed that our comrades were being over run in their trenches and bunkers. We could see absolutely no return fire from our troops. We figured that they were being wiped out. At the last minute, the friendly force opened fire with every weapon on the hilltop as the enemy fire faltered, withered, and went silent. Shortly after, the machine guns raking our hill ceased to fire along with the incoming Willie Peter (WP) as we called white phosphorous.

Shortly after that, the chaplain held a memorial service in a little draw close to our hill. We were in No Man's Land but hidden in the draw with BAR men positioned around the troops in worship and prayer. The National Guard chaplains were right there with us. The service was for Chaplain Crane who had been killed earlier.

One of the least desirable activities was the listening outposts that consisted of single soldiers dropped off down a finger leading to our outpost. About dusk, a squad would assemble an at intervals of about 100 to 200 feet, a man would be dropped off for the duration of the night. This was a scary activity because your mission was to alert the outpost in which case, you would probably cease this mortal life. Before dawn, the listeners would move back to the position until the next night.

A Short Rest
and Back to a Reinforced Squad Outpost

The new outpost was just a few hundred yards in front of the mainline of resistance or MLR, a euphemistic term for a front line that was a series of foxholes and bunkers manned by troops spread out every hundred feet or so. There was no depth to the front line and a concerted attack could punch a hole through the line at will. However, effective massed artillery could be shifted anywhere on the front and literally destroy any Communist intrusion. In the rear were reserve forces that could be rushed to the front to plug any breakthrough.

Patrol—13 Men and a War Dog

Our new position was a small knoll with two bunkers and a rifle pit to the rear. It had been a Communist position; however, they had moved out so fast that they left most of their mortar rounds in the original cans, and the bunkers were strewn with potato masher grenades which I tossed down the hill. Occasionally, we could see Chinese soldiers in the open down near the railroad leading to Kumsong in the valley below. We were in that position from the last day of April 1952 through May. For May Day I was ordered to take a reconnaissance patrol down to a knoll overlooking the railroad tracks. It was a particularly hazardous night because it was a great Communist holiday and in previous wars and battles they had celebrated with attacks.

The patrol had 13 men and a war dog. We left at dusk and as on every patrol, our greatest fear was a sudden ambush. The eruption of burp gun fire from any direction would make us extremely tense with our hearts pounding and breathing with our mouths open hoping to hear better. We passed through a mine field without incident and reached our objective, setting up a perimeter of defense on the knoll. In the swampy land below us, the frogs were chirping loudly as the dog rested his head between his paws. When the frogs stopped chirping, the dog rose and pointed in the direction where he detected sound. We watched the dog and swung our weapons into position. A patrol was moving out there but our mission was to warn the MLR of any concerted attack, not routine Communist patrols. As I was leaving the MLR that night, I asked the Lieutenant for instructions if an attack should come. He merely shrugged his shoulders and said, "Do the best you can." I got the sinking feeling that he didn't expect us to return.

At midnight, the dog was tired and had to go back to the MLR with his dog handler. We had orders to fall back to a secondary position half way back. From up on a little ridge we began to receive small arms fire, but the firing was wild. We did not return fire. We became lost in a mine field but by then the mechanisms were probably frozen as the night had turned cold. We lucked out but were concerned about the firing on the ridge. We found a large pit and all twelve of us took cover in the pit until just before dawn when we returned to the MLR. As we approach the MLR in the early dawn, our point man called out the password. The dumbest guy in the whole platoon was manning the machine gun. He couldn't remember the password and kept saying, "Who der?" Finally we heard two clanks on the machine gun and knew that this dumb guy was going to mow us down. The point man jumped up and shouted, "Don't shoot, its me, Baby San." Baby San was his nick name. The point man, Maupin, was later killed in an ambush.

Time to Rotate Home

Near the end of May, I was rotated out of Korea, glad to go home, relieved that I would not live in fear, but feeling guilty leaving so many buddies who were not coming home with me. It was a bittersweet mixture of emotions. Some of those guys would later fight on Heart Break Ridge while I was safe at home.

Home, Education, Marriage, Family, Career,

Santos Vincente and I rotated together back to Sasebo, Japan and then to Camp Stoneman near San Francisco. I came home on the Greyhound Bus to Los Angeles and took the streetcar and bus back home. I was so anxious to see my father that I dropped my duffel bag in the street and ran from the bus stop home. What an emotional experience to be home in the United States. It was a sacred and holy feeling. But I wasn't finished with military service, I applied for OCS Artillery and Missile School at Fort Sill, Oklahoma where I earned a commission as a Second Lieutenant in the U.S. Army Artillery. I reverted to the National Guard for the next few years where I was assigned as Ammunition Officer and later as Battery Exec Officer. I became a school teacher/ counselor and married my wife while still in school. We both worked full time and went to school full time because the Veteran's Educational Bill was not as generous as it was for World War II vets. Unfortunately, most of the country did not think of Korea as a war. It was merely a minor police action. It took years before the politicians and the public recognized it as a war.

Dave Pressey, 2002

PHOTO COURTESY OF CHUCK BENNETT

I am quoted in the book, The Longest Weekend, A History of the National Guard in Korea where I said, " I would never again experience the closeness and comradeship of those that endured Korea with me.

For those that survived, we still share the comradeship cemented by a common fear and equal suffering. There was nothing spectacular about us except we did our duty as good soldiers without recognition or reward except from our comrades"

LEE STANWORTH

—THE AIRCRAFT CARRIERS

Warfare is a constant kaleidoscope of change. New armament, new tactics, and new instruments of war are constantly changing the balance of power and forces on the battlefield or at sea. Sometimes the changes appear minor and without significance until a startling victory occur. The lowly lime, rich in vitamin C, transformed the British Navy into a potent world-class naval force. Putting steel plates on sailing ships in the Civil War revolutionized naval warfare.

For almost eighty years afterwards, the common denominator in all navies of the world would be the battleship. It became the symbol of national power. But for many years, a quiet revolution was taking place in the minds of naval strategist and planners. The first was the idea of the submarine, a relatively weak and vulnerable craft that depended on stealth to achieve success in the battles of the sea. Submarines were small ships that operated in extreme conditions.

They were particularly threatened when operating as surface craft. With limited armament and limited deck guns, most surface naval ships and hostile aircraft could easily destroy them. Quarters were cramped and the men often slept with the highly dangerous torpedoes and surrounded by diesel fuel tanks. But even with its limitations, the submarine was to become one of the most effective instruments of modern naval warfare.

Military leaders are not always the most progressive in accepting new ideas and strategies. History is replete with sagas of military leadership that was too timid or failed to adapt to new tactics. History is replete with nations that succumb to the notion that they are invulnerable because they won the last war. And nations are vulnerable when its citizens become too preoccupied with the good-life to be willing to fight for their country.

Billy Mitchell was one of those great military visionaries who was almost relegated to obscurity by the intractable military minds governing weapons development between World War I and World War II. General Billy Mitchell was convinced that the key to national strength and a global navy was to create a naval air force where aircraft carriers became the floating island bases from which to strike enemy forces. Much of naval doctrine centered on the continued dominance of battleships. This was true of Japanese as well as American planners. But even as the bombs rained down on Pearl Harbor destroying our battleship centered navy, the submarine, the dragons of the salty deep, and the aircraft carriers, the behemoths of sea and air, became, almost inadvertently, the key to all future victories, especially in the wars in the Pacific Ocean.

The aircraft carrier is almost the opposite of the submarine. In size, the aircraft carrier is a floating city. It is a floating munitions dump. It houses vast stores of aviation and naval fuel oils. It is capable of fighting at great distances from enemy installations and fleets. It is a floating bomb of gargantuan dimensions. Fire is one of the main hazards of an aircraft carrier whether in peace or war. Carriers can give close in tactical air support to front line troops or they can carry out strategic missions such as Jimmy Doolittle's raid on Tokyo in World War II. Many of our fellow comrades in this VFW Post can attest to the effectiveness of carrier based strike forces that tipped the balance of power repeatedly in the wars of this century. Many of us owe our very lives to this effective naval air power, a power projected from the decks of the carriers.

Lee Stanworth served on the carrier, the U.S.S. Kearsarge.

My people migrated from England and Wales to America as members of the Church of Jesus Christ of Latter Day Saints. They settled the peaceful valley in Central Utah back when Brigham Young was establishing the land. On my mother's side her grandfather was a bishop and her father was a bishop and her brother was a bishop. My father's mother came from England to the area around Delta, Utah. They lived in what we would call poverty. My uncle farmed for eighteen years before he had a paying crop. They survived because they were strong and determined.

My father spent his youth in and around Delta. When he was about twenty-one he volunteered for the Marine Corps. He landed in France at the end of WW I, but he never had a chance to use his rifle because the Armistice was signed. He then got a job on a dragline, and was here in Santa Paula working after the San Francisquito Dam broke. He helped clean up the mess after all those people were killed. I went to school with the son of the guy who had built it, Bill Mulholland. Most people don't know anything about that disaster which killed some 500 people—mostly in Ventura County!

When I was about nine years of age WW II started. My cousin was aboard an aircraft carrier on maneuvers away from Pearl Harbor. He would correspond with me through the war. He became a Chief Petty Officer and was a Career Officer. I found him to be a hero like my father.

At age twelve my father bought a house in Canoga Park. We moved there from West Hollywood where I was born on August 14, 1932. I was the oldest of four kids, two boys and two girls. My father delivered ice, and he used to get me up at 4:00 in the morning to help him, then afterwards, I would go to school.

Korea—
"Don't go over there if you can help it!"
In high school at Canoga Park some of the young graduates joined the Marine Corps on their graduations in 1949. By 1950, when I graduated, some of those young

men weren't coming home because they were foot soldiers and they died in Korea. The ones that did come back, said, "Don't go over there if you can help it!" So when I graduated from high school I worked for a couple of years delivering lumber. Some of my school friends were being drafted into the Army but I decided that I didn't want to be a foot soldier, so I joined the Navy.

"You're in the Navy, Son!"

The first day at boot camp in San Diego, I got a letter from the draft board saying that I was drafted into the Army! I asked my Chief Petty Officer, "What do I do now?" He said, "You're in the Navy, son!" That was what I wanted, because I just didn't want to live in a foxhole. When I finished boot camp in San Diego I was sent to Norman, Oklahoma to learn about basic aviation.

Lee Stanworth after basic training, 1955

Aviation Electronics

When I finished two months of training, they told me I was going to Memphis, Tennessee to learn aviation electronics to be an electronics technician. I spent a year there in Memphis. When that training was over, the Chief Petty Office came to me and said that I had the physical requirements and that I had done well in my year of schooling in electronics. Now they wanted me to sign up for six more years and they said that they would train me in Pensacola, Florida, to be a pilot in the Naval Air Corps. I said "Six more years! I'm in love with this little gal back home in Canoga Park so I think I'll pass on the offer." It was a mistake really, because she didn't wait for me, and I could have ended up being an airline pilot. Anyway they sent me to Point Mugu, where I worked for a year in electronics until I was assigned to the U.S.S. Kearsarge.

PHOTO COURTESY OF U.S.S KEARSARGE YEARBOOK, 1956

Aircraft Carrier U.S.S. Kearsarge and Three Lumbering Pot-bellied Guppies

The complexities of an aircraft carrier demand that the whole ship have a system of missions and duties integrated so tightly that the ship functions like a living, breathing organism. I belonged to CAG – Five Group with a specific mission in support of the three lumbering pot-bellied guppies. These AD5W's provided aerial support platforms for reconnaissance against hostile air and submarine attack. They were the eyes and ears for the defense of the carrier. They carried both radar and sonar devices. They had another unique task, which was towing the target sleeve for the ship's gunnery practice and the CAG's. It carried three people, and I always sat in the back, operating the sonar and electrical systems. I made about 50 flights off of the carrier, and it was a thrill every time! Taking off of an aircraft carrier, which is only 60 feet off the water, is interesting. Because these weren't jets, they would drop after leaving the deck, and disappear from sight until they could pull up.

Flying over Mt. Fujiyama.

Visiting Hot Spots

We were there to help quell some of the activities in the China Sea. The Red Chinese were trying to take Taiwan. Essentially, the carrier is an offensive weapon in war and an extension of national power backing up diplomacy in times of peace. Most of the time aboard the U.S.S. Kearsarge we were in the trouble spots of the Far East. But we got the opportunity to tour Japan, Mt. Fujiyama, Tokyo Bay, and Hong Kong. We also went to the Island of Corregidor, which is in the Philippines Islands. It had been totally destroyed by WW II though. You couldn't find anything that didn't have 50 caliber holes in it! One time while in Japan I went to this shrine from when the bombs had been dropped, and it was no bigger than my living room, but it had 264,000 people buried there. That atomic bomb had leveled the whole valley. It was starting to get built up again, and the people were pretty forgiving. Amazing. I do remember going on leave though and I took a train by myself to view the countryside. Some people were still pretty upset. Their families had been burned, and one guy started pushing me around. I couldn't understand what he was saying, but I knew what was going on. A lot of other people just grabbed him and made him stop. But we didn't know what he went through. Nobody does.

Life on a Floating City

All in all, it was a great tour. Our opportunities for travel certainly coincided with the Navy-recruiting slogan, "Join the Navy and See the World." Life aboard a carrier is pretty good; it's literally a floating city. I never saw 80% of it! It can be dangerous though. Five of our men didn't come back. One night when we were out near Hawaii, a pilot came in too low and he flew right into the back of the ship. He hit right where they stored all of the pyrotechnics, so all of it exploded and he, of course, died. So we had to go into port while they fixed the carrier.

Another time I watched a young kid in maintenance walk straight into a prop. It just chewed him up and spit him out. Body parts just went everywhere; it was terrible!

After the Military

Eventually my tour was up, so I decided to get out of the military. When I got back we went to Disneyland, because it was the first year it had opened. I lived near Woodland Hills Junior College, so I went down there for a semester or two until Uncle Sam offered us the GI Bill.

I decided to go to Utah to Brigham Young where I met my wife. She was smart; she worked in the men's dorm hamburger shop! She had a date every night, and her calendar was full. When we met, I asked her out, and she threw away her calendar! It was just like that for both of us. Her name is Darlene, and we have six kids together—three boys and three girls.

I went into business for myself, and I am now in my upper 60's and am still working as an independent businessman. I used to be a Bishop in the Church of Latter Day Saints and I've also been active in the VFW Post 11461 where I have served as chaplain.

Bruce Vail

–*Coming of Age in the Cold War*

In the 1930's and 1940's Ojai was a sleepy little rural town far removed from the big cities, the nation, and global events. There were barely 1500 people in the valley and everyone knew each other. There were a few health spas known to the locals and the wealthy. The country club was a focal point of a tiny tourist industry.

But most of the Ojai Valley was wilderness, cattle pasture, hay ranches, and the still present orange orchards. The high school was situated where the present Junior High exists. The so-called Y with the shopping centers and medical complexes as well as the present day Nordhoff High School was a huge pasture for grazing cattle. The town of Ojai consisted of the pool hall, a tiny theater, and a soda fountain. The pool hall and theater remain today as they were sixty years ago with some slight modifications to the fascias.

The road to Ventura was long and twisting. The oil fields were the chief economic activity after agriculture. Many of the residents of Ojai who did not work on the farms and ranches worked the oil patch. As today, the high Topa Topa bluffs and Nordhoff peak ringed Ojai. Each winter saw the occasion of snowfall across the ridges of the massive coastal range. The summers in Ojai were scorchers with days of 105-degree heat not being uncommon. Today the climate is much more moderate with warmer winters and cooler summers after the construction of the Casitas Dam and the filling of Lake Casitas. All the four roads in and out of the Valley were winding and twisting. None was designed for heavy traffic. But it is the same today ,for the roadways have changed little except for Arnaz Grade and the short section of the Ojai Freeway.

Bruce Vail was raised in an idyllic world except for global events far removed from Ojai. The Spanish Civil War was fought in the last half of the 1930's. Little did anyone suspect that this was a prelude to the greatest conflict in the memory or history of mankind. Hitler, Mussolini, and Stalin used Spain and the Spanish people as guinea pigs for their experimentations in modern warfare. Except for a mild economic upturn, the Spanish Civil war was scarcely noticed in the towns and hamlets across America.

Ojai remained a sleepy and tranquil place until that momentous event at Pearl Harbor plunged the United States into global and the eventual East-West Cold War. This is how world events changed the life of Bruce Vail.

I was born on March 23, 1928 in Long Beach, and we moved to Ventura when I was six months old. We then moved to Ojai from Ventura when I was five years old. Most of the population of Ojai worked in Ventura for the oil business, and my father worked for Getty Oil Company out on the Avenue as a refinery operator. There were three boys in my family, and I was the middle one. At that time, the population of the valley was only about 2000 people! It was all orange groves, no avocados at that time.

The "Y" was a huge pasture for grazing cattle. The town of Ojai consisted of the pool hall, a tiny theater, and a soda fountain. They had a packing house out at the end of Blanche Road for the oranges and the railroad came up here just for the purpose of shipping oranges.

We lived in Meiner's Oaks, and there were only about 50 families there at that time. Harry Hunt's father was the local Sheriff and he had a real good rapport with the kids. Everybody knew everybody. We hated the fact that the town was so small because whenever anybody got into trouble, the whole town knew it!

Troops Set Up A Training Camp at the Ojai Valley Inn

WW II was brought close to home when 5000 infantry troops detrained at the intersection of Highway 150 and Highway 33, where the bike path is now. The troops set up camp at the Ojai Valley Inn and started training at the mouth of Matilija Canyon. You could hear the rumble and roar of 60mm mortars and 75mm guns exploding just a mile from the Nordhoff Campus and occasionally the chatter of machine gun fire. I remember seeing hundreds upon hundreds of infantrymen marching to Ventura, training. Eventually, the Ojai troops were shipped to Attu and Kiska to halt the Japanese invasion of Alaska.

Rationing at Home

Because of the war there were shortages of protein foods, butter and fats, gasoline and oil. So the government started a system of rationing. Every individual was issued coupon books with designated allotments of food. New appliances and cars were nonexistent because all manufacturing activities were converted to the production of war materials. Our next-door neighbor was a WW I Navy chief who had been assigned to a destroyer, so my older brother, Richard wanted to go to work on a destroyer when it came time to go into the war. He and four other buddies from high school, all went down and enlisted in the Navy. He never came close to a destroyer though. They put him on The Missouri, which was a battleship. He was there in Tokyo Harbor when the Japs surrendered.

I had friends and acquaintances that were captured by the Japanese. One guy I knew was captured on Corregidor by the Japanese and sent to Japan as slave labor. In the process, American submarines sank the prison ship and as the ship was going down, the Japanese shot all the prisoners who tried to escape. Another guy we knew was a prisoner of war in a Japanese coal mine.

Graduation and 18? —You're Drafted!

I started the first grade at Ojai Elementary School, and then I went to Matilija Junior High and then to Nordhoff High School. They were right next to each other at that time. I graduated from high school in 1946. During the summers I worked for Shell Oil doing manual labor because there was a shortage of manpower due to WW II. When it was time to graduate from high school, eight of us guys went down and joined the Navy. During WW II, if you were 18, the day that you graduated from high school, you were drafted the very next day! So we decided that we'd beat them to the punch. We went up to Santa Barbara, and when we got there, they told us that since the war had ended, they were discouraging people from enlisting. This was June of 1946. So when the Korean War came along, guess who was number one on the list?

Korea—Army Draft Beats the Navy Choice

So again in 1950, I decided to join the Navy. The Navy recruiter would come to Ventura on Wednesdays where he had an office in the library on Main Street. I went down and filled out all these papers, then went home for lunch. While I was eating lunch, I went to the mailbox to get the mail, and wouldn't you know it, but I received a draft notice! They had me scheduled to go into the Army. So I showed up at the Greyhound bus station in Ventura, and there were five of the guys that I had graduated with, all going in the Army with me.

They sent us to Fort Ord for basic training. When we finished basic training, they told us that there were two schools that we had to choose from. One was at Camp Carson in Colorado. They said, "If you know anything about skinning mules, and you really want to skin some more mules, then volunteer to go to Camp Carson!" What it was, was pack artillery. Nobody volunteered for that except one guy. They sent the rest of us to Fort Benning, Georgia.

Advanced Combat Training at Fort Benning

The school lasted for six months, and it was advanced combat training. I said, "Oh boy, that's it, we,re going to Korea." Our maneuvers included encounters with water moccasins, rattlers, and all sort of critters. It was so hot and humid in Georgia. During the early months of training, I learned the fine art of mortar fire using the 60mm mortar, the same weapon I had heard thumping away in the hills of Ojai during World War II.

Armored Units of the 4th Infantry Division during the winter of 1951 in Grafenwehr, Germany

PHOTOS COURTESY OF BRUCE VAIL

As our training progressed we were thinking that we were going to Korea. One day they said, "Oh, by the way, I guess you'd like to know where you're going? You're going to Germany." They put five whole division out there facing Czechoslovakia and East Germany, but they didn't tell us what was going on.

A Worried Truman
Sends Us to the Czech Border

All of a sudden, we realized that something was up. We thought that since the American Army was engaged in heavy combat against the Chinese in Korea, that that was where we were going. As it turned out, Harry Truman had decided that there was something going on with the Russians, so they put us up on the Czech border facing thousands of Soviet tanks. For miles, that was all we could see. And we were thinking, "Great, so I'm gonna stop a Russian tank with an M-1 rifle!?" We found out later that since the Chinese were giving the American forces such a hard time in Korea, that Russia was getting ready to rattle their sabers. That's why they had amassed all those Soviet Army divisions in Europe. The American forces planned to destroy the three bridges across the Main River if the Soviets attacked the American sector in Germany.

Schweinfurt, Germany.

When we arrived in Scweinfurt, it had been flattened. There was nothing left of it still. Any building taller than five feet had been destroyed during WWII. And this was five years later. The Germans hadn't even begun to recover. There were very few men between the age of 20 and 50. Most had perished in the war. They still felt that they were on the right side of the World War II issue. Towns that had been temporarily under Soviet control after World War II had horror stories about the abuse visited on the German civilian population by the Russian military. We were stationed there, but most of the time we were out in the boon-docks.

Two Winters of Foxholes and Paperwork

I was trained as a mortar-gunner back in at Fort Benning and also as a supply sergeant. They had gone down the line when we were at Fort Benning and selected people to go to supply school. I didn't want anything to do with it because of all the paperwork and red tape. But as it turned out, it was a good place to be while we were in

Germany. When I wasn't in supply, I was digging foxholes, making sure the Russians could see us. We spent two winters there.

It was real easy getting into Czechoslovakia. The train went right across the border. I remember one time four of us used to go to this tiny, tiny town out about 30 miles east of the base. We had to get on the train to get there. We had been partying, and we got on the train and we missed the stop. Now if you were American, you didn't dare get caught in Czechoslovakia. As luck would have it, the conductor on the train said, "You guys don't belong here, you're in Czechoslovakia!" So he put us back on a train heading back, real quick! Boy were we lucky!

Sgt. Kiefhuber with a 57 recoiless tank rifle, 1951

Another thing I remember was, one morning I got up to shave, and I had red spots all over me. I went down to sick call. The Medic took one look at me and he said, "Go to your room, get your shaving gear and your tooth brush and come back here immediately. Don't talk to anybody!" I had the measles, and when you have 5000 troops, you could have an epidemic real quick! They shuttled me out the back door, put me in an ambulance all by myself and sent me down to Wertzberg. They had taken over a huge hotel and we were using it as a hospital. I found out why some of these guys were continuously going to sick call. That hotel was beautiful.

Those Lousy Troop Ships

When our enlistment was up they sent us back on a troop ship with 5000 people aboard it! Those troop ships were something else. They stacked us four-high in hammocks. That old ship we were on would only do 11 knots, flat out! But we finally got into New York, and they flew us from New Jersey to the West Coast on DC-3's. While we were at the airport waiting to board, the airplane we were supposed to get onto, burnt to the ground right in front of us! I turned to a friend who was from Santa Paula, and I said, "You may get on that thing, and my duffel bag may get on that thing, but I'm going to go over the fence. I'm going to hitchhike, and I'll see you back at Fort Ord!" Well, about then the MP's showed up and they rounded us up and put us on that plane. Needless to say, we were relieved when we were finally on approach to the dirt airstrip at the Monterey Municipal Airport. But even landing was a hair-raiser because the pilot was barely able to stop that plane before we got to the end of that airstrip. It wasn't built for DC-3's; it was built for little Piper Cubs! I survived and I got out of the Army after my enlistment expired.

Corporal Bruce Vail on leave in Amsterdam, 1952

Back Home; Edison Company, Marriage, Kids and Avocados

I came back to Ventura where I got a job with the Edison Company, routing electricity at the control station. I met my wife in Ventura. I walked into the Santa Cruz Market, and Mary, the wife of one of the guys that I worked with, said, "I've got someone I want you to meet." So we were introduced.

Lavonne was baking for the school where she worked She had an apron on, and she had flour in her hair!" We went on a blind date thing to Santa Barbara, and things went downhill from there! We dated for about a year, then we were married in June of 1955. We've been married over forty-seven years and we have one daughter and two grown sons and four grandchildren. We lived in Ventura until 1985, when we bought some property on Fairview Road at the peak of a little hill. I retired in 1988, We planted avocados on the property which keeps us quite busy!

Bruce Vail, 2002

PHOTO COURTESY OF CHUCK BENNETT

Though retired, Bruce is like most of us of that generation; he still works hard every day. He is as lean and tough as when he faced the Russians on the Czech border. His ranch off Fairview Road is at the peak of a little hill where every day he looks down on the old mortar, artillery, and machine gun range from WW II. Realizing the unpredictability of the "luck of the draw'. Bruce is ever grateful that, unlike some of his friends and acquaintances from Nordhoff High School in the quiet and tranquil valley of Ojai, he was blessed and came home to a long, happy, and satisfying life.

THE VIETNAM ERA
■■■■■■■■■■■■■■■■■■■■■■

*T*wo forces converged to produce one of America's most horrific and divisive wars. The first force was rooted in the colonialism of the French Empire, a nation committed to "Liberty, Fraternity, and Equality" except for the one fifth of the world occupied by France for the benefit of the Motherland! Such disparate positions and inherent contradictions led to numerous colonial wars after World War II. French Indochina was caught up in this new wave of Asian nationalism. Vietnamese native leaders attempting to emulate the ideals of liberty, fraternity, and equality in their native land were quickly silenced, imprisoned, or declared outlaws. The repression promoted a growing rebellion.*

It had been demonstrated that the average French citizen was not interested in politics that went beyond rhetoric. The French had no stomach for the fight. Surreptitiously upon the occupation of a defeated Germany, French officials began the recruitment of ex-Nazi soldiers and other German nationals seeking a place to hide from the pending war crimes trial after World War II. Many of these men became the cannon fodder for France's colonial wars. A French Foreign Legionnaire became a faceless being. Certainly, France would not cry for the fallen Legionnaire. Led by French Officers, supplied with U.S. military hardware, and the ranks filled with foreign mercenaries, France attempted to impose a military defeat on the colonials.

At that time, it is reported that the man most admired by Ho Chi Minh was none other than our General George Washington. Like George Washington, Ho Chi Minh felt that he was struggling to throw off the yoke of foreign oppression.

But there was a second force at work in the Vietnam psyche, it was the force of world communism, a sinister ideology bent on world conquest and domination. The Soviet Union under the communist ideology was the only colonial power that remained unscathed in the colonial revolts in the aftermath of World War II. The Soviet Union, unlike the United States and our other allies, did not demobilize. Instead, the Soviets continued with a massive build up of men and arms. Taking a lesson from the Nazis, they developed a propaganda machine coupled with subversion. This machine infiltrated every known country.

With the conclusion of the Yalta Conference and the Potsdam Conference, the Soviets had a license to steal, steal the freedoms of conquered and suppressed peoples throughout the world. Vietnam was no exception. It was an ideal scenario whereby Communist agents could infiltrate a movement for national independence. It was an opportunity to bleed free nations dry of resources and manpower while using the Vietnamese as fighting surrogates. The United States had a difficult decision. North Vietnam became a puppet Soviet State while South Vietnam became a so-called democratic state. This was because the bureaucratic administration of South Vietnam was generally corrupt and lacking unity and the will to fight against Communist infiltrators and fifth column agitators.

South Vietnam became the scene of civil war, a civil war underwritten by the now Communist North which in turn was a client state of Red China and the Soviet Union. The prevailing political theory in Washington was that the fall of South Vietnam would lead to a domino effect in South East Asia. If South Vietnam fell, Malaysia, Burma, Singapore, Thailand, Laos, Cambodia, and perhaps Indonesia would fall under Soviet influence and power.

Gradually, the United States became enmeshed in the war. However, the politicians had no clear strategy for winning. As in Korea, the American military became bogged down in a war the politicians would not let the military win. President Johnson, for still unknown reasons, confined ground operations to South Vietnam. No advances into Laos, Cambodia or North Vietnam were allowed. So there is where the Viet Cong went to rest and resupply. Here is where the Ho Chi Minh Trail was established to bring supplies and weaponry from China and Russia. Tactically these movement restrictions left no area of real strategic importance for the North Vietnamese Army (NVA) to have to defend. Consequently, with no frontlines to hold, the NVA could pick and choose the areas to attack and simply melt away afterward. Battles were fought in the same areas over and over.

Micro management of tactical field situations became common. American military personnel became the victims of an inept political machine in Washington that planned to win the war with technical superiority. As a result, we sent as many as 525,000 men in one year, yet only fielded 50,000 to do the actual fighting on the ground. In a long protracted war, this ultimately created a very costly conflict as well as mental exhaustion of the public back home. Over 2.8 million Americans served in our country's longest war.

The longer the war lasted, the more home-grown American Leftists were able to sway public opinion. Riots and demonstrations broke out across the nation. The soldiers, sailors, and airmen who fought the war, bled and died by the thousands, became the targets of the radical students and war protesters. Those Americans who bore the brunt of the hell we call Vietnam, the men who carried out the will of the politicians elected by the people, became victims for an event over which they had no control.

President Lyndon Johnson resigned under pressure leaving a new president to get us out of the mess. The new president was Richard Nixon, a man greatly feared by friend and foe including the Soviets because Richard Nixon was unpredictable. The Communists were afraid of him. Withdrawing from a fire fight is a tricky business. Withdrawing from a war is even more difficult. Withdraw we did, but not without paying a frightful price in human destruction and carnage. Recently, President William Clinton, one of the most vociferous war protesters of the Vietnam era authorized a delegation to North Vietnam to normalize relations. Many veterans have mixed feeling about this action. The final chapter is not yet written.

But whatever is said about the war in Vietnam, it did serve notice on the Soviet plan of world conquest. As in Korea, it showed that America would fight if necessary. It showed that a line of blood had been drawn in the sand. Today, the Soviet Union is a ghost of its former self. Some people believe that Korea and Vietnam were the turning point. Ultimately, our servicemen and women turned the tide against this baneful and unwholesome ideology called Communism.

CHUCK BENNETT

—VIETNAM; PLATOON LEADER AND COMPANY COMMANDER THROUGH THE 1968 TET OFFENSIVE

Infantry is the cutting edge of all warfare. Infantrymen are the ones who must take and hold the ground in direct confrontation with the enemy. While holding ground they are usually at the receiving end of a vast array of weapons and tactics that are used to dislodge or defeat them. Ground combat is an irrational experience and survival is often the "luck of the draw" or "by the Grace of God." Intellect and split second decisions by trained and experienced leaders enhances survival, but even under the best of circumstances, the life expectancy of Infantry leadership is short.

If Infantry warfare is the cutting edge, Infantry platoon leaders are the ultimate leaders for they must lead in the face of fear, confusion, and the ever present irrationality of the battlefield. The experience is so different from any other human experience that only those who have endured the trauma can grasp the ultimate pathology of ground warfare. This is the story of Chuck Bennett who survived, but barely.

I had just graduated from Norland High School in North Miami, Florida, 1965. The Vietnam draft call was getting serious. I wanted to be an artist. I had just completed the "Draw Me" mail order school of art and I was hot to get a job. I was willing to be a "go-fer," sharpen pencils, anything to get my foot in the door. My High School pal, Paul Brown and I loaded up my '55 Ford with probably a hundred canned goods, tent, and our sleeping bags. We were going up the coast, the Boy Scout way, ultimately to Minneapolis or bust! I wanted to personally meet some of my art instructors. Being the oldest of six, I'd never seen a bigger smile on my Mother's face as she waved good bye to the first one out of the nest. I swear I could hear a huge sigh of relief as we drove away.

Poor Paul didn't last past Jacksonville. He was pining for his on and off again girlfriend and took the Greyhound back home. I kept on. At every major city I stopped and phoned an advertising agency. I almost always got an interview. They would look at my drawings and slowly wag their heads saying, "Yes, some of this is OK, but if we hire you, it will take us a year to train you and then you'll be drafted!" That was probably their kind way of saying, "Your stuff stinks." I eventually got the "draft" part of the message.

The old Ford made it to Minneapolis in the dreary, icy wet fall. Even though I came from Wisconsin originally, I found that town's fall weather to be miserable. I did enjoy all the people I met along the way, but my car's U-joint kept going out by then and I kept climbing under it dropping the drive shaft and repacking it until my car appreciation turned to a hate relationship just about the time I arrived at my grandparents in Janesville, Wisconsin. It was there that I was flat broke and decided to volunteer for a two year draft and get it over with. The slick Army recruiter got me to extend a year to learn something useful while I was in—communication. Supposedly, kind of art related, or something?

Off to Fort Lost-in-the-Woods Misery

I took my first train ride going to basic training at Fort Leonard Wood, Missouri, soon to be known to us trainees as "Fort Lost-in-the-Woods, Misery." September is a lousy time to take basic training there. It was getting damn cold in that mostly treeless, rock-infested rolling hill country. I well remember my Drill Instructor (DI), Sgt. Morehouse. He appeared to be directly from Hollywood casting for a DI—a taller Robert Mitchum. He did not think much of me. Most of us rotated into some kind of leadership position eventually. Not me. The highest I ever got was

Road Guard. This privileged duty allows you to triple time (running faster) up to a road crossing in advance of your double-timing-everywhere-we-go (running in formation) platoon. You get to stand there at parade rest, red-faced in spasms of apoplexy as the platoon cruises by and then triple time again to catch-up back into ranks.

After a battery of tests, my name was called to join ranks with a few others in the company to get the pitch to go to Officer Candidate School (OCS). I really couldn't believe my ears. I was much too young. I did the ultimate no-no and went up to the First Sergeant, who was calling out the names, and asked if he was sure he called my name—in front of the whole company. This is not a smart move in any man's army. I don't think I ever completely recovered from the full blown results of not listening attentively.

My Advanced Individual Training (AIT) was at Fort Jackson, North Carolina. Afterwards, I was held there until an OCS class opened up. They gave me Corporal stripes so I could give orders with some authority. In fact I was still the lowliest pay grade. I learned the in and outs of the mess hall—things like the automatic potato peeler and pumping the kitchen's huge grease pit—learning how to crack hundreds of eggs, one in each hand—doing menus, ordering food, and cooking for 250 people. I didn't know at the time, but this was about as good a time as my three years in the Army was going to get.

A Six Month Wonder at Fort Benning, GA

I believe I was the youngest in my OCS class and I was thoroughly intimidated. I'd made up my mind that I would give it all I had knowing I was up against college kids and NCOs mostly who had many years in the service, or at least some college. I had one other ace in the hole besides a good attitude. I had been on the high school five-mile cross-country track team and while I was one man away from a Letter on my jacket, our team won All-State. The Army could never exhaust me running.

OCS was constantly about keeping you so busy that you always had far too much to do. Personal stress was always high. You had to organize yourself and be a team player to survive. The bookwork was severe. I was in the Seventh OCS Battalion that had recently opened up. We were part of the rapid expansion of OCS from just the 5th Battalion that had been graduating four companies of officers every six months since the Korean war. President Johnson's enlarging war effort expanded OCS to the 8th and 9th Battalions before I left for Nam—very sad for the quality of officer who was being rushed through the ever-faster expanding vortex. My Tactical Officer (similar to the Drill Instructor in Basic) was Second Lieutenant Judd L. Clemmens who had Airborne Jump School Wings and had been a Staff Sergeant in an Armor outfit. Every Tactical Officer gets to choose his successor when they themselves leave for Nam. Nobody was more surprised than I was to be the chosen one. A supreme compliment to be what some would consider a prison sentence extension—OCS for another ten months in my case.

Graduating OCS, brand new Lieutenants, Lendhardt and Bennett, come back to the program as Tactical Officers—each in charge of a platoon of OCS candidates. Bennett obviously doesn't understand how serious the job is.

This meant I had to get up an hour earlier to get the platoon up and go to bed an hour after they bedded down. Most of that evening time I spent interviewing individual progress and typing up reports. Oh, great! Actually I loved the job seeing so many individuals who had already changed a lot to get to OCS and then make additional positive changes to get through it. I felt enormous responsibility to turn out adequate platoon leaders and worked my platoon members hard.

Jungle Training in Panama

The Army kept me in OCS as long as they could. Then off I went for two weeks of jungle training in Panama. Jungle training was scarier than Vietnam at times. I trained with other Army individuals, companies of Marines, and numerous Seal Teams. Those that came in groups for this additional training were far more effective and successful than individuals arriving and teaming up with strangers. We suddenly had to rely heavily on each other. That in itself taught me quite a lot.

Panama's deepest jungles are awesomely beautiful and dreadful. The jungles I tramped in Vietnam were not as thick nor animal-infested as Panama. We always slept on the ground in Nam. We always slept in totally enclosed hammocks in trees in Panama. The netting kept snakes off as well as mosquitoes—someone in our group always had an animal, usually a snake, in their hammock material when they awoke.

After an especially grueling day we got a live chicken to kill and potato looking raw roots to cook for dinner (no matches). Our unedible dinner was followed by a nighttime jungle walk. Only in Panama have I experienced trudging through dead leafy vegetation that exploded in whitish green phosphorescent showers. The sprays looked somewhat like the splashing "angels" we would make as Boy Scouts swimming in the St. Johns River in Florida at night on hot summer camp-outs. The triple canopy jungle blocked out all night light so you just followed the trail of phosphorescent light from many feet moving up and down and across a pitch black steep valley with many fumbling, mumbling, falling, cursing soldiers.

This was also my first experience with jungle rot. If your skin stays constantly wet in this environment, it will first turn a deep red then eventually black and then fall off. I've seen it mostly on feet and around the crotch area. Forget wearing underwear. You want to be aired out as much as possible.

The overnight escape and evasion course really capped off the experience. Vietnam was going to be like this plus live ammo?

Vietnam and the 25th Divisions' Wolfhound Regiment

When I went to Vietnam I had no practical hands on Company level experience as an officer. Along with the expansion of OCS Battalions, the rise in rank was also shortened to one year from 2nd Louie to 1st and only one year to automatically make Captain. The day I hit Nam I took off the butter bars and put on silver. I didn't know it, but I was, at that moment, the senior Lieutenant in my new Battalion, the 1/27th Infantry Wolfhounds. The 1/27 and 2/27 Wolfhounds were the infantry combat assault Battalions for the 25th Division. The Wolfhounds were formed and got their name from their war service in Siberia, being the first to fight the Russian Communists in the bitter cold and forgotten end of WWI.

There are those that would argue that being a Ranger, Special Forces, Recon or even a LRRP (Long Range Recognizance Patrol) is more dangerous than being a platoon leader of a bunch of mostly draftees. Well, we could talk.

After the nineteen mile truck ride to Cu Chi Division Base Camp, northwest of Saigon, I got the ceremonial dump off the back of a deuce-and-half into the muddy ditch as we crossed into Wolfhound home base. This was just a small wedge in a huge circular perimeter that took in the 25th Division Base Camp. It must have been a mile across. Wringing wet and muddy, but drying out quickly in the heat, I got my gear, was issued a weapon and ammo, shown to a musty bunk with no other officers around. The 1st Sergeant was forward too, I think the highest rank in the Delta Company area was an E5.

"Incoming" on the First Night and My First Look at Death?

I got my first "Incoming!" experience that night. Being by myself in the Officers' Hooch I ran out in my skivvies looking for a foxhole thinking, "Dummy, why didn't you think about this before now?" As I madly circled the hooch I realized there was no bunker outside the officers quarters! About 10 meters away was the Company HQ and I was sure they had one. Luckily, I could run. As each foot hit the ground I was thinking, "dummy, dummy, dummy." I dove into the Company HQ bunker as a huge round landed in the company area. It was over almost as fast as it started. While I was hesitant to go out again, I heard loud conversation outside and looked out to find men furiously working with a man on the ground. Evidently he was running just behind me and caught what I presume to have been a clothes line at neck level. It must have flipped him since his neck was purple and bulging. He also had shrapnel in him and was bleeding in numerous places. My first look at death?

I was contemplating how lucky I was and how insane war was at this point and how unprepared so called prepared soldiers, like myself, are to fight it. The reality of any moment in war can never really be anticipated in training. In retrospect certain aspects of war are funny in a macabre sort of way. I will tell you that war at the platoon and company level is sickening when you can back up and get a birds-eye view of it. On the ground you are bouncing and blanching from pillar to post. Having as much memorable training as possible, helps keep your wits about you—and you alive. One must always be thinking ahead and around corners.

I never knew if he survived since I was helicoptered to the forward base camp at daybreak the next morning. The helicopter I was on from 25th Division Base Camp was one of the helicopters to be used in the pending 1/27 Battalion assault —very efficient, but hell on a brand new platoon leader. "Yaaa, he'll fit in soon enough." Damn people who think this way. I'm going into hell with no orientation and I'm immediately responsible for my platoon level results!

A Combat Assault Before Meeting My Platoon

I meet my 1/27 Delta 4th Platoon Sergeant as the choppers are revving up for take-off. He says, "The CO (Commanding Officer) is on that chopper. We are on these choppers, I'll be on this chopper behind you. See you when we land." He left out the part that we were on a full combat helicopter assault into a live (firing back at us) LZ (Landing Zone).

The choppers all start climbing carrying the Battalion to "the river." There is no ability to talk over the chopper noise. I get a few curt nods and some icy smiles from members of my platoon as we lift off and swing in a big wide ever-rising 360 degrees—I think? I madly try to find the river on the map, plop my compass on top to orient north and it dawns on me, "What difference does it make? I don't know where we are now or where we are going!"

I don't know who or how many are in my 4th platoon. Most haven't even seen me much less met me. Still I try to get my bearings as we whop, whop, whop loudly—choppering towards a wide wandering blue ribbon over a seemingly endless mixture of forest, swamp and rice paddies. Finally I have North on my map coordinated with my compass as the helos begin to descend and, on que, all begin a circling attack run to confuse the enemy commonly called "Charlie." Forget Charlie, what about my bearings? And my wits? Attack helicopters on each side begin dropping tons of smoke ahead of us. The increasing roar of the attack is punctuated by the firing of helicopter belly rockets and the staccato of their automatic 40mm grenade launchers into the jungle of trees and swamp lighting up with explosions. I feel I'm in the middle of a very noisy B-movie asking, "Is this the part where I die?" That thought would wander in and out almost daily for a year.

I had a sample of this style of attack back at Fort Benning, but this was real. The men grab their gear and move to the open helicopter doors and hang both feet out onto the landing skids. "Some balls," I think reflecting that in the States we wouldn't dream of doing something that crazy! Minutes later I understand what a serious target a chopper full of soldiers is, and how you want off ASAP! I'm the last one off and land almost waist deep in swamp.

Checking Out the New Lieutenant

I could tell who most members of my platoon were right away. We were the last to land and my men were mostly waiting to see what I would do. I could not believe that they weren't racing to get under cover! They were looking at me as if to say, "What's this F-ing new 'LT' going to do next?" A quick look around and waving and yelling loudly, "This way." Heavy with gear, rifle up, I'm stomping water like a big fat duck trying to take off for the nearest woodline. Surprise, surprise—that's where the rest of Delta Company went. I could not believe how slowly my platoon members moved, even with loud encouragement.

Suddenly the chopper noise and firing is gone. Everything seems suddenly quiet. My radio telephone operator (RTO), whom I had barely met on the helicopter, looks like a drowned rat. I wonder if the radio will work? I meet my Company Commander over the radio, get my bearings, connect up with 3rd Platoon and move on line towards the river. I could tell already that I had a great platoon Sergeant.

For all the landing fireworks, it turned out to be a cold LZ (Landing Zone)— no Viet Cong anywhere. There were well worn trails everywhere so trying to stay off them for fear of booby traps was hard. This river area was Charlie's historically favorite stomping ground and we weren't too worried since we figured they wouldn't booby trap their own heavily trafficked river edges. We decided to walk waist deep or deeper at times in the man-made canals that were going in our general direction and gave us good upper body protection. We were in no hurry, my platoon Sergeant said, as this was an exploratory mission for the battalion. Everyone is very skeptical about me and I redouble their reasoning about an hour later.

Blood Sucking Leeches

Wading around in this waist deep water I get introduced to blood sucking leeches. With your fatigues bloused in your boots you are usually OK until the water gets to waist level and they can swim right between the buttons on your front and waist area. They are painless, so you can't tell when they attach themselves. You can't just pull them off or the teeth remain in you and you get infected without a doubt. We had one go up a guy's penis—now that must have been a painful operation to remedy that. We were always extra careful and as soon as we ever hit the land, everyone dropped their pants and used their Zippos to burn them just enough that they would let go. One of my men slept with one of these on his leg and awoke with an incredible two inch by about ten inch blood filled leech.

Probably My Most Stupid Move as Platoon Leader

We came upon a whole series of what looked like very old above ground sod bunkers looking like black igloos. (Probably made by chopping and pulling up layers of very thick root material.) They were about 10 feet in diameter and four feet high with firing slots on two or three sides, and a pipe out the top. We were told to clear these bunkers as we came upon them. My Platoon Sergeant and I were waving the men up and out of the canal and converging on two sides of the bunker. Again I'm frustrated how slow and methodical these guys are dragging each other up and out of the canal.

I grew impatient as I was deciding how to clear this bunker without sending someone on hands and knees through this little hobbit hole opening, or lobbing a grenade in the front door and having it miss. I get this brilliant idea to drop a grenade down that pipe sticking out the top. And since I was on the side without a shooting slot, I was the safe bet to be the one to do it. First mistake! Platoon leaders should not do these kind of jobs! I yelled, "Fire in the hole, everyone get down—fire in the hole!" I popped the pin on that grenade and started counting as I found out that #2, it wouldn't fit down the pipe. #3, it didn't look like anybody got down. #4, while I was concentrating on clearing the bunker, platoon members had almost surrounded the bunker by now. #5, "What's the F-ing new LT gonna do now?"

There I was on top of this bunker holding a live grenade with this imaginary blinking sign over my head. You can imagine what it said. The only luck I had (five, four, three...) was that I had played baseball up through Pony League. I yelled, "Live grenade" and threw like I'd caught a ball in deep left field and was throwing for home plate. Needless to say that among those who cared, morale plummeted. None as deep as mine. This was not a Platoon Leader's job. Yes, lead a charge where the whole platoon must be inspired but not clearing a bunker. At a minimum, as a new LT, I should have discussed it with my Platoon Sergeant—a very experienced E6 at 26 years old. "Dinky Dau," and other expressions were projected my way. I guess I was at that moment prime lieutenant for a fragging. By evening I had met everyone and was mutually allowed back to square one, "Giv'em a chance, the next Lieutenant could be a whole lot worse!" It took a few days to recoup from that, mostly by visiting with each platoon member many times as I had done as a Tactical Officer in OCS—and listening carefully.

Typical Day-in-the-life, Hunting VC

Life in one of the Wolfhound assault battalions for the 25th Division quickly fell into a routine of lack of sleep bordering on exhaustion. We were expected to accomplish tasks of a full strength company, and we never attained even two thirds strength while I was there. Days of no VC action and dull routine were punctuated every few days or so by minutes and sometimes hours of shear fear and horror. We never got the "big picture" down at platoon level. We were always just going from here to the next suspected hot spot.

A typical day in this draftee/volunteer army was one of two directions. You were either coming off nightly ambush and had perimeter duty for the day or you were going out after nighttime perimeter duty and going on daily maneuvers. Even in the heaviest of monsoon rains you would be able to sleep anywhere, anytime with just a poncho over you. To get out of the puddles I would lie on my back across the spreading roots from a tree trunk or junk lying around. My steel pot served as a pillow. I'd be asleep in about 30 seconds.

Reveille was first light and most often someone coming by for a head count. Shower was your neck towel, soap, and a little water in your steel pot. Breakfast was often "A" rations—that is fresh bacon, eggs, pancakes etc. I met a Marine from 'Nam shortly after I got back to the world. I found out there are three reasons to go Army when the next one hits—You don't have to hump a 70 pound back pack full of everything you'll survive on; you will eat a lot better; and the army rarely goes beyond artillery support! I remember a couple times of low crawling through the chow line as nearby friendly jets or artillery barrages were pounding away. Our Battalion Commander, Lt. Colonel Condina, who refused to be intimidated by such things, had a large chunk of spent artillery go through the meaty part of his left shoulder on one of these occasions.

Leaving the Battalion perimeter we would step around the tanglefoot and concertina wire on a pre-dedicated path and clip a loaded magazine into our weapon. At least every month someone was hurt or shot doing this. I watched as one of the men in my platoon had his shoulder broken when an M79 grenade launcher was breeched to unload it and somehow re-closed and it fired. Luckily for all of us that day, those grenade launchers take ten meters travel to self arm.

Montagnards—Vietnam's Indians

In the three months before the infamous TET offensive that I was online, we walked the flat lands of rice paddies in the south and the steep three canopy jungles, in some places, in the North even working with the Montagnards for a short time. These are the Vietnamese equivalent of American Indians. Those women, of all ages, saw no reason to cover their tops. Montagnards loathed the VC and were happy to work with us.

Rooting Out the North Vietnamese Army

The worst areas by far were the thick forests near our 25th Division, home base of Cu Chi. This was where we always seemed to find the NVA. To avoid booby traps we had to stay off well traveled paths or roads. Humping the boonies was very slow going and noisy because brambles and vines were incredibly thick at times with vines climbing well up into the trees. Instead of fanning out in a typical tactical formation at times we had to go in two rows staying in sight of each other. The two point men would machete and, often as not, climb up "the wall" until it collapsed under their weight. This was extremely tiring on the point man. We rotated point often because of the exhaustive work. I was third man back with the RTO.

PHOTO COURTESY OF CHUCK BENNETT

We worked with tanks and APC's a lot during the short dry season. A gloved door gunner's hand rests on his M60 machine gun as our helicopters lands in a secure LZ. Note the C-ration can affixed under the belt feed of rounds going into the gun. Whatever works for you!

How we made contact was usually up to the point man. If he was careful, awake, quiet and really wanted to live, we had a fair chance of surprising Charlie. If not, the single VC in the spider hole would blast away our point man.

Our Ideal Fight
—Contact, Artillery, F4 Jets, and Gun Ships

After enemy contact, a team would go in and scout out the area ahead. If we received more fire, we were up against a larger fighting force. We would then call in an artillery strike that would bracket an entire area with rows of shells landing like two marching teams coming together across a football field and meeting in the middle where we thought the enemy was. We started on the enemy outreaches so if the enemy started running away from the first row of bombs, he would run into the second. If it was early enough in the day, we might get lucky and get Air Force F-4 Phantom jets—usually in pairs. Artillery would stop as they arrived on target. We would carefully identify our location with colored smoke grenades. We established the direction the enemy was heading and let the pilots do their job. Each pass over the enemy usually involved dropping napalm canisters or a barrage of cluster bombs—napalm is jellied gas that would throw up a wall of flame. We lost most of the third platoon of Charlie Company to a napalm delivery mistake. Cluster bombs were circular and when dropped at high speed would open an outer enclosure into two halves like butterfly wings. This slowed the bomb traveling somewhat horizontally and allowed a pin to drop that ignited a shower of hot shot like a cloud of locusts that spread over the target area.

Depending again on the time of day, availability and the results of the jet pilots visual "recon" of the area, helicopter gun ships would come in—also usually in pairs. The sleek two-man Huey Cobra with the huge shark face painted across the nose did not start arriving until about the time of TET, still months away. We often had a front row seat to all this action.

"Kit Carson Scout" Attached to Us

We had a Chieu Hoi, a "Kit Carson," which was a captured and reformed Viet Cong attached to us for a short time. The men couldn't imagine a more hated person to have amongst us and this guy could feel it. He was very useful whenever we came up on enemy base camps, tunnels, and captured VC. So we didn't kill him right off. Just under the surface was the seething revenge continually building up against VC for our buddies who were being picked off continually by constant sniping. There was little ability to respond quick enough as they ducked into tunnels and other pre-planned escape routes.

When the attack choppers came in one day, they came right over us and ol' Kit just had a fit much like a person going into an epileptic attack. He was on the ground in contortions. I have seen and felt the deepest of riveting immobilizing fear. We knew his fit was not made up since it is hard to stage losing all your bodily fluids at once from both ends. We never saw him again.

PHOTO COURTESY OF CHUCK BENNETT

The Air Force would drop 350 and 500 pound bombs at night and pock mark the landscape with holes ten to fifteen feet deep and some times fifty feet across with a shallow pond as seen here from a helicopter.

Constantly Breaking in the New Guys

After only a few weeks on line I found the experienced men did not want to get to know the new guys for a number of reasons. It took a week or so to find out if the "FNG" (f-ing new guy) would fight, walk anybody's slack (protect your backside)—and get you killed, or was he to be trusted. Very demoralizing for the new guy to find that fellow soldiers had no interest in his welfare.

My first few enemy encounters went OK; nobody got hurt and we were maneuvering squads pretty well. I felt a developing trust among most of the platoon. It was about this time that our Battalion ran into what we were told was a Battalion-sized Viet Cong Base. It took some two or three days of constant pounding to clean it out, and the Battalion ran out of their resupply of Captains to be company commanders. That is when I found out I was the senior Lieutenant in the Battalion.

First of Five Times as Company Commander

My Delta Company Commander happened to be the senior Captain in the Battalion. He and I began the first of five occasions while I was a field officer for me to move to Delta Company Commander and Captain McCoy to move to command the company who needed a replacement. This meant I had four platoons and two RTO's, one for Battalion net and one for my company network. Platoon Leaders get only what the Company Commander passes along from the nightly review and planning meeting with the Battalion CO and his team nightly—in the big tent.

The "big tent" usually had four by five foot map boards with acetate overlays full of pins, flags and pointers with "the Big Guy" sitting at the table up front and all "Need to Know" people in folding chairs throughout, just like in the movies. I wish I could say we learned really important information here. Here again I was the FNG and I paid very close attention, writing furiously. What you soon find is that the meeting was all about best guessing from intelligence tidbits collected locally and from Brigade or Division level S2. This was the first time I could see the names of whole valleys and territories, theatres of operation—not that I could remember much of it. Nor did it seem to matter. What mattered was where we were going tomorrow and to accomplish what? How were we going to get there and where all the friendlies were. Where was base camp going to be that night?

Keeping to Our Priorities

Others would, and did, argue that killing VC was the Company Commanders biggest job. I found the biggest job to be how I maneuvered my platoons and kept contact with the Battalion's companies on my left and right. All of this was first to keep us from ever mistakenly shooting at each other which happened more than a few times. Second was killing VC. What brings this message home was when the Company Commander has to write that last letter home to Mom and Dad explaining just why and how their Johnny was killed.

The NVA's (North Vietnamese Army's) Ideal Fight—End of the Day, Surprise, Dense Foliage, Ambush, Lots of Wounded

I think it was my second time as CO of Delta when our company was on the very left flank of a Battalion sweep across a mostly grassy swamp-like area. It was a rather dry area, at the time, with dotted areas of woods. We were coming up on a solid woodline as sunset approached. We began the tedious hacking into brush to keep us all visually on line and in sight. My third platoon was hit with ferocious firing as everyone hit the ground. Suddenly second and fourth platoon were also getting fire and we knew we were up against something big. While each platoon had a point man at the front of an upside down wide "V" formation, third platoon had arrived upon the NVA obliquely and at least four were down and not responding, and more were slightly wounded.

Third platoon radioed that we were almost on top of them and couldn't pull back because we couldn't leave our wounded. We couldn't call in artillery. This was a full in-your-teeth DO SOMETHING. It would be dark in about an hour. "Delta three calling six, over." Roger three, watcha got, over?" "I can see the bunker clearly in front of us and want to take it, over." "Have you intel on your left and right, over?" "No, we are maneuvering right to get out of direct fire and plan to attack from the side, over" "Where's 3-5 (his platoon sergeant, second in command), over." "Don't know—he's not responding, over." "Be sure you've got a number two to support you as you get in position, ID your squads, call before you go in there, out." "Roger, out." Just to help me keep a clear head, the

Battalion CO is yelling on the other net, "Delta Six, Delta Six, Mustang Six, What the hell is going on?"

I have read that all officers were rotated in combat areas in order that all officers possible could attain the much treasured Combat Infantry Badge (CIB). I know of no policy like that except for Battalion level Commanders. The Army was full of Colonels desperate to get combat experience. This one was a true hot shot that craved contact with the enemy and was literally on top of any action in his little glass bowl helicopter as fast as he could get there. Amazingly he never got hit and it wasn't because Charlie wasn't trying.

Since we are in contact with the enemy, and they are well dug in and not maneuvering, it matters little what you say over the net. It's history unfolding and there is nothing Charlie can do with the info in time to change the outcome. Charlie Company, on our immediate right begins a flanking action to scissor that side as Bravo and Alpha companies are maneuvered toward our left. There was really little hope they would make it there by dark.

My third platoon leader had been with us at least a month longer than I, and I felt he was experienced. Charging a bunker seemed nuts to me, but he felt strongly he could do it successfully. I could only imagine the rage and adrenaline the rest of his men felt. All my platoons were continuing to move forward slowly, with my fourth platoon now also taking casualties. Making sure Second Platoon would not be firing to their left flank, I let third platoon attack. The Lieutenant and his Platoon Sergeant both died in that assault. Bullets crack as they pass within feet as I continue crawling forward against this bunker complex. Not two minutes later the glass bubble lands and the Commander is standing over me wanting a report. I'm thinking this dumb b ____ is going to get shot as sure as I'm kneeling here giving my report. From above he had seen the NVA disappear into tunnels as fast as the action had started. He informs me, "Good job, Captain McCoy is assuming command again. A new Captain is on the nightly resupply to take over Bravo Six." Whew, fine by me.

It's raining. As usual for Wolfhounds, it doesn't matter. At this "Stand Down," the Chaplain is commemorating the almost thirty Wolfhounds who have given up their young lives in the past number of weeks. We are reminded that for every death usually five more have been wounded.

Bronze Star with V Device

I was very near 4th platoon and told my Platoon Sergeant I was back again, and asked who is missing? Two that he knew of. Based on the Battalion CO's comments, I told him to pull our men back and I was going forward to find the missing men. One of them was one of our married men, with four kids. Because I asked for volunteers, I could not get anyone to go with me. It was pitch black when I found the second man and pulled them both out. Both were dead.

It was intense putting out our claymores, trip wires, flares in the pitch black. Then whiteness with wide-area night flares while we were digging sleeping pits and sand bagging at least the sides for some protection. Nobody got much sleep that night. The next morning we swept a sizeable underground base camp and hospital with paraphernalia strewn everywhere. Evidently they had evacuated rapidly—probably at the beginning of our sweep early the day before—and left a sizeable force to ambush us as we appeared sure to stumble on their camp.

My Platoon Sergeant wrote me up for a medal which I received at our next Stand-Down—Bronze Star for Valor. My Platoon Sergeant, an E6, career man, and the married man who died, were both twenty-six. A few weeks later I find out the most thorough soldier anyone could ask for, my platoon sergeant, had successfully pulled enough strings to get him off line. Good for him, lousy for us. I became the oldest man in my platoon—age twenty!

Working with Burnout and Draftees

There is a horror of war that is rarely talked about because it is so inhumane to those back in the states who are cool, comfortable, and rested, on the couch. Day after day of rarely more than four hours sleep, merged with moments of high levels of fear and sudden death around the corner has a definite effect. As new fast friends are instantly removed with a sniper bullet or land mine, the rage builds. America's draftee Army is trained and built to fight a conventional war where massive firepower and men en mass can sweep through and overcome obstacles.

Stand Down was also the time to award medals. 1Lt. Chuck Bennett receives his Bronze Star for Valor from Lt. Colonel Condina. Fellow Platoon Leader 2Lt. Roger Horn (r) stands ready to receive a medal too.

But in Vietnam, we are a rather noisy, large group of men that may surprise Charlie through a rapid helicopter assault or otherwise. But once on the ground, Charlie's' spies are everywhere and we are very soon found out, and watched. Charlie learns how to hit and disappear quickly while we can only react like a big bull swatting a fly. But this fly is able to stick us like a Spanish Picador. And we soon become enraged. Having been in similar territory at about the same time, I can very well feel what must have been going on in the minds of court-martialed Lt. Calley and his platoon for atrocities at My Lai. It is not pretty. It is a horror to me now to remember that American troops can so quickly begin to think along those lines.

They say the soldier finds God in the foxhole. I would suggest it must also be a Supreme Being that the soldier believes in. We must believe in a God above us, not a "natures god" or that we are ourselves godlike that we have our own morals because we are atheist or agnostic. These beliefs lead us to the situation Calley's men soon found themselves. This is where the Fascist and Socialistic "Nazi" (meaning National Socialists) took too many of us.

When You No Longer Care...

It is incredible to know that even in this fearful environment some of the men began not to care about living or dying. I think some Prisoners-of-War react this way. One particularly hot dusty day, before the Monsoon rains, we were crossing dried-up rice paddies obliquely heading toward a very tall, thickly-treed hedgerow. As the first crack went by our heads I looked right to see our Company Artillery Forward Observer take a bullet in the neck, collapse and die almost immediately. You'd have thought everyone would instantly drop behind the nearest ridge that divides the paddies into rectangles that usually hold the water for the fields of rice.

Many did try to shovel dirt with their nose. A number just kept walking as if in a trance. I had to yell to get them down. As platoon leader, I asked my best machine gunner to move further left to get a better strafing field of fire across the front of us as we moved toward the firing coming from the trees. He slowly stood up, grabbed a few bandoleers from others and slowly plodded fully upright to the next rice paddy over, plopped down and started short bursts obliquely into the treeline. I had men actually holding their arms up hoping for that slow-healing "million dollar wound" that would send a bullet through a bone guaranteeing a quick trip back to the "world."

"Naaa, that's too incredible."

One really hot and sticky burn-out-day we had been crossing swampy miles of lousy area. We are struggling up onto the embankment of a dirt road and from out of nowhere a bright red 1965 Mustang, with ragtop down, goes roaring by about sixty with a young American guy and girl, smiling bright and hair blowing in the wind like a TV commercial. In a flash they were gone. "Did you see that?" "Naaa, that's too incredible. Didn't happen."

Bigger VC Base Camp and a Purple Heart

My platoon literally stumbled upon a Viet Cong bicycle manufacturing, storing and repairing facility near the

Cambodian Border. We got our platoon picture all on bicycles in the military Stars & Stripes newspaper, and our Company spent a few days clearing extensive underground rooms. A few days later we came upon a huge stockpile of rice. How big was it you say? It was easily the size of a three-bedroom American suburbia house in width and length including a pitched roof! Now how do you destroy that much rice? We reported it and left that problem to others higher up. Hopefully it went to hungry "good guys." We knew we were in the thickest of Viet Cong Country and were taking our careful time.

Want to manage this surly bunch? Bennett's platoon makes the Stars & Stripes military newspaper with this photo taken by S&S photographer after a soldier stepped into a huge underground bicycle factory. We bad, we nationwide!

Next we came upon a lightly forested but very brushy and viney area that was like a huge briar patch. You couldn't see very far and it was very slow hacking our way. Couldn't we just go around it. No, Charlie could be in here—and he was big time! We had to go with each platoon in two single files in sight of each other and in sight of the platoon on either side. Keeping my platoon together was easier than keeping contact with platoons on either side as they often moved away from you at the same time. As you see yourself losing contact, you want others to slow down and there's a lot of phone talk about who's losing whom and how to correct it. The day quickly wears away in time and frustration. I only learn later that we were again almost on top of another Viet Cong Base Camp as the firing erupts when the first grenades are lobbed our way. Again, we are caught on Charlie's terms, at the end of the day.

Bleeding from the Mouth—Not a Good Sign

My first reaction is remembering one of Charlie's tricks is to pop up out of a tunnel, and fire or throw a grenade in opposite directions to get two sets of friendlies to start firing at each other, both thinking they are firing at the enemy. While we had never experienced it, we had sure heard about it happening often enough. I instantly keyed the net (keeping the talk button held down) yelling, "Stop firing, I think you're shooting at us!" Two more grenades landed right in the middle of our platoon. One next to my squad leaders foot as I watched most of it disappear and felt something hit my chest. "Lieutenant, Lieutenant, you've got blood coming out of your mouth!" "Get me the Platoon Sergeant," I said taking my map out of the plastic case and handing the compass and map to my RTO whom I had taught to use.

After making sure we were not firing on each other, our return fire became voracious as the platoon moved the fight past me and forward toward what I later learned was a very large entrenched base camp. In my mind, it could not have been more cleverly located and protected from the Americans. The difference was—we were Wolfhounds! We go anywhere.

The sun was giving up its last large throws of light as machetes were chopping away the underbrush and tree branches overhead. I could hear the chopper coming and could only hope it was a Medevac for the wounded. Through the continual sporadic firing it hovered overhead and turned on its spotlight and then abruptly pulled away as the machete chopping intensified. The chopper must have taken rounds; possibly the area was not big enough to land. Soon enough the thundering noise and dust was back, with night spotlight on that said "shoot me, shoot me." This time the Medevac landed on the ground almost upon us.

A Mental WHAM!

Over and over I think; relax, stay calm. The less blood you move the less you lose. I'm lucky in one small way; there is little pain with this sucking chest wound. I try to go comatose mentally as the helicopter lifts off into the night. Now I don't need to think about the safety of my men, or tactics. Just concentrate on myself, on staying alive. The damp sweaty air changed to cool and refreshing as the helicopter rose quickly way up and over the fighting. I was on the lowest litter in there, and through the open doors, I felt gifted as another sunset winked momentarily through the darkening cloud strata and blessed my eyes as we headed toward even more people who might also help save my life.

Any soldier may be a bit off on exact details of life in a combat zone over many months, but when you think you are dying—even thirty plus years later, you can still distinctly remember almost every moment. Did they get my Squad leader on board with his blown away foot? How about the two others with shrapnel wounds that I know of? It didn't matter now, even though I cared a lot. I had just been taken out of the picture. I held my plastic map case over my chest hole to keep the air bubbles from coming out. I didn't know much about first aid but I knew that wasn't good. I could still taste the blood in my throat. I figured I was dying and because I wasn't in great pain and I wondered what I should be thinking about? You may laugh—there are lots of ways for every one of us to freely choose to go out of this world. In hindsight, I had a real carnival of thoughts as a twenty-year old. Mostly because that was my life up until then. This was my first experience with death. I had really thought I was becoming invincible. WHAM, did I have an epiphany!

Dustoff to Cu Chi and the 25th Division's 12th Medevac Hospital

I was in somebody else's hands now. I had done my duty. Now I could only hope that others would do theirs.

The Medevac helicopter dropped on the pad with a thud. Hands grabbed my rack out of the copter and I was on a gurney being wheeled into the Cu Chi 12th Medevac intensive care tent within seconds of landing. God, I thought, it doesn't get better than this. I'll be under a Doctors' stethoscope in minutes. And there I lay in a corridor of connected tents.

While I was the most important, with a sucking chest wound, to require a helicopter medevac—blown off feet don't count enough for helicopter pilots to risk their lives in a hot fire zone—here, I wasn't so important. I was somehow triaged off to another line of gurneys because, I guess, I hadn't turned a pasty yellow yet. After a long while, an "I don't care—I'm too tired"—looking nurse stabbed a thermometer in my mouth as she continued through the tents of human wreckage. I felt as though I was in basic training again. How do I make myself important? I don't look devastated. I'm a whole person yet I've got this hole in my chest and I'm afraid to move around too much.

So, I just lay there. I'm just one on a gurney among two haphazard rows of gurneys with an isle down the middle. Hours seem to go by as others are selectively interviewed and moved forward. Finally someone with a foreign accent suddenly appears in my face with a clipboard. "Who are you?" I tell him. "What is wrong with you?" I've been hit through the chest with shrapnel from a grenade. Uneeremoniously he says I must know where the shrapnel has gone and immediately sticks his index finger deep into my chest. I barely feel a thing. He says nothing and leaves.

Intensive Care

I am moved to intensive care; I guess it was near midnight. Really, I am moved into the house of horrors.

They assume I've lost a lot of blood. My arm is plumbed with big needles attached to bottles on a stand. After awhile I can no longer lie in bed. My night nurse brings me a stool to sit on so I can prop myself against pillows at the top of my bed which has been cranked to an upright angle. We get to know each other. She is a saint, a sweetheart, and a true soldier. I don't think I've seen a Doctor yet. Maybe Mister Fingerpoker was a Doctor? So this is how it is at the end of the line. I'm feeling very expendable. I'm thrown in this trash heap called an intensive care ward and forgotten. Nobody thinks about this part. Hours go by. I still can't sleep. Finally, my leaky lungs seem to settle down and I slowly get into this sitting upright bed and finally sleep deeply.

The House of Horrors

I slowly awake to the dim morning light in this intensive care Quonset Hut (a half circle of all corrugated roof building on a plywood floor about a foot off the dirt). The smell is indescribable—a cross between maybe scented bleach and a sickly sweet death odor after a few hours in the heat. A large tall Black man, maybe 240 pounds is wheeled in on a gurney with his right arm propped up about thirty degrees wrapped in gauze between splints. His whole right side is also wrapped up. They put him directly across from me. He seems barely conscious and they pull a privacy curtain around him.

A rocket hit his locker and blew him off his cot right here in Cu Chi base camp. They took the arm off before he went to Japan.

I look up and down the line and am just shocked at the look of imminent death over a long room with so many faces staring at the ceiling—so pasty and yellow. I learned that no matter how serious the wound, if the soldier wasn't allowed to acclimate his new wound in Vietnam for a few days, he would surely die in the Japan hospital that they used to be immediately flown to. After "draining the wound" for a time, they could be flown out and have a better chance of survival.

A Viet Cong is Lying in a Bed Next to Me

As I looked to my immediate left I see a Vietnamese boy, who couldn't be more than fourteen years old. Both legs were gone right up to his groin area. The gauze wrappings were saturated and oozing like so many others in this room. His seemed more so. I looked to see a soldier stationed at the foot of his bed with an M16 with a full magazine locked and loaded in the weapon. This was not normally allowed inside the base camp. I smiled and asked the soldier why he thought such security was necessary for someone with no legs? I was told that he had already tried to escape twice and the second time he got away over a quarter mile.

Why We Lost the Vietnam War

Twenty some years after my Vietnam experience there was a long article in the Sunday Los Angeles Times about how the Vietnam War couldn't happen again mostly because of business trends. This was also when candidate Clinton was saying, "It's the economy stupid!" I wrote an editorial, that they printed, wherein I remembered my bedside young Viet Cong. Hitler knew it, FDR knew it, Ho Chi Min knew it, this Viet Cong kid was an example of it— It's not about big business, it's the hearts and minds of the people—stupid!

The only alternative to convincing people is to bang them back to the stone age. This is what we came close to in World War II. It is a little known fact that the German people where reduced to wearing paper clothes and eating only rutabagas in some areas. The frustrated civilian population rebelled; that helped force that war to stop. It is the attitude of the folks at home that finally matter.

My Lung Fills up with Blood

As my first day in intensive care wears along I'm taken into a darkened room and laid onto a platform bed that looks like it could take a full body x-ray with the huge machine looming over it. They find a small piece of shrapnel under my shoulder blade. They decide to leave it. Later in the day my breathing becomes noticeably shorter. In fact I am now taking many short breaths just lying in bed. A deep breadth is impossible. This information finally gets some hospital staff excited about me. I'm moved out on another gurney to a pre-prep area outside the operating room.

Blood Spurts Everywhere

I finally see a Doctor. He says we have to drain at least one lung. We are going to put a tube between your ribs up into your lower lung cavity. I'm sitting up on the gurney with my legs hanging over. He says take a deep breath, hold and push from inside your chest. I have another sweet nurse in front of me who I can tell is watching me carefully to see how I react. She talks pleasantly to me as the Doctor sticks a knife between my back ribs and slips in a plastic hose. As I push air from inside blood is spurting out my chest hole. The young and pretty nurse is talking casually as she cups her hands in front of me to catch my erupting blood that spurts everywhere and is contained nowhere. I think, how messy this all is, yet how relaxing, they are all keeping me without any medication. Back to intensive care I go, thinking how primitive my hospital care has been.

Next day I was feeling better. My chest hole gets sutured up. A few days later I'm allowed to walk around outside, still with a tube in my back and arm rolling the IV stand with me. My Battalion Commander, Colonel Condina, stops by. He offers me the dream of every career Lieutenant—Command of a front line Company—a Captains position. I liked Colonel Condina from the day he arrived. He didn't know I was in this man's Army to sooner get on with my art career. More importantly, I had just re-realized how fragile life is. Since he offered rather than assigned, I respectfully asked to decline the offer. I was surprised at the surprised look on Condina's face. I saw that he thought I would leap at the offer because I had been so thoroughly gung-ho Army up to this point.

HQ CO 1/27 Wolfhounds, Bn Rear Cdr

The next day I shuffle around the outside on wood planked walkways dragging my wheeled IV bottles just to get away from all the intense misery for a little while. I find out that I'm HQ CO and will be running convoys as soon as I can report back. Wow, even though I will have a lot more responsibility, at least I'm off line.

Signing My Life Away, Again?

Headquarters Commanding Officer I quickly found to be a nerve wracking responsibility. I signed papers assuming control of over a million dollars of equipment. Equipment lists were pages and pages of items like the entire motor pool and all the vehicles; the medics in every line company were my responsibility; all the medical support in the Battalion; mortars; ammo of all types; all types of one of a kind equipment that a Battalion must have; all our resupply stuff. And all of this strewn all over a war zone. I was thinking how could I even inspect even a tenth of this list?

My head in hands, "Oh me, oh my" thoughts and it only got worse when a short heavy set ever ebullient Sgt Gratz dropped by my office, a tent with a wood floor and gray desk, and smacked a fifth of Johnny Walker on the desk. He said, "Yes sir, Lieutenant Bennett, everything's goin' to be jus' fine!" This is my Supply Sergeant? Is this how you join ranks with the Vietnam Mafia?

My First Sergeant turned out to be the perfect match-up for me. He had seventeen more years in the service than I was old! Nobody messed with him. He would find out where I was going to go snooping around next and he'd go over and usually get it squared away before I got there.

We had Inspector General inspections stateside that always made everyone stiffen up and get everything squeaky clean and accounted for. I couldn't believe they were going to inspect us, an infantry line Battalion during combat! They did and we got a special letter of commendation. I understand it had been the first one for a combat arm in the whole 25th Division since they had arrived in

Country. Well, I like to think that. It was a tremendous amount of work by a lot of overworked soldiers.

How to Run Truck Convoys —Untimely and Fast!

My new job also included running truck convoys to the forward base camp whenever they were within driving distance. Convoys out of Cu Chi were always dicey since it was located at the bottom end of the NVA's Ho Chi Minh Trail that came down through Cambodia. I soon enough decided to be the Jeep driver and put my driver in the deadlier jump seat, usually with an M60 machine gun. He liked that. The first time we tried it, we folded the hinged windshield forward out over the hood and laid a few sand bags there to prop the gun on. I don't think we were out the front gate before the glass shattered.

PHOTO COURTESY OF CHUCK BENNETT

Rather than be in the jump seat looking like an officer to be pot shot at, I preferred having more control as driver and let my driver carry an M60 in that hot seat.

The Motor Pool Warrant Officer, some thirty years my senior, was always on my case since I led the convoy on asphalted, but heavily pot-holed roads. I only had one speed—fast. As long as the convoy held together, we were OK. Truck maintenance was hellish and a broken Jeep window just gave him more verbal juice, "You damn hippie types are all alike..." I reminded him, "Wasn't that your crowd that was swallowing live goldfish?" We actually got along well, he loved to complain. As soon as we hit the dirt roads two trucks, with added steel plates and sand bags under the seats, would take over the lead.

These drivers were excellent with keen eyes and we missed hitting most mines by simply going off-road at times.

Two Man Copter, "The glass bubble!"

When the Base Camp was farther forward I would often meet the two man chopper that the Battalion CO flew around in, when it came back to Cu Chi Base for gas. I'd take mail, new maps and intel reports out and often spend the night. The chopper always went back to Cu Chi since it couldn't be left to suffer the many nightly mortar attacks.

Our Battalion Commander flew in this LOH (Light Observ. Helo.—also called a Loach). He would oversee his troop movements throughout the day with no return firepower capability. Possibly the most dangerous thing to be in at times, in Vietnam. Hit this—your down! Bennett, as Headquarters CO and Battalion Rear Commander would come out on this Chopper and often go back to Cu Chi main base on it at the end of the day, or on refueling trips.

The chopper pilots were all crazy, young and adventurous. After a super dull day of sky taxiing the "Old Man" around, they would look at me climbing in with the wry smile, flared nostril, hairy eyebrow—and those eyeshades. The copter would barely be off the ground before he would turn it 90 degrees and aim it at the base of a hundred foot high hedgerow. He would hop over that at the last minute and take me for a Disney E-Ticket ride down on the deck of any nearby waterways lined with huge trees and follow the twisty turns in the general direction of Division Base Camp. He's looking more at me for my reaction than he is where he is going! I guess short of filling my pants, I made his day.

If we kept moving our forward base camp every few days, we were not usually mortared. On these overnight occasions I didn't have a foxhole, so I would sleep near the Battalion HQ Support Bunker. This was usually a shallow hole with dirt-filled ammo boxes on the sides and fence stakes over most of the top with two or three layers of sand bags on top of that. A direct hit on this, even with the smaller 61 mm mortars, would be devastating. I usually slept next to the chow line between the hot/cold food storage lockers for some side protection.

This particular base camp had not been mortared and I suspected a couple soldiers in the HQ tent next to me had been drinking or otherwise were very non-caring. The late night wump, wump, wump of mortars being launched had me up well off the ground and running on this very still night. Looking to my left, there was one of the soldiers about six feet away leaning against the side of the tent, unmoving, with a sleepy smirk on his face. I would have reached the bunker OK except I was running the wrong way. Having lain down with my head away from the bunker, you instinctively roll over and up and run towards your head as you wake up.

Mortars are like grenades—you've got about ten seconds after you first hear them. A quick 180 degrees and I literally dove into the bunker smacking my head and arms into a groaning pile of men. Afterwards, as I rolled over, an officer pointed up to the roof and the horizontal support stakes, the end of one which I had barely missed impaling my head while diving in, in the dark.

Afterwards, the soldier leaning on the tent was still there—very dead. His buddy inside was wounded badly.

When Your Mind Starts Shutting You Down

Feelings and emotions are often very different in actual combat as part of a fighting force versus simply witnessing combat around you. When you don't have an important combat job your personal fear level is likely to go way up there. Being an Infantry Officer, if you are doing your job, you are completely occupied with maneuvering your men to fight well, as well as their welfare. All soldiers have detailed and particular functions to complete and are moving and working as a team. I found as HQ CO Forward I had only a few support people I needed to work with and no real combat role other than being available to fill in where needed. As artillery flack, mortars and rounds come flying through camp I, on occasion, had too much time to think about myself. You can feel yourself freezing into immobility and the mental struggle you have to go through—like awakening from a particularly horrifying dream that you must awake fully from. Back to reality, action and movement.

The Infamous TET Offensive Hits

Lt. Colonel Condina's six month rotation time was up and a new Battalion Commander was on board. One of his first duties was to bring as much of his Battalion Staff to the Forward Base Camp as possible.- All his S1,S2,S3 & S4, their assistants and most of their equipment and radio gear. "To be better connected with the war!" This left me as the only Officer for the Battalion back at Cu Chi, 25th Division Base Camp.

It started as just another mortar attack on Cu Chi. The dense forest all around for miles had been knocked down with huge heavy equipment so you could see long distances in every direction. I often wondered if that was smart. I'm told the VC use this knocked down area like Brer Rabbits briar patch as new growth spurted up through the downed trees lying there. They began sending us rockets the size of telephone poles. They would cradle these self propelled missiles on the fallen trees and send them erratically into our Base Camp. No bunker I'd seen could withstand their direct hit. This night their bombardment went on for hours and numerous VC sappers popped up, for the first time, from tunnels well within our huge perimeter. I didn't find out about this until the next day. I was far too busy concentrating on moving our Battalion. As we left the bunker we saw next to us a huge forty foot diameter by fifteen foot deep hole that had been our HQ EM living quarters hooch about twenty feet away. Luckily all those men were at the forward battalion base camp or in our bunker.

PHOTO COURTESY OF CHUCK BENNETT

Doing a Major's job, 1st Lieutenant Bennett and a skeleton crew at Wolfhound Battalion Rear accomplished miracles doing never before attempted sorties, sending huge amounts of Battalion supplies Northward, and back again rapidly during the 1968 Tet Offensive.

Thus Began 60 Hours of No Sleep

Intelligence reporting went ballistic with the massive attacks going on throughout the Country. The Wolfhounds were assigned to go way up North to Pleiku. For those at the Forward Base Camp this meant gathering their gear as usual and boarding helicopters. For us at Battalion Rear, this was a whole different monster. Pleiku was a plane ride away. Battalion didn't know how long we would be there and they wanted to be prepared. They wanted massive amounts of resupply. This meant huge sling loads hooked to the belly of huge Chinook double-bladed helicopters that were also full of troops taking off not from Cu Chi, but from Tan Son Nuht Airbase next to Saigon. My skeleton crew worked like the exhausted maniacs we all became. All of us doing jobs we had never done before. No sooner do we get to Pleiku and bed down the Battalion around 0200 in the morning when the word comes down to break camp, we are going back!

Watching Soldiers Die in the Butcher Shop

There is something almost as bad as the anguish and mentally freezing in combat. That is getting a radio call that the Wolfhounds are fighting Charlie, and Dustoffs (helicopter Medevacs) from my old Delta Company are coming in. My job became identification of dead and wounded as well as contacting relatives and next-of-kin. We were always visiting and helping our wounded in intensive care. My route during these emergencies were surgery, intensive care and the morgue.

Surgery was justly called the butcher shop. I watched numerous operations through the plastic portals of the swinging doors into surgery. Sadly, doctors and nurses many times are clueless to the wounds as they receive a barely-alive soldier on their operating table. The procedure far too often was to simply open him up completely. Clothes are completely stripped off. He's sanitized. A nurse takes a shaving type razor and takes off all chest hair in a few blood spurting swipes. The knife comes down from the chest cavity and all the guts are soon out on the table as everyone is looking for shrapnel and holes. A Major had caught a piece of shrapnel the size of a match head into his heart. They never found it and he died. I watched a good friend in my platoon tragically almost make it after being patched up from numerous shrapnel wounds. In their hurry they missed the hole in his back and he died. Life becomes cheaper as you constantly witness this, and a numbness sets in.

Discovering Buddies at the Cu Chi Morgue

The morgue was a large very dark tent even in the daytime because the canvas walls wet from being sprayed.

I would have to wait with tremendous trepidation behind a curtain in an outer room where I could hear the corpses being unloaded. They wouldn't let any direct light in so it was somewhat eerie with water dripping through slippery wet slats of the floors that let the water out rapidly. As I soon enough saw, corpses were still in their fatigues, stiff by now, and propped up in a somewhat standing pose at about a 30-degree angle against posts with angled slabs to support them as men fire-hosed off the grunge and blood of war. I never knew who I would find here and it was gut-wrenching duty almost every time.

Could it get worse? Yes. If I didn't get here soon enough, usually the next day after the sun was up and very hot I would be taken to the corpses loaded into those big shipping containers like you see Semi-trucks hauling on our Freeways. In here, in the dark, unbreathable heat are bodies stacked up in wooden bunks five rows high, one row on each side of the container. I could never force myself to walk more than a few body lengths into the container.

Because it was usually the next day, at least here I usually knew who I was looking for and was somewhat better braced for it.

Writing Those Deceased Letters to the Family

I spent a lot of time researching the reason for a soldier's death and personalized the account as best I could. Often I would get a letter back asking for more information or personal items. I probably wrote some forty of these letters, some of them for line Company Commanders.

Leaving Vietnam, Just as Thankless as Coming

You are supposed to get at least seven days' notice with orders to pack up and process out of Country. You would think the HQ CO could get that handled for himself. I reminded the Bn. CO I was just days and counting. They all seemed oblivious. I had three days left in the Army and I was out loading helicopters with the Forward resupply. I still had no paperwork. After finishing, I went over to this new in-Country Major and handed him my own hand written statement of name rank and serial number (in case anybody cared) and that I was going home and getting out of the Army. I was giving my responsibilities directly to him. Saluted and thanked him for his full name.

I walked out the Cu Chi front gate with a big duffel bag of gear, hitched a ride on a huge earthmover down to Saigon. Put my name in at the Tan Sun Nuht airport for a ride home. I just knew I'd have a problem here. Not so. Onto the plane I went.

Back in the World—a Changed Person

Twenty-some hours later landing and getting off the plane at Oakland California for out processing didn't feel like returning home. The military "hurry-up-and-wait" was still everywhere. The noise was loud as usual in these big hangar areas. Amazingly, Army Out Processing had their copy of my papers that I'd not seen yet. I was supposed to have a final Dental exam. They'd get back to me on that. Sign here sir and you are out of the Army—September 1968.

It was not until I passed through the doors of that noisy hangar and saw my dear Aunt Rita, who lived in San Francisco, and all those new American cars in the parking lot, that it really hit me—I was actually home in one piece.

Crossing the Bay Bridge, in a nice air conditioned car, glimpsing the Golden Gate Bridge and the San Francisco skyline, I inhaled a sob and then couldn't resist crying.

"The period between October 1967-1968, a time coinciding with Chuck Bennett's tour of duty, was the most violent twelve months of the Vietnam War for American forces. Because the 25th Division was so deeply involved from start to finish, they suffered badly. Throughout the war the 25th lost 4,500 men killed, the second highest total suffered by any division in the army."

Dr. Eric Bergerud
Authority on the 25th Division, author of
Red Thunder, Tropic Lightning, and Fire in the Sky

JULIO CONTRERAS

—*FROM A FAMILY OF PATRIOTS*

Freedom is not free. Someone had to pay the price. Periodically, the price must be paid over and over again. Seldom is the cost of freedom equally distributed. Seldom is the price of freedom fairly extracted in proportion to the benefits received in society. The Vietnam War was a political disaster. It was a war in which the pampered and the privileged escaped their duty while patriots bled and died. It was a war in which the shrill rhetoric of the pampered intelligentsia worked at cross-purposes to the ultimate national interest. It was a war in which unbridled and irresponsible freedom of speech almost led to national anarchy. Eventually, the bored, the pampered, and the vocal radicals became a fifth column undermining national unity. But nevertheless, the men and boys who fought in Vietnam as well as Korea established a defense against the contagion of world Communism eventually leading to the collapse of the "evil empire."

Family Roots That Go Way Back!

My family came from the early colonists who settled California during the days when Spain ruled this area. The family came from three different backgrounds of warrior races: the Yaqui, the Apache, and Spanish conquistadors. My mother was born in Santa Ana, my father was born in Los Angeles, and they met in Carpinteria. I was the second child, and the first boy. They had six boys and one girl. My brother Manuel was only eleven months younger than I was, so we were really close. We were together through everything.

Tuberculosis=Quarantine for Mom =Foster Home for the Children

Our father died when I was twelve years old, and our mother had to go to the hospital with tuberculosis. Back in those days, they quarantined you for three or four years when you came down with TB, so we had to be put into foster homes.

My bother Manuel and I went to live with a woman named Elizabeth Barnes. She was responsible for putting me on the right track, for the most part. She showed me how to believe in myself. She fostered many children on her ranch. I think that there were about eight kids there when I was with her, all sets of brothers.

Tennis Team Captain Helped Prove My Worth

Since we lived on a ranch, I had to milk cows and do chores. We had to make the ranch work. Anyway, she was the reason why I decided to play tennis. She encouraged me and I practiced real hard, and I made the team the first year. The second year I became the number three player, and the third year, I became the captain of the team! She made me realize that I could do anything that I really wanted to, and that really changed me.

Dumpster Diver Turns up a Millionaire

When I graduated from high school, I left my foster home because my foster mother wouldn't let me have a car. I was seventeen years old. She went into Solvang to get some pastries, and I jumped in my car and took off. I slept in my car in Santa Barbara that night. The next morning I got up and went to look for a job. On my way, I walked past an old man who was digging in the dumpster. I thought he was a bum or something, and I said, "Good morning!" He grumbled, "What's so good about it! What do you want?" I started to back away, and then I decided, "No, I'm not going to let him do that to me!" So I went back and said, "My name is Julio, what's yours?" He turned around and he had a smile on his face. He said, "I'm John Lutkenhouse." He shook my hand, and it turns out, that he was a millionaire! He was looking for lumber for one of his companies.

Julio Contreras (left) with his Mother and brothers at Camp Pendleton California, 1967—during happier days before three brothers would pass away.

He then asked me to go hire six men to build a home for him on the Riviera in Santa Barbara. At first I thought he was kidding! I didn't know then he was a millionaire. All I knew was that he was digging in the dumpster. I told him that I didn't have any experience building houses, but he said, "It doesn't matter, you want to learn don't you?" So, I hired some men and managed the project for him. I learned all the skills of building a house, although I honed in on the electrical end of it.

Need a Little Discipline? Try the Marines

After working for him for a couple of years, I decided to go into the Marines. He didn't want me to go into the Marines; neither did my foster mother, Mrs. Barnes. I needed an outlet though because I had started to get into trouble with the gang of guys I hung around with. I saw some violent stabbings and shooting, and things of that nature. I knew I needed to get out of there and into something with some discipline. The Marines did the trick. It saved me. It gave me discipline, I got to travel, and I got to serve my country.

Brother John was the First One Killed in Nam

My little brother followed me in the Marines. John was the first one to go, and he was killed in Vietnam. He was in Khe Sahn on a patrol and was ambushed. The whole unit was wiped out. It was very, very difficult for the whole family because he was only eighteen years old. He had always made us laugh. He had his hopes and dreams just like all of us, and he was a great photographer. I had only been back from Vietnam for a month when he was killed, and up until that time, the family didn't understand the seriousness of war.

Next was My Brother Charlie

Charlie was the best Marine I had ever seen. Out of his class of 300 Marines, he was #1. There was nothing he couldn't do, and that's why he became a drill instructor. He went to Vietnam with the air wing and was on a helicopter. He made it back alive. But shortly after he made it back, a drunk driver killed him. He was 26 years old, young, and extremely athletic. We had been very close.

Then Brother David

Then my brother David went into the Marines and was an MP at Camp Pendleton. He spent four years in the service, then got out and got a degree. He wanted to go back into security. But he came down with a kidney infection and he died from it at the age of 35. So I only have two brothers left.

My First Tour, Gulf of Tonkin, 1964

My first tour was "sea duty" aboard an aircraft carrier in the Gulf of Tonkin. I was attached to a Marine unit over there, and we handled the brig. We escorted all the top figures. Generals, Admirals, etc. My job was to train pilots in weaponry in case they were captured. If they were shot down, all they could rely upon was their little 38 revolver. I was an expert with a 45, so I trained them. I also did funeral details for the pilots who were shot down. The first time I went over to Vietnam, I went over on an aircraft carrier. It was November 1964.

Fire Team Leader with the New 5th Marines

After eighteen months I was sent back to Camp Pendleton, where I became cadre in the newly organized Fifth Marine Division. I was assigned as a radioman and later as a fire team leader with a rank of Corporal.

A fire team in the Marines is a basic element of every marine squad with three fire teams making up the total squad.

"We Reported You Dead!"

We then shipped out to the Philippines where I trained in underwater demolitions and as a scout swimmer, which was an equivalent to a modern day Navy Seal. From the ship we would get on a raft, go into shore, and find the most comfortable, safest spot for the troops to land. The first time we did it, I got lost! They let us off at 3 0'clock in the morning, and it was pitch-dark. The guys who I was with all got separated because the current was so strong. Luckily, I was able to find them, but when I got there, they said that they had reported me as dead. I said, "Well, as you can see, I'm alive!"

I also instructed sailors in "drown proofing" and rescue procedures. I would be dropped off four miles at sea, scout for a safe landing area, and direct rescue of ship personnel.

While on R&R, the Whole Village is Burnt to the Ground

While I was there, I met a girl who was the daughter of the mayor of a little town called San Miguel, just outside the military base. I was on R&R, so I went to her village with her. The people lived in little huts made out of sticks. Anyway, I went back to the base to get my pay, and while I was gone, the village was overrun by HUKS who were their equivalent of Communist guerrillas. They had burnt the entire village to the ground, taken all of their belongings, and killed some people. This had happened over and over, and the people were just desperate. When I returned, the Mayor came up to me and pleaded with me, "Julio, will you please teach us how to fight? We will give you all the fish that you want; that's all we can give you, because we have nothing else." I felt so badly for them, because these people had lost everything. I said that I would teach them.

I spent quite a bit of time with them and I taught them everything that the Marines had taught me. I was fortunate that I had gone to get my pay that day, or I might have been killed there in the Philippines. You just never know.

Jungle Training by Moros

While we were there, the Moros trained us in jungle warfare. We actually fought against them earlier in the Spanish American War. But they were very knowledgeable about survival in the jungle. It was very enlightening because we would be going to the jungles of Vietnam. They taught all of us who had O-311 status, which meant that we were going to be going into the front lines as infantry.

Second Tour, Defending DaNang Airbase

It was late 1965, or early 1966, when I was sent back to Vietnam to defend the DaNang Airbase. My second tour of duty consisted of aggressive patrols with occasional firefights, sniping, and mortar fire. The casualty rates were mainly due to daily sniping and mortar attacks rather than from major assaults. During that tour, I started as a rifleman, and then worked my way up to fire team leader. Then I became the squad leader before being sent back to the States.

A Third Tour? Friendship Matters...

I went over to Vietnam twice, and I was getting ready to go over for a third time because I was so close to the guys in my unit. We had been through so much together, and I wanted to be with them when they went back. I could count on them, and they could count on me.

There is no skin color when you are in a situation like that. My best friend was white. He was from Wisconsin. His name was Richard Siegler. We were such good friends. He ended up getting his shoulder blown off over there, but he made it out. He actually moved to Los Angeles to live, just to be close to me. That's how close we were after going through everything together over there in Vietnam and in the Philippines as well.

I had another friend named Usury. When I was getting ready to reenlist, he came up to me and said, "Julio, don't do it. You have been over there twice. You have more than done your time, don't do it." I said, "I guess you're right." He said, "I know I'm right!" He talked me out of it. He really did a sales pitch on me! If it hadn't been for him, I would have gone back.

War and Patriotism Seems to be a Cycle

A lot of people couldn't handle the violence of war, and I can understand why. Most people over there were brought up without violence. But I had seen a lot of action here before I ever went over there, which ended up being a plus for me. The violence wasn't shocking to me. The difference was that I wasn't getting arrested in Vietnam. I was serving my Country instead of trying to stir up trouble for my own selfish needs. The experience really gave me a new focus, and it woke me up!

Patriotism was gone for so long in this Country, and I think it is coming back. I can't tell you how sick I was because of the apathy. Upon arrival at the airport in Goleta, we were treated like dirt. In my United States Marine uniform with my hard-earned ribbons, I stepped out on Hollister Street. People were cursing at me, giving me the middle finger.- So many men have been lost; had died to defend what we have here. Then to not appreciate it, it just killed me. We used to march in the parade and people wouldn't stand, or clap. I was wondering, "What's happening? What's going on? Don't they realize why they are blessed with what they have?" You want to make them aware, but you can't.

People Learn Appreciation From Devastation

Unfortunately, people learn from devastation. I know that I learned from it. I mean, my brothers, they are true heroes. They gave their lives for this Country, for me, for our family. I know that there are many loved ones out there who have given their lives for their families. I just want people to know that we are thankful for what they have done for us. They served for us even when they could have come up with a good reason not to.

One of my brothers could have had a good reason for not going. It would have been very easy for me, or them to go to Canada or Mexico. But the men who served went because we all owe something to this Country, for the freedom that we have. My brother Manuel just moved back home to Ojai, and it's so great being together again!

Family. Freedom. This Country.

That's what's important. A month before I went into the Marines, John F. Kennedy said something that really hit me. He said, "Ask not what your country can do for you, but what you can do for your country!"

I just hope we don't forget that.

Julio Contreras proudly carries a heavier load representing everything his deceased brothers stood for about patriotism—and he too stands for.

Julio has been Commander of our VFW Post 11461 in Ojai three different times and marches yearly, down main street, in our small town's family style Independence Day Parade.

A common theme of so many Vietnam veterans is the disgraceful way they were treated upon returning home. Julio felt that he and his family, who had sacrificed so much in the Nation's cause, should be respected. Upon arrival at the airport in Goleta, he caught the full fury of the university radicals. The pain of that degradation has left its mark on Julio, but he still has difficulty understanding the unfairness of the system, a system that required so much from some and so little of others.

Julio met and married while on leave and he had three daughters. The youngest daughter contracted leukemia and died at the age of four. This was the saddest and most difficult tragedy faced by Julio who had already faced the tragedy of losing three brothers. It is said that the worst tragedy of life is losing a child. A divorce left Julio with the responsibility for raising two daughters. Upon remarriage, his wife Danna became a mother to the girls and helped him raise them. Julio earned a degree at Santa Barbara City College and received a vocational teaching credential before embarking on a career as an electrician. Over the years, he has taught vocational school as well.

In all that Julio does, he emanates a sense of duty, fidelity, loyalty, patriotism, and responsibility. He stands tall as a proud Marine when he carries the colors down Ojai Avenue each Fourth of July Parade. He was unbowed before the Communist in Vietnam, he was unbowed before the university protesters upon his return home, and he continued a productive life in the face of almost insurmountable tragedy. Julio has been Commander of our VFW Post 11461 three different times.

It is evident that the key to the Contreras' family is their heritage and their courage in facing life's challenges, trials, and tribulations. Julio is always there for the Post, the cause of veterans, and his veteran comrades. He is there in remembrance of all veterans, but particularly the three Contreras brothers, members of a truly patriotic family.

■■■■■■■■■■■■■■■

JERRY DUNCAN

— *SOLDIER, SAILOR AND SEABEE*

The name Duncan brings to mind the wild freedom loving tartan clad clans of the ancient Celtic race. From the dawn of the historic age, the Duncans manned the field against the armies of Imperial Rome driving the invaders from their sacred soil. In the Darker Age the Celtic race saved the faith spreading the Cross across the northern tier of Europe's nascent states.

As the British nation coalesced, the clans gave their fealty to the British crown marching forth with skirling bagpipes and the staccato of beating drums. There is mysticism in the Celtic nature; mysticism driven by a martial pride mixed with a gentle and compassionate soul.

I was born and raised in South Philadelphia. Growing up, I would go down to the ports and talk to foreigners coming in. I was fascinated with their lives. They seemed like they were from worlds away.

OK, Merchant Marines for Me!

When I graduated from high school I immediately went down to join the Merchant Marines. But the problem was that you couldn't get a seaman's card if you didn't have a job, and you couldn't get a job if you didn't have a seaman's card! So I went down to Sun Oil in Chester, Pennsylvania and got a letter of promise for a job, then I came back to the Coast Guard and got my Merchant Seaman's papers. I was 18 at the time. With a Seaman's card, you are at the bottom of the ladder.

I got on the S.S. Delaware Sun, which was the first supertanker of its day. We went to Venezuela to pick up some oil. The ship was having a Coast Guard firebox inspection. The ships burned oil to turn the turbines, and everything was all automated. The ship only had a crew of about 40 men even though it was huge. It was about as long as a football field!

"Tie a rope around him (me) and pull him out after fifteen minutes."

I was the new kid on board, so I was a wiper in the engine room. They would turn off one of the engines, tie rags around my feet and a mask over my mouth, and I had to go in and sweep up the oil ash. They would tie a rope around me, and time me. After fifteen minutes, they pulled me back out. It is the finest, dirtiest stuff in the world.

Eight months after doing that, I still had black stuff coming out of my pores. It was killer stuff! I was ready to quit. To add to it all, the supertankers loaded and unloaded in eighteen hours. You didn't have the time to look at anything, which was not my idea of seeing the world.

I came back and was put on an old ship, an old, old diesel. We went to Port Arthur, Texas for another load, and in the process, somehow or another, I missed the ship when it left. I was burnt out anyway, so I hitchhiked to California and looked for work. This was 1959 and there were no jobs, so I decided to join the Navy.

OK, Let's Try the Navy

My twenty-six year military career began in San Diego, where I had basic training. From there I was transferred to Port Hueneme for construction electrician school. I liked Hueneme right off. It was all open country, with nothing but open fields for miles. If you wanted to do something, Santa Monica was the place to go.

Jerry Duncan with his Seabee Detachment in Dalat, Vietnam

Climbing Some of the Highest Antennas in the World—Looking for Women Behind Trees...

From there, I was sent to Midway Island for my first duty station. Midway was something else. It was nothing but goony birds and a woman behind every tree. And there weren't any trees on Midway! I got to climb some of the highest antennas in the world—up into the clouds, to change high-voltage construction lights.

From there, we went to Adak, Alaska where we were involved in typical Seabee construction activities.

Driving the Commandant in New York —My Early Combat Training

Shortly after the Adak assignment, they shipped me to New York to be the driver for the Commandant of the 3rd Naval District where I learned "driver protocol." Driving in New York City is a scary proposition even for an old Seabee. Tailgating isn't wise, yet, if you don't tailgate, you'll never be able to drive in New York. New Yorkers will grab any opening and cut off any driver given a chance. New York driving is not for the timid and weak. It might even be considered a prelude to combat training!

I remember one time when I was driving the commandant and a junior officer. I noticed that the commandant kept chuckling to himself, and the young lieutenant kept holding on to the back seat with white knuckles, punching his shoes against the floor as if he could stop the car. It was pretty funny.

Building One of the Largest Airfields in the World

I went back to Adak and then to Okinawa for additional construction assignments. I had intelligence clearance, so I did a lot of work with foreign nationals, escorting them in and out of secure areas. The Vietnam War was going full blast though so I was sent to MCB. They were competing with RMK, which was Ladybird Johnson's construction company, in making one of the largest airfields in the world, at Chu Li, Vietnam.

It was a hellhole! They had Navy Chiefs busting concrete bags open, putting them on the ground, watering them down, then putting matting down. It was the longest concrete pour in history. It was very strange, the whole thing, coming over on a commercial airplane, getting off, and bumming a ride to where I was going. There was no real briefing of any sort to tell me what I was doing!

Loaded Clips and Weapons onto a Private Plane to SF—No Way!

It was all very bizarre, and I hated the work and the weather over there, so when I got a call asking whether or not I wanted to volunteer for a Seabee team, I, of course, said "Yes!" First of all, it would get me out of that hellhole and I would go back to the U.S. for training. I went down to supply, to turn all my stuff in and they said, "We have to issue you your gear here, so that when you go back, you have all your own gear."

Besides everything that I brought to Vietnam, weapon, shovel, canteen, they issued me another set of gear for the Seabee team, which is very extensive. Canteens, bayonets, two sea bags, full military pack, etc. I left there, loaded for bear. I had an M-14 with full clips of live ammo, and I got on a military hop to Okinawa. There was a typhoon going on there, so I slept on the airport floor for three days until it passed. I was carrying an unbelievable amount of gear, so when I went to get on the aircraft, which was a civilian Northwest flight to San Francisco, they said, "You can't bring that weapon on this flight!" So I went back into the airport to a trash can, emptied the clips out, broke the weapon down, and handed it to them to keep in the cockpit!

I arrived in San Francisco still in the stinking, sweaty uniform I was wearing when I left Vietnam. I hadn't showered in about four days; there wasn't any place to shower. I was ripe and I was sweaty, and I was starting to get really upset with the madness of it. I had all this gear on my back, so when I got to the bus station, I just fell on my back onto all this gear. It was absolutely nuts! I had a helmet, weapon, everything, walking through civilian airports and bus stations in uniform. Not to mention the fact that people were anti-military right about now, with Vietnam and all.

I got on a Greyhound bus and people were making anti war comments, I had all this gear, and I couldn't find a place to put it. I sat down next to a lady, and five minutes later, she got up and left. At this point, I just didn't care! Finally, I got to Port Hueneme at 2:30 am, exhausted, and reveille was at 4:30! They were three weeks into training when I got there. The original electrician had broken his leg, and I was there to replace him.

SERE: Survival, Evasion, Resistance and Escape

For sixteen weeks they crossed trained us. We learned how to drive a bulldozer, grader, do welding, and wire electrical circuits just in case one person on the team was killed, the team could still carry out its mission. After we completed that, they shipped us off to Coronado, near San Diego for "SERE" School. SERE stood for survival, evasion, resistance, and escape.

They had replicated a Vietnamese prison camp. Anyone who was in a position where they could be physically captured was put into seven man units. Then we were sent out to the "boondocks" without food or water. We had to survive on whatever we could. This camp had been running for quite a while; this was 1966. So there wasn't a whole lot left up there by the time we arrived.

Would We Eat the Mouse in the Rattlesnakes Stomach?

They ran us up and down mountains for three days, trying to just wear us down. We were exhausted and starving when a rattlesnake crossed our path. A couple guys passed by it, but when the last two of us got up to it, we jumped all over that snake! We skinned and cleaned it, and then sat down and had a conference on whether or not to eat a mouse that was in its stomach. We decided not to because we were told that they had rabies. But, boy, I'll tell you, rattlesnake, with pepper on it, cooked, is very much like chicken. To this day, my mouth waters, thinking about how hungry we were!

At the end, we came to an area where they pointed down to a place called "freedom village." They said, "If you make it without getting captured, you'll get a sandwich." We were all channeled into this area and all of a sudden, all these vehicles started coming at us. The instructors were very well trained and they were dressed up as Chinese Communists. Eventually we were captured and taken to a "prison camp" constructed just like one would be in Asia.

Getting Us to Helpless and Hopeless

The first thing they did was slap us around. They had us take our clothes off, so we were standing there stark naked. We didn't know what to expect, which was the whole object of the training. They got us in the back of a truck, naked. They transported us to the POW camp. They had us crawl, totally naked under a field of barbed wire to where the guards were. We were supposed to smuggle anything in that we could, that could be turned into a weapon, with the exception of real weapons because these guys got "weirded out", and they would try to kill people.

After we got through there, I was told to go and report to a guy at a desk. The programming is, to escape. Instead of going where I was told, I went into one of the hooches and hid under a bunch of gear. I was there two or three hours when I hear "Prisoner Number 307!" I just stayed there until they found me and pulled me out by my collar. This time they whacked the hell out of my commanding officer! The game plan was to turn us "trainees" against each other. Eventually, all leadership and comradeship was gone.

When night would come, and we were all just exhausted, they would start the interrogation process, one at a time. They would take you into a dark room with light shining into your eyes. You couldn't see anything except the outline of the interrogator's face.

Into "The Black Box" on Hands and Knees

They would slam you down into a chair with a guard on either side of you, and they worked on any weakness they could find. Your faith, your family, anything. The guy would work himself into a rage, until finally, he'd walk up and whack you. We didn't know it, but the chairs were cut off in the back, so you would just go down. We were so exhausted that we had no resistance whatsoever. Then they would drag you out and put you in "the black box," which really psyched some of the guys out. You had to get in on your hands and knees, and you are head down. Then they slid this lid over you and close you in. Me, I was back in the womb, so it was actually kind of a nice break. Other guys just flipped out, and they would have to take them out because they didn't want any mental breakdowns.

After that, they would take us out and have us stand at formation, and they would say, "Who's in charge?" They would go down the line, and rough each guy up, until there was no one left. Escape was not an option, because everything had been tried. Finally towards the end, after eight or nine days, they filled a big cauldron with water and rice, and it smelled so good. The commandant was yelling and screaming at us because some of us hadn't confessed to being aggressors. He was in a rage, and he walked up to the rice, and dumped it all out on the ground.

Couldn't Finish Eating Even an Orange and a Little Oatmeal

That was just the bottom! Anyway, when they finally briefed us and let us out; they gave us an orange and a little oatmeal. We couldn't even finish it because our stomachs had shriveled up. Two thoughts kept running through my head while I was going through the SERE training. "This will end, it's only for a time." And, "This is my own government that is doing this to me." It was an eye-opener, but we made it through.

Got a Problem?

From there, we were sent to Vandenberg Air Force Base, to weed out our own people. We were going to be living together for months and months in very isolated conditions, so any personality conflicts had to be worked out first. They gave us an assignment to build a bridge over a ravine. They sent us lumber though, instead of timber. We had our own generator, tents, refrigerator, grader, bulldozer, and weapons carriers.

The Difference in Lumber and Timber

When we were finished, ready to go, they sent all the equipment over the bridge. The grader was first, and then they had a dump truck, a deuce, with a trailer on it, the refrigerator, the tents, and the guys on top of that. As we started to go over, I said, "It's not going to hold!" So, I got up on the edge. Sure enough, the bridge just twisted and gave. The truck slid down the ravine onto its side, the bulldozer went upside down. Nobody got hurt, thank God. That ravine was really steep though.

The next Seabee team that came through was given the project to get the dozer out of there. Everybody was devastated, especially the commanding officer. But they gave him lumber instead of timber! That was the beginning, not a good omen for the team. Then they sent us to Vietnam into the central highlands near a beautiful city called Delat.

Delat in the Gorgeous Vietnam Central Highlands

Dalat was where the rich French colonials used to go tiger hunting. It was absolutely, unbelievably, gorgeous and very much a hands-off during the war. Now we were thirteen kilometers outside of that little tiny camp that was built by the Japanese and used when they were over there putting huge transmission lines in as part of World War II retribution. The Viet Cong overran the camp in 1954 when the French were there. It was right at the base of a huge dam in a valley. Anybody who wanted to could throw grenades down onto us, and all we could do was to throw them back as best we could. It was nerve racking! There were two Army advisors there who kept an eye on the provinces for intelligence purposes, and there were two Vietnamese guards, who were totally worthless.

Jerry Duncan with Montagnard bows and arrows, central highlands of South Vietnam.

Montagnards

But during the night, the Montagnards would come, and they would bring their kids with them. The Montagnards were similar to the American Indians. The Vietnamese hated them. They were people of the land, and they just couldn't grasp city life. They were slash and burn farmers, nomadic. They smelled of fire. I remember, we would get movies in our camp, and the Montagnard children would come and just sit there, absolutely amazed. The look on their faces was amazement as they tried to comprehend movies like West Side Story.

I would watch them rather than watching the movie. They were so loyal; you could really depend upon them, just a wonderful, remarkable people. There would be four of them awake and one American. We also had an interpreter, who was a Montagnard, who was educated by French Trappist monks.

French Trappist Monks

The monks lived in a huge, beautiful monastery. They were wonderful people as well, really a pleasure to work with. They hand pressed beautiful tiles. Many times on Sundays, which was our day off, we would go in with our dozers and do work for them. We were there to help rebuild towns for American supporters.

Sometimes we would go into town for supplies; the look of hatred on the faces of some of the people was quite evident. I just knew that they were Viet Cong. The hatred was liquid. But there was a hands-off policy in that area because it was a very rich farming valley and the Viet Cong was getting food because of it. Right before we went over there, we had run into some Girl Scouts and they asked us if they could send us some cookies. We said, no, but that we could use clothing and toothbrushes. So while we were over there, we started getting supplies regularly. A Navy recruiter named Vince Erickson organized it. We clothed a lot of people over there. It was cold up there, which was nice, not to be in the hot tropical weather.

Duncan helps distribute supplies to the village on Don Duong in the Central Highlands of South Vietnam. 1967.

Ambushed in Phu Bai

We were then moved to Phu Bai, where North Vietnamese regulars ambushed us. Marine Corps detachments moved in for an aggressive counter attack, but they didn't have us on their maps, so they accidentally fired on us, killing about five Americans and wounding scores of Seabees.

Tet of 1967

I stayed there through the Tet of 1967. You don't hear as much about it as the Tet of '68, where the Viet Cong attacked the American Embassy and just about every major city. The North Vietnamese lost an unbelievable number of troops in the Tet of '68, but they won the war politically because the American media and leadership lost the will to win.

Home to Machine Guns on Pennsylvania Avenue

Leaving Vietnam for the second time, I got orders to Washington D.C. State Department because I had clearance already. I got off on Pennsylvania Avenue, right into the riots! Talk about a bizarre feeling. There were people walking around with machine guns, military on all the streets.

From there, they sent me to Tel Aviv, Israel. We were responsible for debugging all of the construction over there. Then I was sent to Moscow during the height of the Cold War. There were all sorts of things going on over there also. There were tunnels, espionage, and all manner of clandestine activities. Russia was one of the most paranoid countries in the world. There was a lot of anti-war propaganda too. When we were over there, you didn't speak. You had to point, and then go to a special room to talk.

Too Much Fun—You are Off the Party List!

One night we were out in town, and we met some Bulgarians who played music. We invited them over to the

American Embassy for a small get together. The next thing we knew, there was a huge crowd! There were Secretaries of this Embassy, and that Embassy, all stashed in this room! We were just packed in. We had the Bulgarians playing, vodka from the Marine bar, impersonators, actors—it was a great party! We were questioned the next day, as to who was there, and we didn't know. We were in big trouble. Needless to say, we were put on the list and nobody was allowed to attend our parties anymore.

I came back from overseas and got booted out of the program because I got married. We ended up getting a divorce anyway. I then got orders to go back to Vietnam. All this time I was an E-6. I had passed the Chief's test three times, and each time they said that they didn't have an opening. Meanwhile they had pulled in civilians and gave them the rank of E-7, and they weren't getting out. I decided that I really didn't want to go back to Vietnam, especially if I was going to remain an E-6, so I got out.

California National Guard and Los Angeles Race Riots

I served five more years in the Naval Reserve, and joined the Santa Monica Police force and the California National Guard. I worked for the police department for ten years, then in 1989, I went back into the service for a while, and my last major military action was in the Los Angeles riots where I commanded troops from Inglewood, many of whom recognized rioters from their own neighborhoods. The National Guard was inept in supplying munitions for the suppression of the riots, so soldiers supplied themselves. I helped locate one soldier's mother and led her to safety. Los Angeles was one scary place to be during the riots; it was a war zone.

After retirement, I moved to Ojai where I raise my fourteen-year-old daughter, Amber.

PAT NOLAN

— DOOR GUNNER; SHOOTER SURVIVES ON A SHORT LEASH

Pat Nolan occupies an architectural office in Meiners Oaks. It is a quiet office except for a phone that seems to be constantly ringing. Stacked about the offices are plans, notes, and construction manuals and directives. Well-used and worn building and safety codes line the bookshelves. Centered in one room is a drafting table.

Within the Ojai Valley, Pat has a reputation for being a well-qualified designer with a degree in Architecture, a degree that is displayed on the office wall along with other certificates and licenses. As a student, Pat excelled in algebra, geometry, trigonometry, and calculus, subjects so familiar to engineers and architects. He must have been a studious fellow at Cal Poly in San Luis Obispo where he was on the Dean's List. The quality of work produced at this office is such that reputation builds the business. Meticulous attention to detail so necessary in planning along with an in-depth knowledge of government codes and regulations are Pat's stock in trade. By nature, Pat is a quiet and unassuming fellow who truly knows his business and understands the dynamics of the construction industry.

In contrast to the professional designer and planner, Pat Nolan's background is quite different from his present occupation. Pat is a Vietnam veteran who participated in some of the bloodiest fighting in the Mekong Delta where he was a door gunner on attack helicopters. Pat was the consummate modern warrior participating in the violence of constant warfare in the Mekong Delta region of South Vietnam.

In his youth, Pat was a service brat and followed his father from one duty station to another, mostly naval bases on the East and West coasts. The father's service included World War II and Korea on aircraft carriers. Most people from that background follow in the parent's footsteps or reject the transitory life of the military altogether. The constant change of life style, schools, and living conditions do not auger well for the children. Frequently, academics suffer for the children of career military personnel.

In contrast, Pat was a studious and an accomplished student. Pat was introduced to Ventura County when his father was assigned to Point Mugu Naval Air Station. Pat attended Hueneme High School for a time and Ventura Community College for a semester. But Pat was restless and he had a burning desire to serve his country in a combat arm known for "gung ho" macho guys, the paratroopers. Much to the consternation of his parents, he enlisted in the airborne Infantry program.

This was at a time when the war was raging in Vietnam. Pat could have avoided the draft because he was in college, excelling in architectural and math studies. Pat had no desire to use college deferments to avoid military service. He was not looking for the easy and comfortable whether as an academic scholar or as a professional soldier. He wanted the challenge of real action and true service. The nature of paratrooping is hazardous in peacetime, but extremely lethal in wartime. His mother was frightened and concerned. His father thought that the U.S. Navy was a better choice than jumping out of planes and living in a muddy foxhole.

Modern armies need intelligent and well-motivated soldiers. When army personnel saw Pat's math and scholastic background, they wanted to enroll him in an officer candidate program, but Pat had a one-track mind. He wanted to be a soldier. He wanted to be a tough paratrooper jumping out of planes and making assaults. As I interviewed him, he was quite reluctant to state the motivation behind his choices. Still waters run deep and underneath his quiet exterior, Pat has the soul of a patriot-warrior. The bottom line for his motivation was patriotism!

I was born May 5, 1947. My dad was in the Navy all of my childhood. He served as an aircraft mechanic for aircraft carriers. My dad served in WW II and Korea, and he spent twenty years in the military. When I was a kid, his stations were always changing, so I moved back and forth my whole life. While my dad was stationed in California, we stayed four years at Point Mugu, and then we went to Imperial Beach. And that's when he got out of the Navy.

PHOTO COURTESY OF PAT NOLAN

Private Pat Nolan, basic training graduate, Fort Benning GA, 1967

No Arguing
—I'm Army Paratrooper!

We liked it up here, so in 1965 we moved back to Ventura County. I graduated from Hueneme High in 1967. But I was tired of school and Vietnam was going full blast. I was young and adventurous so I got involved. I decided to go into the Army, which didn't make my Dad too happy. I went to basic training at Fort Benning, Georgia where I trained as a paratrooper. And from there, they sent me straight to Vietnam in 1967.

The Mekong Delta in a Hut the Japanese Built

The summer of 1968 was a pretty big one for the war. They sent me to Camrahn Bay, assigned to the 101st Airborne. Then they changed orders and sent me down to the Mekong Delta. It was so hot and humid in that jungle! I lived in a hooch that the Japanese had built when they had occupied Vietnam and there were probably about six or seven of us in there.

Fly it in or be Ambushed on the Ground

The only way we could get to our station was to fly in using helicopters. You couldn't drive anywhere because it was all Viet Cong-controlled. Any supplies had to come in by convoy or by air. I never saw a convoy though. We just knew that convoys would get ambushed because there was only one road leading to and from our base.

PHOTO COURTESY OF PAT NOLAN

"Slick" infantry squad level transport helicopters flying to battle in 1968

Chopper Door Gunner Goes Where the War is—Every Day

I was a door gunner in a chopper, and each day we flew to where the war was going on. I was in the helicopters for a year.

I was a gunner on the slicks, which are troop carriers. We'd just carry troops into a LZ or Landing Zone and drop troops off, back and forth, back and forth - I switched to gun ships still in the capacity of a gunner. I stood on the rocket pads of the chopper tethered by a leash to keep me from falling as the chopper flew in direct support of ARVN (Army of the Republic of Vietnam) ground units.

In that exposed position, dangling hundreds of feet off the ground and exposed constantly to enemy fire, I fought the war against the Viet Cong. Obviously, the life expectancy of a door gunner was very short. The gunship would give cover fire for the helicopters that were dropping troops into the LZ. We'd come back and do air strikes.

All Over the Delta and Cambodia

Then I was stationed in a place called Sac Tran. The only way you could get there was by air because they didn't allow you on the ground where you'd get killed. When we got a mission we'd fly off, and we'd be gone about three or four days at a time. There were four people on the helicopters, two pilots, a crew chief and a gunner. We picked up downed pilots, wounded guys, and we flew everywhere in the Delta that there was to fly. We flew into Cambodia and picked up dead bodies on the battlefield, where they'd just been left out there by the South Vietnamese.

How A Helicopter Base Fights Off Night Attacks

In the Mekong Delta there were only three helicopter bases to cover the whole area. But, all three posts were overrun during the TET Offensive. At night, two choppers guarded each chopper base. One was a "Gun Ship" that flew over the base. The other chopper was called a "Firefly". The "Firefly" dropped flares lighting up the whole area so the gunship could break up any enemy attack. Choppers had no place to hide. They were very exposed in the air or on the ground. Mortar attacks against our base happened two or three times a week so the helicopters would take off to deliver fire on the Viet Cong positions surrounding the base.

We'd use our machine guns taken off of the helicopter to fight with on the ground. You mounted them when you took off, but then you unmounted them when you got back home. We used M60 machine guns.

Typical Helicopter Unit and Tactics

In my camp, there were two helicopter units and each helicopter unit had slicks and they also had gun ships. Each helicopter unit had probably five gun ships each, and five or six slick-ships each. Then we had the Medevac ship, and two or three Air force people.

We usually ate C-rations, pineapples and bananas. I'd trade my C-rations for pineapples and bananas. It's all jungle where we were and pineapples and bananas grew all over the place, just wild.

Looking back on it all, the most difficult thing about being in Vietnam was losing friends. As far as flying and going into battle, firing machine guns and stuff, the helicopter is the greatest roller coaster in the world. There's never a dull moment. It was actually kind of thrilling all the time. The morale in the camp was pretty good. People didn't necessarily want to be there, but they weren't running around, cussing or groaning all the time. I don't know if we ever felt we were accomplishing anything though. We were a little bit, day by day, but you didn't really know what was going on as far as what the ground troops were getting into. It was just like a job, like a never-ending thing. You just were doing something a little different each day. It was exciting though.

All Systems Normal—Chaos Everyday

It was all pretty chaotic over there. You never knew from day to day, where you were going or what you were going to do. According to the indoctrination that I got, we went over there to stop Communism—more or less the same old thing. But once you're over there, you don't even think about why. It's immaterial. The only ally that our unit had to work with over there was the South Vietnamese Army. And actually, they'd just as soon shoot you, as anybody else! When you'd fly, you'd either fly at two thousand feet, or three feet. Nothing in between, because you are an easy target.

Captured Vietcong,1968

Receiving Friendly Fire? Fine, We are Returning Friendly Fire!

We flew back from an operation once and the pilot noticed we were getting some fire out of the tree line down below. We called in, and they said, "Don't shoot back, because there were 'Friendlies' or South Vietnamese soldiers down there." The pilot radioed back, "Receiving friendly fire, returning friendly fire!" and went down and shot them up. The one nice thing was that I didn't have to call in and say, "I'm getting shot at, can I shoot back?" I was given clearance to make the judgment call if I needed to shoot or not.

M-60 Gunner in Attack Mode...Body Count

When in the attack mode, the M-60 gunner shot anything that moved. Body count was a big thing with the commander's back in Saigon. We averaged a body count of ten kills a day, but this was difficult to determine. Usually the fire was directed into trees or brush where a body count was impossible to ascertain. Frequently, the ARVN on the ground would take credit for what ever they found. Wherever the action, that is where we would fly in support. The military command would emphasize the number of enemy killed and de-emphasize the friendly forces killed. One day, the Ninth Infantry Division lost 10 KIA's, "Killed In Action." But the official report listed only two American KIA's. I was part of the rescue force extracting the dead and wounded, so I know that more men died than we heard about.

Shot Down Twice

Every helicopter was shot up or shot down as we carried out our missions. I was shot down twice while I was over there, yet somehow I survived to fight another day. One time we crash-landed at 90 knots. The rotor blades hit the earth and caused the chopper to flip over, killing our crew chief.

PHOTO COURTESY OF PAT NC

Infamous TET, the Lunar New Year—1968

Downtown Soc Trang after Tet1968—building full of holes

In 1968, when the Viet Cong launched the Tet Offensive, the enemy was slaughtered in the vicious fighting. That was followed by our base being overrun by Viet Cong. We stayed there though, and the Viet Cong didn't do too well. They overran us, but they were killed in the process. I don't think they were too bright when they did it. The Viet Cong losses were so great that it was unreal—the U.S. clearly won the battles throughout Vietnam during the Tet Offensive. But by then, the anti-war factions were undermining everything that we were over there fighting for. All those lives of U.S. servicemen were lost for nothing!

PHOTO COURTESY OF PAT NOLAN

Here's lookin' atcha. Pat Nolan playin' poker on R&R.

Now for Something Entirely Different —Freezing in Tanks, in Germany

Anyway, after a year, my tour was up in Vietnam and they needed to send me someplace. I think that they figured they'd keep me as far away from California as they could, so they sent me to Germany in October—and I about froze to death, going from the jungle, straight to snow and ice! They put me on a tank to boot! The only thing that I knew about a tank, was, "That's a tank right?"

What I did know was how to shoot machine guns. So in three months' time, I was tank commander of an M60A1 Armed Tank! Back then they were still worried about the Russians and the Czech border. If the Russians came across the Czech border, we were to be the first line of defense for Europe. I was stationed in a place called Baumholder, a place on the top of the mountain, out in the middle of nowhere.

You Want Me to What?

I was there for 18 months and then my enlistment came up. They offered me $10,000 to reenlist, which was a lot of money back then. They said that they wanted to send me to OCS (Officer's Candidate School) Flight School, and they told me how I could beat the Army out of four years because you'd have to reenlist for six. Once you finish OCS they discharge you as an enlisted man, and reenlist you for two years as an officer. Vietnam was going on full blast then, and I knew exactly where they would send me again, and I wasn't going back! So, I thought about it, laughed about it and forgot about it!

Back Home to Oxnard and Ventura College...

When I got out, I went back to Oxnard, as my family was still there. I went back to college at Ventura College, and I worked for Abex Aerospace in the summer as well as Allis-Chalmers. Then I transferred to Cal Poly. I had always wanted to be an architect ever since I could remember. There isn't any one thing that sent me in that direction, but I was always good at mechanical drafting, which I don't even do anymore, thanks to computers! I met my wife in Oxnard, while I was still in school, because I came home on the weekends. We met in the tavern where my mother tended bar; it used to be called the Pirates Den on Hueneme Road. The guy who owned it had been a friend of the family for years. Nadine and I dated for about a year and a half. Then we got married about a year after I graduated from college.

No Work for an Architect

After I graduated, I tried to get work as an architect, but there were no jobs available in California. So I ended up going to work pulling lumber on a green chain at a sawmill in a town called Sweethome. It's a little place east of Albany, Oregon. I only stayed in the lumber industry for about eight months and then I came back to California. We moved to Oxnard and I got a job as a cook. My wife and I had four kids from her previous marriage. There were three boys and one girl. We never had any kids together because we had our hands full with those four!

I finally got a job in Ojai drafting, but I was still working as a cook. It was tough back then, but we made it through. My wife and I have been married for 25 years now! The kids all lived here in Ojai until the girl recently moved to Arizona.

About War and Politicians Getting People Killed...

Looking back on my life and my time in the service, naturally, my experience in the war changed my thoughts a bit. You don't really know what war is until you have experienced it. Nothing anybody can tell you can explain it to you. One thing I am sure of though is that we definitely need a strong military and we need to get the politicians out of there. They can kill more people than the enemy does. I don't think Vietnam taught them that.

They're still playing politics. It might have taught them something, but they still stick their fingers in those matters. Like when they went into Iraq, the politicians stopped them dead in their tracks and wouldn't let them finish going in. They didn't go in and finish the job, plainly, because of politics. I just hope we learn our lessons and don't have to repeat another war like Vietnam.

I just hope.

Pat Nolan remains active in the Veterans of Foreign Wars Post 11461 and is frequently a part of the Color Guard of Veterans marching down Ojai Avenue in the 4th of July Parade.

Pat scorns the media image given Vietnam veterans and by his own life and achievement, he demonstrates that good soldiers make good citizens. He resents the negative image of Vietnam veterans portrayed by the media.

He believes that the down and out so-called Vietnam veteran portrayed in the media were not veterans at all or had never served overseas. Recent studies indicate that this is largely true. By the Grace of God, Pat Nolan survived the war and returned home to be a constructive builder and contributor to his nation and the Ojai Community. And even now, underneath Pat Nolan's quiet and reserved demeanor, one still finds that patriotic heartbeat of an American Citizen Soldier.

BIBLIOGRAPHY

■■■■■■■■■■■■■■■■■■■■■

Everett Alvarez Jr., **Code of Conduct** (New York, New York: Donald I. Fine, Inc. 1991) 235 Pages

Carl Becker, Sidney Painter, Bert Loewenberg, Yu-Shan, James Blakemore, **The Past That Lives Today** (Morristown, New Jersey: Silver Burdett Company) 854 Pages

William Brebitsky, **A Very Long Weekend, The Army National Guard in Korea** (Shippensburg, PA 17257: Whitte Mane Publishing Co. Inc., 1996) 293 Pages

John Carey, **Eye-Witness to Histor**y (Cambridge, Massachusetts: Harvard University Press, 1988) 706 Pages

Martin van Creveld, **Technology and War** (New York, New York: The Free Press, A Division of Macmillan, Inc. 1989) 342

James D. Delk, **The Fighting Fortieth, In War and Peace** (Palm Springs, California 1998) 424 Pages

Robert Goldwin, Editor with Robert Lerner and Gerald Stourzh **Readings in American Foreign Policy** (New York, New York: Oxford University Press 1959) 496 Pages

Joseph C. Goulden, **Korea, The Untold Story** (New York, New York: Times Books 1982) 690 Pages

Gene Gurney, **A Pictorial History of the United States Army** (New York, New York: Crown Publishers, Inc. 1966) 815 Pages

Walter Phelps Hall and William Stearns Davis, **The Course of History Since Waterloo** (New York, New York: Appleton-Century-Crofts, Inc. 1951) 1083 pages

Joseph C. Harsch, **Pattern of Conquest** (Garden City, New York: Doubleday, Doran and Co., Inc. 1941) 309 Pages

Jim Dan Hill, **The Minuteman in Peace and War, History of the National Guard** (Harrisburg, Pennsylvania: The Stackpole Company 1964)

William F. Mc Cartney, **The Jungleers; A History of the 41st Infantry Division** (Washington Infantry Journal Press 1948) 208 Pages

Samuel Eliot Morison, **History of the American People** (New York, New York: Oxford University Press 1965) 1153 Pages

John W. Pratt, **A History of the United States Foreign Policy** (Englewood Cliffs, New Jersey: Prentice-Hall, Inc., 1960) 808 Pages

David Rees, Consultant Editor, **The Korean War, History and Tactics** (London, England: Orbis Publishing 1984) 128 Pages

Richard L. Rubenstein, **The Age of Triage** (Boston, Massachusetts: Beacon Press of the Unitarian Universalist Association, 1983) 301 Pages

Robert Scheer, **How the United States Got Involved in Vietnam** (Santa Barbara, California: Center for the Study of Democratic Institutions 1967) 80 Pages

Barbara W. Tuchman, **The March of Folly** (New York, New York:Random House, Inc. 1984) 447 Pages

William L. Shirer, **The Rise and Fall of the Third Reich** (New York, New York: Simon and Schuster, 1960) 1245 pages

T. Walter Wallbank and Arnold Schier, **Living World History** (Chicago, Illinois: Scott, Foresman and Company 1964) 7668 Pages

INDEX

B29 Ground Crew Chief XI
Bank of A. Levy 129
BAR 278, 293
Bast, Hank I
Bastogne 68
Bath, England 110
Battle of Okinawa XI
Battle of the Bulge X, 60, 61, 68, 104, 129
battleship 298
Bay Bridge 356
Bedcheck Charlie 284
Beechcraft 67
Belgium X
Bennett, Chuck I, II, III, VII,319, 322, 339, 349, 350, 356
Berlin 31, 97, 106
Berlin Airlift 256
Bertholet, Colonel 62
Biak 202
Bible 23
bicycle factory 341
Bishop, California 222
Blacks 115
Boeing 165
Boise, Idaho 67
Bomb Day 128
Bonesteel, General 11
Boston 96
Bougainvillaea 52
Bouquet Canyon 14
Boy Scouts 18, 253, 320, 323
Bozeman, Montana 255
Brazilians 79
Breech, Harold 131, 136, 139, 140
Bremerhaven, Germany 255
Bremerton, Washington 206
Brendesi 92
Bridge of No Return 6, 10
Brigham Young 299
Brisbane 121
Brisbane, Australia 124
British 13, 79, 199, 367
British Long Tom 80
Bronze Star 18, 19, 227
Bronze Star with V Device 338
Brooklyn Navy Yard 53
Bucher, Commander 10
Buckley Field 135
Buffalo Soldiers 259
Bulacan Province 150

bunker 248
bunkers 17, 292, 293
Burbank Theater 111
Burbank, Luther 197
burial detail 211
Burma XI, 189
burp gun 287, 294
Butte, Montana 253
buzz bomb 28

C

C-104 189
C-119 241, 247
C-47 51, 163, 189
C-rations 170, 223, 280, 281, 285, 331, 386, 245
Cal, John 141, 143, 144, 145
Calcutta India 187
California 75
California National Guard 17, 269
California National Guard Artillery 16
Calley, Lieutenant William 339
Calvary 220
Cambodia 316, 385
Camp Carson, Colorado 59
Camp Cooke 16, 237, 270, 271
Camp Fuji 42
Camp Kerns, Utah 66
Camp Lee, Virginia 116
Camp McNair 241
Camp Pendleton CA 39, 40, 359
Camp Polk, Louisiana 187
Camp Roberts 118, 175
Camp San Luis Obispo 237, 264, 265
Camp Stoneman 119, 128, 295
Camp Swabb 42
Camp Walters, Texas 76
Camp Zama 241
Camrahn Bay 384
Canadian 182, 185
cannibals 123, 202
Canoga Park 299
Canole Valley, Italy 79
carbine 270, 284
Caribbean 91
Carper, Gene 219, 226
Carpinteria 357
carriers 141

Casitas Dam 306
Casitas Springs 14
Catarroja, Sebastian 3, 147, 152
Catholic 53, 149, 288
CBR 31
CCC 198, 203, 204, 253
Celtic 367
Central Highlands 377
Chaplain Crane 293
Charlie 331
Chemical Surety Group 11
Chiang Kai-shek 188
Chicago 175
Chief Petty Officer 299
Chigasaki, Japan 239
China XI, 3, 185, 189, 217
China Sea 302
Chinard Institute 102
Chinese 9, 17, 248, 249, 251, 279, 290
Chinese bodies 292
Chinook 353
Chosin Reservoir 218
CHP 234
Christian. 291
Chu Li, Vietnam 370
Church of Jesus Christ of Latter Day Saints 299
CIA 11, 224
Civil War 14
Civilian Conservation Corps 197, 198, 199
Clark Air Force 58
claymores 338
Clinton, Ohio 76
Clinton, President Willim J. 317
Cluster bombs 332
Coleman County 22
Colorado Springs 8
Colton, California 236
Combat Infantry Badge 336
Communism 8
Communist 12
Company Commander XIII, 319
Concord 267
Concord, New Hampshire 102
Condina, Lt Colonel 339
Confederacy 21
Congressional Medal of Honor 231
Connecticut 53
Constabulary Corps 30

222, 232
Typhoon 239

U

U-2 spy plane 5
U-boats 89, 91
U. S. Army Command and
    General Staff College 8
U. S. S. Pueblo 8
U.S. Air Corps XI
U.S. Army Air Corps XI
U.S. Army Military Police XII
U.S. Army Nurse Corps X
U.S. Marine Corps XIII, 41
U.S. Marines 41
U.S. Merchant Marine 89
U.S. Naval Armada 210
U.S. Navy XI
U.S.Army Coast Artillery XI
U.S.S Olmstead 139
U.S.S. Argentina 28
U.S.S. Bonhomme Richard 208
U.S.S. Boxer 7
U.S.S. Bunker Hill XI, 206, 209,
    212
U.S.S. Enterprise 212
U.S.S. Essex 208, 212
U.S.S. General Freeman 190
U.S.S. General Walker 224
U.S.S. George Washington 61
U.S.S. Helena 50
U.S.S. Kearsarge XII, 301
U.S.S. Lane Victory 92
U.S.S. Louis Pasteur 67
U.S.S. Mount Vernon 119
U.S.S. Pennsylvania 93
U.S.S. Pueblo 6, 9
U.S.S. Randolph 208
U.S.S. Tutuila 54
U.S.S. United States 77
UCLA 71
United Nations 29
United States Postal Service 190
University of Pennsylvania 107
University of Southern California
    102
USAFFE 151
USC 129
USO XI, 55, 154, 156
USS Breton CVE 23 15
USS Gunnison 15

USS Norris DD 895 15

V

Vail, Bruce 305, 312, 313
Vandenberg Air Force Base 16,
    237, 270
Ventura 14, 36, 154
Ventura College 156, 162
Ventura County 55, 157
Vero Beach 53
VFW 228
VFW Post 11461 III, V, 3, 19,
    46, 55, 63, 93, 146, 216,
    252, 391
Viet Cong 316, 327, 334, 341,
    346, 375, 377, 385, 388
Vietnam 5, 11, 18, 42, 43, 316,
    360, 371, 375, 383
Vietnamese 315, 331
Villa Franka Airport 83
Virginia 117
Volcano 194

W

Waist Gunner 95
Wake Island 90
Wales 299
Wallace, Vice President, 1942
    184
war brides 31
War Dog 294
Warren, CA Governor Earl 241
Washington D.C. 3, 103
Washington D.C. State
    Department 378
Washington Naval Conference
    141
Watts, California 15, 75
West Point 58, 103, 226
Westinghouse Corporation 76
Wheeler's Gorge 38
Wiklanski 289
Willawalla winds 90, 173, 179,
    182
Williamsburg 117
Willie Peter (WP) 293
Wisconsin 320, 363
Wolfhounds XIII, 324, 329, 337
Woodward, General 9

World War I 103, 228
World War II 5, 89, 103, 393
Wyoming 225, 261

Y

Yalta 217, 316
Yamanaka 232
Yap Island 208
Yaqui 357
yellow jaundice 182
Yokohama 17, 38, 273